BLESSED

Co-author Roy Collins has been a sports columnist for over 17 years and is a personal friend of George Best. A chief sports writer on *Today* for ten years, followed by the *People*, Roy writes for the *Guardian* and *Sunday Telegraph* and has co-written the autobiography of Frank Warren.

GEORGE BEST

WITH ROY COLLINS

BLESSED
THE AUTOBIOGRAPHY

EBURY
PRESS

This edition first published in Great Britain in 2002

19 20 18

First published by
Ebury Press
Random House, 20 Vauxhall Bridge Road, London SW1V 2SA

Random House Australia (Pty) Limited
20 Alfred Street, Milsons Point, Sydney, New South Wales 2061, Australia

Random House New Zealand Limited
18 Poland Road, Glenfield, Auckland 10, New Zealand

Random House South Africa (Pty) Limited
Isle of Houghton, Corner of Boundary Road & Carse O'Gowrie,
Houghton 2198, South Africa

Random House UK Limited Reg. No. 954009

www.randomhouse.co.uk

A CIP catalogue record for this book is available from the British Library

ISBN 0091884705

Typeset by seagulls
Jacket design by Gyles Lingwood

Front cover photograph © George Best column,
Night & Day, The Mail on Sunday
Back cover photograph © Peter Robinson, courtesy of Empics
Other photos © George Best unless otherwise stated

Printed and bound in Great Britain by Bookmarque Ltd, Croydon, Surrey

Papers used by Ebury Press are natural, recyclable products
made from wood grown in sustainable forests.

For the boys of '68, who helped
fulfil one of my dreams
and my beautiful wife Alex,
who continues to fuel those dreams.

ACKNOWLEDGEMENTS

To my Father and family, Alex, Professor Williams, Akeel Alisa, Dr Graham Lucas, Belfast City Hospital, David Goff and Andrew Gouck at Gordon Dadds, Natalie Jerome, Jake Lingwood and everyone at Ebury Press, Roy Collins, Phil Hughes, Paul Collier, all at GeorgeBestofficial.com and to all my well-wishers over the years. Thank you for your continued support.

CONTENTS

PROLOGUE
THE 'OTHER WOMAN'

I was in such agony that if someone had offered me a pill to end it all, I wouldn't have hesitated to take it.

Death would at least have ended the dreadful, persistent pain – the worst I've ever known – which felt as though a knife was being twisted in my stomach. But despite weeks of this pain, weeks of throwing up and coughing up blood, which is the most frightening sign that you are really seriously ill, I refused to accept that I was in need of urgent hospital treatment.

My wife Alex, as you can imagine, had been growing increasingly frantic in her pleas to me to go in, sometimes trying to cajole me and at other times threatening to leave me to suffer alone. Just like you do with a kid. Also, unbeknown to me, she had begun crushing up vitamin pills to put in the little bit of food that I had been managing to eat, though I rarely kept anything down for long. She also began crushing up tablets of milk thistle, which helps to clean out the liver.

Given the amounts of booze I've put away, it was like trying to dilute a vat of scotch with a thimble full of water but you could understand her doing it. She had also been reading all the medical books she could get her hands on and knew that everything pointed to me having cirrhosis, though without being unkind to her, I think anyone could have worked that out.

I knew it myself but there was always something inside me, that little inner voice, which said that it didn't matter whether my condition was caused by booze or something else. If I was going to die, I told myself – and I did think it was a distinct possibility – it had to be something, so why blame the booze? Everyone always blamed the booze. Slowly but surely, though, it started to sink in that I could get treatment, could do something about this pain and that it would involve going off the drink. Of course, that's the bit that I didn't want to accept so I kept on pretending.

If I ever had any doubts about my condition, I only had to look in the bathroom mirror to dispel them. I had noticed my skin starting to turn yellow, the first traces of jaundice which comes with cirrhosis. My face was pinched and I had begun to lose so much weight that my clothes looked as though they had been bought for someone two sizes bigger.

I'd started to feel ill just after Jimmy Tarbuck's 60th birthday bash in February 2000. The invitations read:

> *Men – dinner jackets; women – posh frocks; food – upmarket fish and chips*

And that's what was served up at Tarby's golf club for celebrities like Cilla Black, Ronnie Corbett, Russ Abbott, Robert Powell, Michael Parkinson and Adam Faith. It was a fantastic evening but I had not been on my best form for a while so I'd decided to book a week at Forest Mere health club in Hampshire.

For years, this had been my pathetic answer to a lifetime of drinking to excess – going to a health club four or five times a year and believing that it balanced out the drink, even though I often knocked back wine when I was in one of those places. Sometimes, I would actually come out in a worse state than when I went in but I still convinced myself that I had been doing myself some good, sorting out my problem. Unfortunately, there is no solution to alcohol.

You can't make it go away.

I also got another sign at Forest Mere that things were seriously wrong. I was about to step in the shower one day when

I noticed a little spot on my leg, the sort of thing we all get. Automatically, I scratched it and it started to bleed. And bleed. And bleed. It's something everyone has done at one time or another but it was unbelievable that this little spot was producing so much blood. Before I knew it, the floor was covered in it and I was surrounded by blood-stained toilet paper and tissues which I had used to try to stop it. Eventually, Alex managed to get a plaster on it but for the next couple of days, the blood continued to seep out. It was a sign – but not one I cared to take any notice of.

As for the drink, I wasn't really interested in trying to make it go away. Quite the opposite in fact, as true to form, I looked for the solution to my stomach problems not in a bottle of medicine but one of brandy. I was not supposed to drink the stuff in normal circumstances because it wasn't good for my blood pressure, though some of the bar staff at my local pub in Chelsea, the Phene Arms, would always slip me one.

Now, I began to drink more and more of it, sometimes starting soon after I got up, on top of the daily wine lake I was putting away. And, of course, the more I drank, the more the pain eased. So with the logic of an alcoholic, I reckoned that more was better. Naturally it helped, but as the pain was caused by my liver screaming for mercy, it was making my condition even more chronic.

But I wouldn't go into hospital because I knew what the 'treatment' would entail. No more of my own medicine.

Alex and Phil Hughes, my agent and friend, who have both seen me through some pretty bad times, realised long before me that this was something serious. Or, at least, they accepted it long before me. They were now begging me to go to hospital on a daily basis but I continued on the brandy self-help diet and rolled into the Phene every day. It had become as familiar as my own living room.

Then, when I was sitting in my usual seat in the corner one afternoon, something amazing happened. The pub door slowly opened and I looked up to see one of the old regulars who hadn't been in for a while. I didn't recognise him at first because he was so frail and thin and when I realised who it was, I was absolutely shocked. His skin and eyes were completely yellow and his cheeks were almost hollow. Needless to say, he had just been diagnosed with cirrhosis.

Now, my skin had started turning yellow but it was nothing like this guy's. He looked ten times worse than me and how he survived, I will never know. I knew from my jaundice that things were not right but here I was looking at the next stage of my condition, I was looking at me in a few days' or weeks' time, if that long. It terrified me and the timing of this guy coming into the pub also made it seem as though it was meant as a warning to me. It certainly helped me make the final decision to go into hospital.

One thing that had allowed me to keep up the pretence was that I still felt reasonably fit in myself, though I would hardly have described myself as athletic. But all of a sudden, almost overnight, I had no energy whatsoever. I was completely drained and I couldn't do anything. Alex had to dress me, feed me, even take my socks off for me. And all the time, I was suffering this awful stomach pain, literally doubled up with it. My resistance was wearing thin and Alex was stepping up the pressure.

Finally, one day, when I was curled up on the bed like a baby, she told me she was calling an ambulance.

This time, I did not resist.

They took me to the Chelsea and Westminster, which was only round the corner, and they practically had to carry me in. But despite the pain I was in and my dodgy right knee which has never been completely right since my playing days, I wouldn't let them put me in a wheelchair. I wasn't taking the risk of having that picture plastered all over the newspapers the next morning.

The doctors did a lot of tests and also gave me a shot which took away the pain – in hindsight, probably not the best thing to do because I thought I was OK and refused to be admitted. Alex was absolutely furious after the effort she'd put in getting me there. But I thought I would go home and take some time off the booze, as if that was going to make any difference at this stage.

And when I say some time off, it could have been a month, a week, a day, or just a couple of hours.

I certainly could not accept at that stage that my long, and often undistinguished drinking career might be over. But if I was going to have to go dry for a while, then I wanted to suffer the horrors of withdrawal in the privacy of my own home, rather than in a hospital bed gawped at by all sorts of people.

Anyone who only drinks socially will at some time have suffered the familiar symptoms of a hangover, the throbbing head, the nausea and a throat like sawdust. But only an alcoholic knows the real suffering that comes when the hangover is finished and the discomforts of withdrawal kick in; the sweats, the palpitations and the panic. Going cold turkey, the drug addicts call it, and that's as good a description as any, seeing that you spend a lot of time shivering, even if you're in bed under a pile of blankets or sitting by a roaring fire.

I've never had the full DTs with hallucinations of mice running up the curtains, which you see in movies like *The Lost Weekend*. But there have been times when I've stopped and, for a few days, felt like shit, sweating and suffering hot and cold sweats. I've also had the shakes so badly that I've been unable to hold anything. And alcohol is such a weird drug that you know that if you have a drink, the shakes will stop, so you're still fighting temptation even as you're committing yourself to withdrawal.

When I was in the Vesper Hospital in California in the early Eighties, during one of my many failed attempts to give up, I also saw people go through horrendous withdrawals as they tried to come off hard drugs, all sorts of people from 14-year-old kids to 70-year-old grandmothers. They were so bad that the rest of us, who were hardly in a fit state ourselves, used to take it in turns to go into their room and try to help them through it. It was frightening to see them.

This time, the horrors were not that bad, though I spent the whole week in our Chelsea apartment, feeling like death. As well as looking after me, Alex spent the time talking to medical people at the Lister Hospital, who told her that the man I must see was Professor Roger Williams at the Cromwell Hospital, a leading expert in the treatment of cirrhosis. She and Phil made the necessary arrangements and on 8 March 2000, I reported to Professor Williams.

It felt a bit like giving myself up to the police, which I have also done in my time, and it is not being over-dramatic to say that there wasn't a minute to lose. I wasn't due to be admitted at that point, it was supposed to have been an initial consulta-tion, after which the Professor would give me a date to come in. But he didn't even need to examine me. He just looked at my eyes, which were now as yellow as that guy in the pub, and told me, 'You're in.'

I had walked into his office at four o'clock in the afternoon and fifteen minutes later I was in bed in the liver unit, attached to a saline drip.

I just felt enormous relief.

Whereas a week earlier, I had been quite happy to go home from the Chelsea and Westminster and suffer, I'd somehow come to terms with the fact that I had to go through the treatment, whatever it took. And I had already suffered enough at home – I'd taken a hell of a lot. But what I hadn't come to terms with was the fact that I wouldn't be able to drink again. Only an alcoholic can see a silver lining in those circumstances and I managed it. Deep down, I knew I wouldn't be going anywhere for some time but I told myself that I'd be in for a few days, a week at most, and then I'd be well enough to carry on as normal and when I felt like a drink, I would have one.

Having been admitted so quickly, I had not packed any hospital things, so the following day Alex went out and bought me three pairs of pyjamas, all identical – the nursing staff must have thought I never changed them. She also brought in the national newspapers, which were full of my obituaries. The papers had obviously got hold of the story late in the day and not knowing whether my condition was life-threatening or not, they'd decided to cover themselves just in case.

It's a funny feeling reading your own obituaries. But most of the writers were pretty kind and reports of my death gave me hours of entertainment.

I wish I could have said the same about the results of my blood tests, which made for the grimmest of reading. The

Gamma GT score, a liver enzyme which gives the clearest indication of damage, rings bells with the doctors if it's over 80.
Mine was somewhere around the 900 mark and the bilirubin
test, which is the yellow pigment associated with jaundice, was
also totally off the scale.

They have a three number system for the sort of liver
condition I was suffering from – if you are assessed at one,
it means you can expect a full recovery if you stay off drink
for a while; two suggests a normal recovery, whatever that
might be, and three is full-blown cirrhosis. I was teetering
between two and three when I went in, which at least gave
me some hope.

Not that Professor Williams was in the mood to encourage
my fantasies of boozing again. He was brilliantly and brutally
honest, telling me exactly what was wrong and what I'd have
to do. Putting it in layman's terms for me, he explained that my
liver had basically run up the white flag and that just one more
drink could kill me. I quickly became friends with him and his
assistant, Dr Akeel Alisa, and, seeing as I was my own worst
enemy, they were just the sort of friends I needed.

Sometimes, in the middle of the night on my own, the black-
ness came over me and that little voice inside me told me that
this was all a waste of time and that I should discharge myself.
Had it been a couple of years earlier, I would definitely have
listened. I would have got up one night, torn out the drip, got

dressed, walked out of the hospital, jumped on a plane and had done with it.

But I didn't. There was something else that told me that I mustn't give up. I had decided that I wanted to be around for a while and if I had done anything to myself, it would have been incredibly selfish and so hurtful to Alex, to my friend Phil, to my dad, to my son, Calum, to the rest of my family and to all the people who sent goodwill messages. Besides, I would be out soon enough and for all I knew, back to my old ways. Professor Williams had made it clear that I couldn't drink again but I reasoned that doctors and their ilk always paint the blackest picture they can.

Drink is the only opponent I have been unable to beat, even though I've tried Alcoholics Anonymous, abstinence and, on a couple of occasions, having Antabuse pellets sewn into my stomach, which last for three months and make you violently ill if you so much as sip a drop of booze. Even they didn't stop me.

Before the pellets I had tried Antabuse tablets in America, which you take orally and, naturally, I had to test whether they really worked, didn't I? I'd gone on a weekend break to Lake Tahoe for a spot of gambling and on the second night, before dinner, I thought I would try a cocktail, just to see if I could get away with it.

I walked into a casino and ordered a large vodka but before I was halfway through it, my face started to break out in red blotches and I could feel my heart racing at 100 miles an hour.

Another time, I went almost a whole year without booze and then, with the logic only an alcoholic could understand, went out to celebrate and began another bender.

When you are an alcoholic, drink is your whole life. Nothing else matters, as I was to prove when Calum was born in 1981 and to my shame, I was unable to stop even for him. Alex is right when she says that before I went into hospital, I was either drinking or thinking about drinking. But I didn't believe I had a problem because I seemed to be leading a fairly normal life and I was earning a living.

It wasn't like the wild old days when I was out of it for days on end. Even when footballers like Tony Adams and Paul Merson admitted they had problems and sought professional help, I didn't relate my situation to theirs. I really thought I had drink cracked because I was doing hundreds of after-dinner speeches and other public appearances in front of big audiences and never blotting my copy book.

Well, only on the odd occasion.

At times, people sitting next to me at dinners would remark about how little I drank. They seemed almost disappointed and I remember saying to one guy, 'Look, if we were to have a competition, you would come second. I just choose not to drink much tonight.'

That was both the old ego rising up inside me and classic

self-delusion, kidding myself that I could choose to drink or not to. One doctor even told me that drink was like a tap that you could switch on or off. As you can imagine, I was really pleased to hear that from a doctor, though I know now that once I turn on the tap, I leave it running.

Even the consequences of my boozing – and some of those have been pretty catastrophic – had no effect on my desire for it. Drink began to destroy my football career almost as soon as it started.

I was 22 when I won the European Cup with Manchester United in 1968 and was named European Footballer Of The Year. It should have been the start of a glittering career but was really the beginning of the end. Drink was the 'other woman' which caused the breakdown of my first marriage to Angela MacDonald James and, at times, has brought on some madness that has put my marriage to Alex at risk.

Drink also led me to Pentonville Prison in 1984 after a drink-driving offence, which would almost certainly not have led to jail if I hadn't headbutted a policeman.

Worst of all, three months into the new millennium, drink almost claimed my life. Yet when they finally let me out of the Cromwell in the week after Easter, following eight long weeks, I still couldn't say that I would never have another drink. Of course, I said so publicly but to an alcoholic, lying comes as second nature. It was also easy to say so because I didn't fancy a drink after all I had been through.

But as I took my first faltering steps back into the real world, looking and feeling a hundred years old, I couldn't admit to myself that my drinking career was over.

And twelve months on, I still can't.

CHAPTER ONE
RUNNING
UP THE HILL

When my mum died an alcoholic in 1978, it annoyed and upset me that a number of journalists started sniffing into our family background, trying to find this reason or that for why she started drinking and why I drank.

An alcoholic doesn't need a reason to drink, though naturally there were lots of factors involved in my mum's drinking and my own. And as painful as some of them are, I will deal with them as honestly as I can in this book, though I have never liked talking about family matters in public. I certainly didn't appreciate the tabloid press trying to insinuate all sorts of things about my mother at a time when I was trying to come to terms with her death.

Yes, she had her problems, like many other mums trying to bring up six children in post-war Britain. But her drinking problems started much later on, long after I had left home. It was tougher for my brothers and sisters but my memories of her as a child are only happy ones.

She was a fantastic mum and growing up was brilliant, it really was. We never had much money but then nor did anyone else on the Cregagh Estate in Belfast, where we moved when I was three and where my dad, Dickie, still lives in our old family home on Burren Way. I was born on 22 May 1946, when everyone was trying to get back on their feet after the war and rationing meant that even the most basic foods were in short supply.

Like most kids then, I spent a lot of time with my grand-parents because both parents had to work to make ends meet. My dad worked shifts on an iron turner's lathe at the Harland and Wolff shipyard, so you never knew when he would be home. Mum worked for a time at Gallagher's tobacco factory, where a lot of my friends' mums also worked. Then she began at an ice-cream factory, which helped develop my love for the stuff, though really I should have eaten enough to turn me off for life because I would walk in whenever I felt like it and pick one off the production line. In Belfast slang, we talked of a poke and a slider – a cone and a wafer in anyone else's language. The family's part-time jobs kept me in treats because one of my aunts worked in a chippy and another worked in a sweet shop.

Literally as soon as I could walk, I had a ball at my feet. One of the first photographs taken of me was outside my granny and grandad Withers's house when I was about 13 months old, with a ball at my feet. It didn't really matter what sort of ball it was – plastic, a tennis ball, anything I could kick around. Sometimes, I would even take a ball to bed with me.

When I started at Nettlefield Primary School, which was close to my granny Withers, I would dash back at lunchtime for a slice of toast and a cup of tea and five minutes later I was back in the school yard, kicking a ball around. It was the same after school. And the bread was only toasted on one side because they used a little electric fire and as soon as one side was done, they would switch it off to save electricity.

Years later, Mrs Fullaway, my landlady at Manchester United, gave me a worried look one day.

'I do butter your bread on the right side don't I?' she asked. 'The toasted side?'

With mum and dad both working, I didn't see them until the evening, when they would often have friends over to play cards, which was what people did before television came along. I would sit and watch them for ages. I had no understanding of how the games were played but I was just fascinated by the cards themselves, the colour of them and the slightly scary picture cards. I would watch for hours until I fell asleep, when mum would excuse herself from the card table for a few minutes while she carried me up to bed.

I would always wake up when she got me upstairs, though, and after a bit of pleading, she would let me come down for another twenty minutes. She was a beautiful-looking woman, my mum, too, though she was also the tough one of my parents. My dad was so easy-going, he would not have dreamed of laying a finger on me. My mum was very quiet, too, though if I stepped out of line, she would give me what she called a good skelping, which is a slapping across the back of the legs.

I was so skinny that she would hurt herself more than me because I was all bone. And she had to catch me first because when I knew a skelping was coming, I'd run upstairs and crawl under the bed and roll up into a little ball so that she couldn't get me.

My sister Carol was born only a year after me and five years later, Barbara came along. I was always close to Carol, I suppose because there is only 17 months difference in our ages. She didn't share my love of football, it wasn't really a girls' thing then. But we used to fool around a lot together in the house, having mock fights, a lot of pushing and shoving, the normal brother and sister thing.

One day, though, it got a bit too boisterous and she hit me right in the solar plexus. It was a punch Lennox Lewis would have been proud of and for a minute or two, I couldn't breathe. She was absolutely terrified and convinced that she had killed me. She still talks about that incident today.

Carol has followed in Grandad Withers's footsteps as the religious one in the family and as its head, if you want to put it like that. When my mother died, she took it upon herself to look after my dad, cleaning the house and cooking for him. And if anyone in the family has any problems, it's Carol they call. She just seems to have this spiritual thing, this peace of mind, and you will never hear her say a bad word about anyone. She lives just down the road from me now so we're always popping in and out of each other's houses and we're probably closer than we've ever been.

My other grandad, James 'Scottie' Best, lived right beside the Glentoran football ground, The Oval. Now growing up in those days, even football support was divided on sectarian grounds, I suppose it still is, really. If you were a Protestant, you automatically supported Linfield and if you were a Catholic you supported Glentoran, or the Glens as we called them. Our family were Protestant, Free Presbyterians to be exact, but because Grandad Best lived next to the Glens' ground, I supported them.

Almost every week I would go with my dad or grandad or some friends and stand by the Oval entrance. That's what you did then, you stood by a turnstile and waited for an adult to come along and lift you over. They got pretty big crowds because everyone had been starved of sport during the war, and the adults would pass us kids over their heads like a human conveyor belt until we got to the front. I didn't have any trouble with the religious bit because nobody wore scarves and we were forty years away from the replica shirt craze. The most you might wear was a club rosette.

My mum and dad were never that religious but Grandad Withers was and out of respect for him, we all went to church on Sunday. The grown-ups went to the morning service and we kids went to afternoon Sunday school, which I enjoyed. I liked the singing and reading the bible and, even now, I still pray at times. When I was first at Manchester United, I actually used to kneel by my bed at night and say my prayers. After church, we all had Sunday tea together, the whole family. It would be salads and spuds and Granny Withers's home-made cakes.

After potatoes, cakes were the staple diet of all our families. My mother's speciality was apple tarts, though at Halloween she used to make these delicious candy apples. When I moved back to Ireland, I asked Carol to give the recipe to Alex, but she hasn't made any yet. My mother just never stopped because she had to fit in all the jobs of a housewife around her work. Sometimes, she wouldn't get home until ten at night, when we'd all be in bed of course. But we would hear her cleaning the windows. We had those big brass handles on the outside and she would be leaning out of the window with a duster and a tin of Brasso at ten o'clock, cleaning them.

If it was a hot summer and they were extra busy at the ice-cream factory, she would have to work on a Sunday, which didn't really meet with Grandad Withers' approval. On those days, my dad would make her a chicken pie, which was one of her favourite dishes, and then he'd heat it and wrap it up really tight so that it would stay warm, and he'd cycle off to the creamery to deliver her lunch. It saw a lot of service, that bike. When their shifts overlapped, mum would take the bike to work in the daytime and when she came home, dad would pedal off to the shipyard for the night shift.

In the school holidays, we would visit Granny Withers's summer cottage in Crossgar, which is on the other side of the Strangford Lough, close to where Alex and I live now. My uncle George Withers, who was a year younger than me, used to come, so he and I and my cousin Louis, who is my mum's sister's boy, were just like three lads together. There was an old barn at the back of Granny's house and we would go round there, the three of us and beat lumps out of each other. We grandly called them boxing matches but they were basically free-for-alls. There was a steep hill that ran down from the house to the main road and I loved running down that at full pelt and I would also run up it, though a little more slowly.

There was no electricity and no oil lamps, the lights were all gas and we had a big stove which kept the place warm. But it was a great life down there. We would get up before the sun and bring in the cows for milking and then collect the fresh eggs, a luxury after the privations of Belfast. We'd help to bale the hay, as well – proper little country boys we were – and the local farmer had a donkey in a field which we used to jump on and ride around. By the end of the day, we were absolutely knackered but also famished.

Our evening meal was a plate of spuds, supplemented by granny's home-made bread and cakes. That was Ireland then – spuds were everyone's staple diet, they were all people could afford. At least there were plenty of them and we had competitions to see who could eat the most. I believe I still hold the record with 23.

I don't remember ever getting any official pocket money but I had my own methods of obtaining some illicitly to keep myself in sweet money. My mum used to collect sixpences, or tanners, in an old milk bottle which she hid under the sink and the coins were slightly too big to go in so she would file the inside of the bottle top until they just fitted. I don't know how she planned to get them out, maybe she was going to break the bottle, but after a bit of practice, I devised a way of fiddling them out. I would only take one at a time, mind, in case she cottoned on, and in any case, a sixpence lasted you for ever at that age.

I was a right little villain, though it all seemed pretty innocent at the time. But I always liked to plan things. In the local shop, they sold biscuits in those big glass jars and just before they closed, they would give you the broken ones, the ones they couldn't sell, in a little paper bag, a sweetie bag they called it. So my mates and I would go in five minutes before closing, pretend to look around and break the biscuits ourselves. And on the way home, we used to pass a big house with a huge apple tree hanging over the wall so we'd pinch a couple of those to eat with our biscuits. Or, at night, we would call in at the local chippy, Eddie Spencer, which is still going, funnily enough, and he would give us the scrapings from the fryer.

I started collecting stamps at that time and if I didn't have any money, I would steal them from Woolworths. Again, I had a plan, picking up six or seven packets to look at and then deliberately dropping them on the floor.

The shopkeeper would start to come over but I'd say, 'It's OK, I'll pick them up,' only I would put just four or five packets back. Of course, they didn't have security cameras then so you didn't have to be a criminal mastermind to get away with such scams.

I also helped out a man who drove around in a van selling fruit and vegetables, for which I earned a few coppers and, on a Friday night I collected the paper money from the people who had their newspapers delivered from the local shop. This also turned out to be lucrative, since people would often give me 15 pence to settle a 14 pence bill. I would pretend to fumble in my pocket for the penny change and then say, 'Sorry, I haven't got it. I'll give it to you next week.'

But I never did and 99 times out of a hundred, people would forget to ask. If I could do that to 20 people, by the end of the night I had 20 pence, which was just over three sixpences. And if someone didn't ask for a receipt, I could pocket 20 pence in one go. How I didn't get caught, I'll never know.

In summer, I would spend my ill-gotten gains at the local funfair. It was one of the highlights of our year when it rolled into town and set up just off the Cregagh Road, in a lovely place called Dallywinkers Lane. Of course, a kid's money doesn't go far at an exciting place like a funfair so when our cash ran out, which was after a few minutes, we had another fiddle going. I loved playing on the hoopla stalls because you could win a prize and we decided to work the odds in our favour by taking along a big stick with a hook on it. Then, while some of us created a diversion, the others would have a few seconds to try to hook something for themselves.

Through the magic of television, I fell in love with another football team. Wolverhampton Wanderers.

After they won the League Championship in 1954, Wolves took on some of the world's top clubs in floodlight matches at their Molineux ground. There were no official European competitions then so these were more than just friendlies. They were Britain against the rest of the world and they were taken so seriously that they were televised live, which was unheard of for games outside internationals. What's more, they were midweek games played under floodlights, which were still a novelty. Though a crude form of floodlighting existed back in 1878, the modern version only started in the 1951–52 season and was still a rarity when I began watching Wolves, the first team outside Northern Ireland that I was able to watch live on television. It was love at first sight.

We didn't have a telly ourselves so when I knew there was a game on, I would go and kick a ball on the wall outside my neighbour's house about ten minutes before kick-off. He was a man called Mr Harrison and, naturally, he would hear me kicking the ball against his wall. He also knew I was a football nut. But he would let me sweat until just before the game started and would then open the door and say casually, as though the idea had just come to him, 'Do you fancy coming in and watching the game with me?'

I was in his house like a shot but the next time Wolves were on television, we would play out the whole charade again.

Mr Harrison only had a small black and white set and TV crews then probably only used one camera, as opposed to the hundred or so they have today. But when Wolves played sides like Moscow Spartak and Moscow Dynamo, it was as though they were playing against aliens. As far as we were concerned, the Russians were bogeymen, they could have come from another planet. And yet here they were playing against Wolves on television.

I was mesmerised by those games. The football was fantastic and there were 55,000 fans locked inside Molineux for every one of them. But it was the floodlights which made them magical for me, made football into theatre. I had already begun a scrapbook on Glentoran, in which I pasted all the match reports from the *Belfast Telegraph*. Now, I turned the book upside down and in the back, I began pasting in reports of Wolves.

I also dreamed of wearing their famous gold shirt, though we had to imagine how those shirts really looked. On Mr Harrison's black and white TV, they could have been pale blue, or light green or even boring old white.

Apart from not being able to watch the football whenever I wanted, I didn't really miss TV because we had the local cinema, which was packed out for the Saturday afternoon matinees. Fortunately, there was a glass shortage at the time, so they would let you in for free if you turned up with a jam jar. And if my pals and I couldn't rustle up enough jars, one of us would go in and slip open the side door for the others.

The shows then were just magical, stuff like *Hopalong Cassidy* and *Quatermass and the Pit*. Epics were also all the rage and the first feature film I saw was *Shane*, starring Alan Ladd. Then I saw *The Robe*, another epic with Victor Mature, and *Spartacus*, which starred Kirk Douglas. I remember reading that the movie cost $12 million to make and employed over 10,000 people, which seemed staggering at the time. *Zorro* was a big favourite as well and when we came out of the cinema, we would fasten our macs around our necks and run home pretending to be him. We also had yo-yo competitions on the stage.

On some Saturdays, I would watch my mum playing hockey, and I would dribble a tennis ball along the touchline during the match. But I never went to see my dad play football, though I know he was a full back and everyone told me he was a dirty little so-and-so. He had no fear whatsoever, that's what they said about him.

There were plenty of hard men from the shipyards and they had a summer football tournament in Belfast at a place called the chicken run. They played so many games on it that there wasn't a blade of grass left and all the players had nicknames. I remember there was one player who only had one arm, though luckily, I don't think he was a goalkeeper. And I remember a guy called Sticky Sloan, he was one of the local heroes. He could play a bit but he was as hard as nails like most of the players. If you didn't get smacked four or five times in a game, you were a big softy.

Sunday morning football didn't exist then, because it was a day for religion and even when Grandad Withers got a telly, we weren't allowed to watch programmes on a Sunday. Of course, when he went up for his afternoon nap, we kids would turn it on low and we would take it in turns to sit on the bottom of the stairs in case he woke up. We thought we were being so clever but I'm sure he knew what was going on because when he got up, he would walk past the telly and touch it, to see if it was warm.

My life at that time seemed idyllic, but as I approached my eleventh birthday, it was all about to change.

I was right in the middle of my Eleven Plus exams. One afternoon I popped into a local shop to buy a ruler for my maths test and the shopkeeper said something very odd. She asked me when my grandfather was getting married.

I looked at her like she was nuts but I must have had my mind on the exam and not heard her properly. It was only when I got home and saw Mum and Dad's faces that I realised that what she had really said was 'buried'. It was a shattering experience for me because I was so close to Grandad George, whom I was named after, and I knew that I was always his favourite.

You never think your parents or grandparents will die, not at that age. They've always been there and you think they'll be there forever. I couldn't understand it and, as I was to do for the rest of my life, I tried to walk away and pretend it wasn't happening. I just walked and walked the streets for hours, tears streaming down my face, until I got too tired and had to sit down. My parents, who had gone spare with worry, found me sitting under a lamppost in the pouring rain at one in the morning.

When someone dies in Northern Ireland, all the family get together and the coffin is left open for everyone to pay their last respects. But on the day of the funeral, only the men go to the graveside, and then to the pub afterwards, while the women stay behind and get the food ready. I didn't look at my grandfather's coffin, I didn't want to see a cold corpse, not when I remembered him as such a warm, lovely man. I couldn't look at my mum after she died, either. I've never seen a dead body and I've really no desire to.

Despite the sadness of my grandad's death I managed to pass the Eleven Plus and my parents were delighted. I was the only one in my class to do so. Me passing was a big thing for Mum and Dad, even though it meant more expense for them, buying school uniform and shoes. Shoes were the biggest outlay for them because with the time I spent kicking a ball about, I must have gone through a pair every fortnight. Like everyone's mum and dad, they warned me not to kick a ball in my 'best' shoes, but like every other kid, I carried on doing it anyway.

So while all my mates went to the local secondary modern school, Lisnasharragh Secondary Modern, I had to travel on my own to Grosvenor High Protestant School, which was two bus rides away.

Things there started going wrong from the start. It wasn't that I couldn't do the work. I was a bright kid and particularly good at maths and English. But I didn't like the journey to school, I didn't like the other kids and I didn't really try that hard to make friends because all my pals still lived on the Cregagh Estate and I would rush home at night to play with them.

The problem with Grosvenor High was that the school sport was rugby, which I had no alternative but to play. I was pretty good, too, and because of my size and quickness, I turned myself into a pretty decent fly half. But rugby could never produce the sort of passion inside me that watching Wolves and those Russians did.

The lack of football was just another reason for my not settling in the school and it wasn't long before I began mitching, as we called it, or playing truant. At times, I would stay away altogether and spend my bus money on sweets but mostly I'd hide in the school toilets as the kids went back to their classes after lunch and then I'd climb over the roof and come home. My aunt Margaret worked all day, so I would hide my bag behind her dustbin and walk around Woolworths and the other shops for the rest of the afternoon.

If I got fed up with that and wanted to go home, I would buy these sweets which, if you sucked them hard enough, would make your throat go red.

'What's the matter? What are you doing home at this time?' Mum would say when I knocked on our door.

'They've sent me home with a sore throat,' I'd say.

'Let's have a look at you,' she'd reply.

I would open my mouth.

'That looks nasty, we'll have to get you to a doctor,' Mum would decide.

The next day I would say I was better, but it backfired on

me in the end because Mum and Dad got so fed up with this recurring red throat that they made me have my tonsils out and I couldn't protest because it would have given the game away.

Truancy was just another way of running away from problems and I always did it on my own. I have always been like that and in later years, when fame became too much, I would go to Manchester Airport and get the first plane out to wherever it was going. It's an instinctive thing, kidding yourself that when you get back, the problem will have gone, though you know that nine times out of ten, it will be worse.

Naturally, I couldn't go on playing truant without the school doing something about it. I knew this something would involve a lot of heartache for my mum and dad and they were devastated when they were called in to see the headmaster. They had no idea what had been going on and they were the sort of people who would have been totally ashamed to be summoned like that.

The school gave me a choice. Either I could drop down a grade or leave. Now I was in the highest grade and it would have been humiliating to drop down but I didn't want to disappoint my mum and dad by leaving so I said I would do it. My heart wasn't in it, though, and about a month later, I told the school that I wanted to leave after all and I joined all my pals at Lisnasharragh.

The first day I went there, the boys were in the corner

picking a school football team and asked me if I wanted to play.

Immediately, I felt like I belonged.

The other reason I had been so unhappy was that Grosvenor High School was in the middle of a Catholic area and the kids from the other schools, like the Sacred Heart and places like that, knew from my uniform that I was Protestant. They used to wait for me and call me a Proddy bastard and try to steal my scarf or cap so that in the end I would wait down the road from the bus stop and time my run to perfection so that I could reach the bus and jump on to the platform just as it was taking off. It was like running the gauntlet. It wasn't very nice but it turned out to be good sprint training for my football. Knowing this had been happening to me had also made it easier for my parents to agree to me leaving.

Religion has never bothered me and there is no way you could ever call my family bigots. But if you were a Protestant, you joined the Orange Order, as I did, and my dad and grandad both had spells as master of our local lodge.

12 July, the anniversary of the Battle of the Boyne, was a big day in our house and all the family would turn out for the parade. The meeting point for many of the marchers would be the master of the lodge's house and I remember how excited we all were when my dad was the master and all these people started gathering in our street.

It was such a colourful and noisy scene, everyone there in their sashes and finery and the pipers and drummers warming up. I know it is a sectarian festival but the Troubles hadn't taken such a violent hold then and, to us, it was just pipes and drums and cakes. And fun. The whole thing was just a carnival. After everyone had arrived at my dad's house, we walked up to the town centre to meet the other lodges and they were coming from all directions, thousands of people, from all over the world, from Australia, New Zealand and America. And they all had their own bands. It was like Mardi Gras.

It was a day out and the whole spectacle was fascinating. As a kid, your first honour on 12 July was the Holding of the Strings – holding the strings that trail from those great banners. So as the men marched with them up the Cregagh Road, we kids would be hanging on to the strings, though on windy days you could have been blown all the way to Finaghy, seven miles away, which is where all the lodges met up.

We used to get a few taunts from the Catholics, calling us Proddy bastards and we would call them Fenians. But that's all it was in my day, just mud-slinging. It was a bit like being a member of the Rotary Club or the Freemasons. It was later that both sides began killing each other and the marches came to be seen as provocation, which I'm prepared to admit they are really.

Funnily enough, given my high profile, I have never been approached by any of the Protestant political groups. They probably knew that they would have been wasting their time because I would never have got involved. The only time the Troubles came close to me personally was when I was in Ford Open prison and some lunatics wrote to me, saying they were going to spring me. They wouldn't have needed to do much springing since Ford was like a holiday camp and if I had really wanted to get out, I could have simply walked through the open gate!

But I would never have put my family under the pressure of going about with some paramilitary group or whatever they were. Creed and colour have never been an issue for me. I just believe in each to his own, unless that involves hurting someone else, which is wrong whichever religion or political dogma you believe in.

On a personal level, the problems I'd had with the Catholic boys ended when I began at Lisnasharragh School. It was also there, when I was about 13 or 14, that I first became interested in girls. But considering the reputation I was going to get later as a Lothario, my career didn't get off to the best of starts. I was pretty shy around girls but there was one girl at the school who was known as the local bike so she seemed the obvious one to go for. Yet despite her reputation, I seemed to be the only one who couldn't shag her and believe me, it wasn't for the want of trying.

So eventually, I started going out with another girl called Liz, a much prettier girl but one who didn't put it about. Again,

not for the want of trying on my behalf and that was probably
the start of it, that thing of me wanting something I couldn't
have. Liz and I did get it on eventually and, in between times,
there was a lot of what used to be known as heavy petting in
all the usual places, behind the bike sheds or the youth club or
in the back row of the cinema.

I didn't have any particular trouble with the teachers at
Lisnasharragh, except for one – a music teacher by the name of
Tommy Steele, would you believe? He had bright red hair and
was always sneaking up behind me and if I did anything
wrong, he would sometimes smack my knuckles with a ruler.
I hated music lessons when I was a kid and I doubt that the real
Tommy Steele could have changed my mind. I was supposed
to be learning the piano and they would give you these paper
black and white notes to take home to help you learn. But as
soon as I got home, all I wanted to do was kick a ball around.
No one I knew played the piano.

Things were developing much faster on the football front,
now that I was able to play at school. And at about the same
time as I had been trying to get to grips with the local bike, I
began playing for Cregagh Boys Club, which was run by Bud
McFarlane, Glentoran's reserve team coach.

Up until then, I had always played in slippers, or trainers
as they would be called now, though in the vocabulary of our
little world, they were gutties. Proper football boots were far
too expensive, though every Christmas I got shirt, shorts and

socks. The Christmas after I signed for Cregagh, however, I tore the wrapping off the present from my parents and found myself looking at a shiny new pair of leather boots with steel toe caps and high sides that came up past your ankles, which is how they wore them then. To me they were absolutely beautiful. If you were tackled by a pair of those today, you would be out injured for a season. But they were the best present I ever had and I would spend ages cleaning them and rubbing dubbin into them to protect the leather before I played.

Those boots were indestructible and to prove it, I've still got them. They probably only cost about 2s 6d but today they must be worth about £50,000, not just because they were my first boots but because I developed this habit, after games, of using a piece of whiting to write down the name of opponents on the sides of them, plus the number of goals I scored against them.

Bud McFarlane was the first one to really encourage me and tell me I could make it as a professional. My dad, though I wasn't aware of it at the time, deliberately didn't try to push me in case it had a negative effect and, for the same reason, he rarely came to the games. Although I was starting to show a lot of talent, many of the old pros often used to say that I was too skinny and too small to make it.

That's where Bud was such a help, believing, like Sir Matt Busby, that if you were good enough, you were both big enough and old enough. My big chance came when I played for Cregagh Boys in a match against Northern Ireland schoolboys' probables. I played really well in a 2–1 win and after being called up into the possibles squad where again I was able to prove myself, I was delighted to be picked in the final 16 for the end of season schoolboys international. Unfortunately they decided to take only 15 players and I was the one left out.

I was absolutely devastated.

As I approached my 15th birthday and the end of my school life, I still didn't know whether I would make it as a footballer and that experience with the schoolboy side didn't exactly boost my confidence. Perhaps I *was* too small, though Bud wasn't giving up. He had a word with Bob Bishop, who ran the Boyland Youth Club, which was the biggest boys' club as far as football was concerned. They were always the best and had already become almost a nursery club for Manchester United. They had become so successful that – luckily for me as it turned out – Bishop had just been appointed United's chief scout in Northern Ireland.

He took me along to a couple of Boyland's weekend training camps and then arranged a match between Boyland and Cregagh Under-15s, packing his own side with players of 17 and 18, men really, compared to us. It was quite a clever idea because they wanted to see if I could handle the physical side, see if I could perform against bigger and more experienced players. If I could, then they would know that my size was not a handicap. I didn't know that the game had been specially arranged for me and I just went out and played in my normal way, notching another two goals on the side of my boots as we won 4–2.

I hadn't actually met Bob Bishop formally at that point. I'd just been one of the lads in those weekend get-togethers. A few days later, however, he turned up at our house. I was kicking a ball around in a field with my mates when my dad called me in and introduced me to Bob. Then, as calmly as he could, he asked me if I wanted to go over to Manchester United for a trial with another lad called Eric McMordie.

Did I?

I ran back up the field and shouted to the other lads, 'I'm going to play for Manchester United.'

They just went, yeah, yeah, sure you are and we carried on with our kickabout.

Of course, I was absolutely delighted and so was my dad. But good old Dad, though he had always believed in my talent, he also knew that things don't always go the way you expect them to in life and in his cautious way, he had decided to keep my options open for me.

So in the final year of school, he had arranged for me to take a course in printing. English and maths were my best subjects in school and he thought that printing would be a good profession to utilise those skills. Plus, he figured that people would always read newspapers and books. I had passed my final printing exam just before Bob Bishop called – and my dad had already lined me up with a job.

Of course, given a choice between printing and playing for Manchester United, there was none to be made. But my dad's choice of an alternative career does seem quite ironic when you consider how many printers I have kept in business ever since!

CHAPTER TWO
DUTCH
COURAGE

As you can imagine, I couldn't wait to get to Manchester United. Wolves might have been the team I supported and dreamed about playing for, but United were a glamorous club and the Munich air crash on 6 February 1958, in which eight of their top players died, had brought them an enormous amount of interest and public sympathy.

The crash had happened in the middle of the afternoon and I remember people talking about it as I came home from school on the bus. I then turned on the radio when I got home and heard all the details. The whole thing had such an air of unreality about it because for most normal people then, flying was a fantasy in itself and Manchester United were the first English team to play in the European Cup. United were on their way home from a 3–3 draw with Red Star Belgrade when their plane stopped in Munich to refuel in snowy conditions and after two aborted takeoffs, it failed to get off the runway a third time and caught fire after crashing through a perimeter fence of the airport.

What made the tragedy even more poignant was that many of the players were so young. When United won the title in 1955–56, the combined ages were so young that the team were christened the Busby Babes after manager Matt Busby. Among those who died was half back Eddie Colman, 21, a local lad whose devastating body swerves earned him the nickname of 'snake hips', and Liam Whelan, 22, who shared the inside right position with Bobby Charlton and didn't even get to play in Belgrade.

But the absolute star of that side was Duncan Edwards, who had the attributes to play in just about any position. He had size, speed, power, was good in the air and was tipped to become the greatest England player of all time. He made his first team debut for United at just 16 years of age and after playing for England at youth level, B level and in the Under-23s, made his full international debut at just 18.

Walter Winterbottom, the England manager, said, 'In the character and spirit of Duncan Edwards, I saw the true revival of British football.' He was just 21 when he died, having already played 15 times for his country and he even astonished doctors in the Munich hospital by hanging on to his fight for life for 15 days after the crash. Had he lived and continued to progress as a player, he would almost certainly have been the man leading out England in the 1966 World Cup, rather than Bobby Moore.

It seemed unbelievable that I was now going to be sharing a training pitch with legends like Bobby Charlton and Harry Gregg, who both survived the crash. Harry was also one of its heroes, climbing back into the plane to drag out survivors until the flames made it impossible. I was in awe of such men, who had become household names – not that I expected ever to play alongside them.

Despite all the encouragement I had received from Bud McFarlane, I was still a shy, insecure kid and though I would later have to learn to be a bit more outgoing, I don't think I ever really changed. I didn't believe I could make it in the big time and neither did Eric McMordie. I knew I could play a bit and that I was much better than some of my rivals in Belfast. But there was a world of difference between knocking the ball past some of my teenage mates and doing the same thing against top international players.

United had offered us a two weeks' trial in order to have a look at us and we believed that after that, they would pack us off home again. We didn't think we were setting off on a glittering new career and a new life when we boarded that boat. We were just determined to make the most of a lucky break which had already earned us the envy of all our friends.

Neither of us had been outside Northern Ireland before and had hardly travelled beyond Belfast. So going on a boat to England was a big adventure and my mum, perhaps wanting me to look less like a little boy lost, scraped together the money to buy me my first pair of long trousers for the journey in July 1961. Maybe she raided the sixpences jar.

I had never even met Eric until he turned up at our house, as arranged, with his parents and we all set off for the docks. My mum was a bit tearful as we got on the boat and issued all the normal motherly instructions to behave myself and to make sure that I phoned as soon as I arrived so that she would know that I was safe.

I'm surprised Mum even trusted me to get on the boat when she and Dad received the instructions from United. You would have thought the club would have sent someone to Liverpool docks to meet us but instead, they had told us to get a cab to Lime Street station and catch a train to Manchester. We weren't sure whether someone was supposed to be waiting for us at the station in Manchester but when we didn't see anyone, we caught a cab to the ground.

We had become a bit emboldened as the day went on and felt like a right couple of big shots when we hopped into the back of a cab at the station in Manchester and told the driver to take us to Old Trafford. But he soon deflated us by asking, 'Which Old Trafford?'

As a couple of kids from Belfast, we hardly knew what

cricket was and we certainly didn't know there was a cricket ground with the same name as Manchester United's. The boat had docked early in the morning, so by the time we got to the right Old Trafford, the players had already begun training. The club's chief scout, Joe Armstrong, took us out there, a place in Urmston, which the club used before moving to The Cliff, where they trained until moving to their fantastic new site a couple of years ago.

After Belfast, everything in Liverpool and Manchester seemed on such a grander scale. Everything seemed so much bigger and, as we discovered when we got to the training ground, this included the people. Joe was a lovely, thoughtful man who was used to dealing with impressionable, overawed young kids and he thought it would ease our nerves if he introduced us to the Irish lads like Gregg, Jimmy Nicholson and Ronnie Briggs, another 'keeper. Unfortunately it had the opposite effect, the size of everyone frightening the life out of me and Eric, especially Harry Gregg. He was six feet tall, which was massive then, and rock solid, built like a brick outhouse.

As if that wasn't bad enough, Joe also introduced us to the junior players, whom I would at least have expected to be our size. But they were a couple of years older than us and had spent those years training and building up their bodies so even they seemed enormous. I'd suffered all those jibes about being too small to make it and now I was confronted by the evidence and I suddenly felt very frightened and a long way from home.

I'd grown up dreaming about coming to England and playing for a big club. But when I was in Belfast, that was just a fantasy which many of us shared. Now I was in the middle of the reality and as in so often the case, it was a lot different to the dream. When you're a kid using your imagination, you just see yourself scoring the winning goal at Wembley and a 100,000 fans cheering you. You don't imagine all the stuff that goes before it, like standing on a cold training pitch with knocking knees as you're introduced to all these big men who were household names.

We also met Matt Busby, who I probably would not even have known was United's manager but for the coverage of the Munich disaster. Busby's chest was crushed in the crash and he was not expected to live. He actually received the last rites twice and was in a critical condition for days. When, miraculously, he recovered, few people expected him to carry on as manager but he went with his depleted side to the FA Cup Final that year in 1958, where they lost to Bolton. His stature in the game was enormous after that so you can imagine how I felt, a 15-year-old trialist from Belfast, when I shook his hand. It was like being introduced to God. Even then, he had that dignified way about him, a military sort of bearing, though with a manner of wanting to make you feel at home. He made some crack about me being the boy he'd heard so much about and said, 'Good luck to you, son.'

After training, we were taken to our digs, Mrs

Fullaway's council house in Chorlton, which was another shock. Our room was nice enough but it wasn't home and trying to deal with another change in circumstances was probably too much for us. In one day, we'd already travelled on a boat and an English train for the first time and met all these star footballers. Now we were sitting down to a meal with a strange woman in a city that was a mystery to us too. Also, we'd hardly had any sleep since leaving Belfast because we were so excited being on the boat that we'd stayed up most of the night.

So after our tea, we went to our room and locked ourselves in. I don't know why we locked the door, we were hardly going to be attacked by anyone but it just made us feel a little more secure after our day of surprises. There was no TV to watch, no radio to listen to so we just sat on our beds, both feeling overawed by everything. As we didn't even know each other, we didn't talk that much, either. I guess we were both just going through the events of our day in our heads.

If we had been good mates, I'm sure we would have started making jokes about all the things that had happened and encouraged each other that it would work out. But we hardly said a word to one another.

'What do you think?' I said to Eric after a bit, maybe just to get a reaction. 'Do you think you're going to like it here?'

'I don't know. What do you think?'

If he'd said something positive, it might have given both

of us a lift but we were both completely overwhelmed by everything. So much had happened in such a short time.

'Do you fancy going home then?' I said, more out of bravado than anything.

'Yes, let's go back in the morning,' he replied.

I'd probably expected him to say no and if he had, we might have laughed it all off. But the fact that we were strangers even to each other had just added to the frightening nature of it all.

So the die was cast. We were two different people trying to come to terms with all these changes of circumstance in our own way and weren't much support for each other. Like me, Eric had only ever travelled as far out of Belfast as Bangor for family holidays. So instead of talking each other out of going home, as mates might have done, we talked each other into it.

After spending an uncomfortable night in a strange room in this, to us, strange and daunting city of Manchester, we were absolutely sure of our decision.

It seemed to embolden us, too, since it wasn't easy telling Joe Armstrong that we had decided to return to Ireland. We certainly didn't call and tell our parents and on the boat back to Belfast, I began to feel very guilty. I had started off determined to see at least the two weeks out and I felt that I had let down Mum and Dad. I'd built up their hopes and they had been so proud, telling all the neighbours that their lad was going to Manchester United. And here I was back after a couple of days.

Eric and I only had a few pence left when we arrived at the docks, just enough to catch a bus home. It was still early morning when I knocked on the door of Burren Way and Mum opened it. Her mouth just dropped open, probably thinking that there had been a bombing or something, and I remember Dad running out past her and saying, 'What are you doing back? What's happened? What did you do?'

Now that I was back, I felt almost as silly as I had when I arrived in Manchester and I wasn't in the mood for talking.

'Nothing, dad,' I said. 'We just didn't like it there.'

'What do you mean you didn't like it?' he said. 'You've only been gone a day. What's happened?'

'Let the lad be,' Mum said to him, more concerned about my bedraggled look, and then turning to me she added, 'Come on, I'll get you something to eat.'

We had some tea and toast, by which time it was late enough in the day for the United coaching staff to have reported for training and my dad went straight out to the local phone box and called the club reverse charges, as he had been told he could.

He was quickly put through to Joe Armstrong. Joe was the top man when it came to dealing with young players and had so much experience with them that he was totally unfazed by what had happened.

'They're not the first to run off and they won't be the last,' he told Dad. 'It's quite normal for lads to get a bit homesick. It can be a bit daunting when they leave home for the first time, though they normally last a bit longer than 24 hours before running away. But your son is welcome back anytime, Mr Best. Let me know when he's ready.'

Dad was relieved to discover that I hadn't committed some heinous crime. But he let me brood on things for a bit. Dad was never one to try to order me about and Mum certainly wasn't going to tell me to go back. This was one decision she was prepared to leave to Dad and me.

'You know, no one thinks you've done anything wrong,' Dad said to me a day or two later, having given me a little time to think about it. 'You were just homesick. But would you like to give it another go?'

When I said I would, he hinted that the club were talking about me going back at Christmas.

'No, Dad, I want to go now,' I said.

I still didn't think it would be for more than a couple of weeks but I was determined to give it a go, both for the sake of my parents and for myself. I felt really silly by this time, wondering what on earth I had been worried about, and was determined to give it another shot.

Dad got the OK from United and two weeks later, he and Mum were waving me off on the boat again – on my own this time.

Things didn't seem quite so daunting in Manchester the second time round and there was no danger of being taken to the wrong Old Trafford. The young players at the club didn't seem such giants, either, just normal lads like me, and I quickly became great pals with John Fitzpatrick, Jimmy Ryan and Peter McBride. They were in the same boat as me, so to speak, all new to big-time football, new to a big city like Manchester, not quite sure what to expect and all a little homesick.

Even so, I wondered whether I had made the right decision in coming back when I discovered that I would not be training every day, like everyone else, as I had imagined. The Scottish and Irish Football Associations had been complaining for years about English clubs poaching their best young players so to discourage this, they put pressure on the FA in England, who decreed that no one from those countries could sign apprentice forms for a League club. So I would have to get a job and train with the amateurs on Tuesday and Thursday nights.

I couldn't believe it. I had come to England to be a professional footballer and I was to get less chance to kick a ball around than if I'd stayed at home.

I would also have been having more fun at home since the first job the club found me was at the Manchester Ship Canal, where I was basically a tea-boy and general gofer, running errands for all sorts of people. I really hated it, though it might not have been so bad if the club had said anything about keeping me on, about what sort of future they thought I had. The two-week trial period ended and I just carried on training, without anybody saying whether I'd be staying for another month, another two months, or whatever. It was really confusing for me, not knowing whether the club wanted me as a player or not and whether they just saw me as cheap labour for the local companies.

Everything was so different from Belfast, the pace of life seemed so much faster and I didn't know what to think. But after a few weeks, I thought that I'd rather go home than carry on the way I was so I told the club that I'd had enough of my tea-boy career.

I didn't know whether they would send me straight back home for my cheek but by then I didn't care. I was miserable with the way things were going and couldn't understand why I was being forced to do such menial tasks when they had brought me over from Ireland to be a footballer. After my complaints, the shipping company moved me to another office at the Canal but it was basically the same job, wasting my time all day, so I complained again. The club then told me to report to a timber yard where, instead of making tea all day, I was put to work stacking wood all day. Well, up to lunchtime on my first morning, anyway, when I told the boss I was handing in my notice.

I told the club that I just wanted to train with all the other players, and when my dad came over after a few months to see how I was settling in, I complained to him too.

'I just want to play football, dad, but they're making me do all these terrible jobs. I might as well be home in Belfast.'

I don't know whether he put any pressure on United but we came to an arrangement to satisfy everyone, with the notable exception of the Department of Employment since it was totally illegal. One of the club's wealthy supporters ran an electrical business near The Cliff, where the training had now been moved, and he agreed to take on John Fitzpatrick and me as 'electricians'. In fact, the nearest we came to any electrical work was clocking on in the morning. Then we'd walk out of the back door and on to the training pitch, returning just before five o'clock to clock off after our exhausting working day.

Unofficially or not, I was now a full-time ground-staff boy, earning the princely sum of £4 1s 9d, of which I sent three pounds home to my parents. Not much when you hear of players today demanding £100,000 a week but at the time, I felt rich. And at last, I was doing what I had come to Manchester to do – play football all day.

Well, not exactly all day. I trained in the morning and then went back to Old Trafford with the apprentices for the sort of jobs that made my previous life as a tea boy seem glamorous. The most important of these jobs was cleaning the professional players' boots. I used to do Harry Gregg's and those of a massive centre forward called Alex Dawson, so I had more leather work than all the other boys.

It might sound glamorous, doing the boots of superstar players but the boot room was a pokey little place, little bigger than a cupboard, with not even a window to let in some fresh air. Remember, these were big, old-fashioned boots and the first thing we had to do was get all the cack off them, using those old wire brushes. Only then could we start putting the dubbin on and then polish them with cloths until we could all but see our faces in them. Dubbin tends to make boots lose their shine but I discovered that a coat of vaseline brought them up a treat. The smell from it all used to get up your nostrils and stick in the roof of your mouth, all the crap and shit and dubbin.

When we had completed that daily task, we'd be given brooms and be sent out to sweep the terraces or whatever other little treat they could find. At least most of those jobs were in the open air and the terrace sweeping did have its compensations. We would find plenty of dropped pennies and halfpennies and Corona bottles, which we took back to the shop opposite the Stretford End and collected the penny return. I suppose I could even have taken them to Belfast and had a night at the movies.

Cleaning the boots of the star players was the closest we got to them. The first team players were a species of their own. They mixed together on and off the park and we youngsters were like the downstairs staff, the lowest end of the evolutionary scale. On occasions, inevitably, I would bump into Mr Busby on the training ground and he would say hello. But he and the first team stars lived in a different world to us.

I've never really got over my shyness, but in those days it was almost a chronic condition. With my thick Belfast accent and my lack of worldliness, I still felt like an outsider and though I got on with the lads, I felt intimidated by most of the adults and particularly, Busby. He also lived in Chorlton, close to Mrs Fullaway's, though in a slightly more comfortable house, and sometimes, waiting for the bus in the morning, I would spot his Jaguar coming up the road and I would try to hide myself in the queue in case he stopped because I didn't want the embarrassment of travelling with him.

He did spot me once and gave me a lift, but I just sat beside him mumbling one-word answers. I didn't know what to say to him and after that experience, I kept an eagle eye out for his car. I was even embarrassed to speak to the conductor on the buses because everyone had trouble understanding my accent and people were always asking me to repeat myself. So I tried to make sure I had the exact money, threepence or fourpence or whatever it was, so that I wouldn't have to ask for a particular destination.

Mrs Fullaway did her best to make me feel at home, too, but she did have one irritating habit which, if I hadn't been so shy, I would have told her about. She would come into my bedroom in the morning and if I wasn't awake, she would tickle my nose to rouse me. It was a horrible way to be woken up and several times, I jumped up in shock but she kept on doing it.

She also fed me generous helpings at meal times, though I remained pretty small and didn't make it into the youth team in my first year, instead playing for the B team. If they had developed the weight training which is now considered a vital part of any football training programme, I would probably have looked like Arnold Schwarzenegger after 12 months. But weights were unheard of then. You didn't really do any work on your upper body, just your legs. My legs were pretty strong in any case and I made them even stronger on the cross-country runs, which I loved.

Fitzy and I were both good runners and loved competing against each other. Some of the other lads weren't so keen and when we turned right out of the ground, they would turn left and hide in some bushes until we got back. Some of them would have a cigarette while we were away and then they'd dip their faces in the little stream that ran by there and sprint back in, looking for all the world as though they were sweating.

I don't think they fooled the training staff and they didn't do themselves any favours. None of that little team made it and it was a lesson to me that you get out what you put in. I loved training anyway and because I was physically strong for my size and had good balance, I rarely got injured or hurt. I was also so good at running that I would have sprint races against my team mates in which I ran backwards and still beat them.

However, I still didn't feel that comfortable in my surroundings. Manchester seemed such a big city and so different from Belfast but I wasn't going to go crawling back to Mum and Dad again and decided that I would knuckle down whatever happened. I didn't, after all, expect to be putting up with this forever because I expected to be sent back at any time. I just didn't want Mum and Dad to think that I'd let them down again. I was helped by becoming big mates with Fitzy, along with David Sadler, who signed for the club a few months after me, plus Jimmy Ryan and Peter McBride. We began going out together, though our idea of a night out then was the snooker hall in Chorlton or, as we got more interested in girls, the bowling alley. That, believe it or not, was the place to pull! The Swinging Sixties hadn't quite got into full swing at that stage and even the Twisted Wheel, which became another of our haunts and may sound like a den of iniquity, only served Cokes. Alcohol was strictly forbidden.

I also became friendly with Mrs Fullaway's son Steve and somehow our friendship survived me pulling his girlfriend. Her name was Maria and she was a lovely-looking girl. I fancied her but was too shy to ask her out so I planned to slip her a note, thinking that if she didn't respond to it, it would at least save me the embarrassment of being rejected.

I took my chance to push the note into her pocket one night when all three of us were walking to the chippy. I'd written that I would like to see her the next day, though as soon as I'd done it, I was wishing I could take it back. But she turned up and we began going out with one another. The relationship turned out to have fringe benefits because her aunt and uncle owned a cake shop and I would go round there when she was babysitting for them and enjoy the twin pleasures of nookie and fresh cakes.

Talk about having your cake and eating it!

Although the friendship between myself and Steve survived Maria, we did have a falling out one night, again after going to the chippy. I was saving one tasty bit of fish until last, the way you do, and just as I was about to reach for it, he jumped in first and put it in his mouth. I gave him a right thump and he hit me back and we both ended up with bloody noses. Of course, we both had white shirts on, which got covered in blood but we told Mrs Fullaway that we had walked into a lamppost.

Fortunately, I never fell out with her or it might have severely curtailed my nightly exploits as the years went by. Manchester United landladies were supposed to operate a strict curfew on their precious charges, which was probably about 10 to 10.30 p.m. in those days. But she didn't say too much if I came in late and, knowing that I probably would be home after curfew, I got in the habit of leaving my bedroom window open. The man next door was a window cleaner and left his ladders in the little passageway, though he probably worked out why they were often propped up against the wall of our house in the morning.

Mrs Fullaway must have got fed up hearing me crash on to my bedroom floor because eventually, she gave me my own key.

It was all innocent stuff and I was working harder than anyone on the training field. I would even go back on my own in the afternoons and work on my skills, trying things with my left foot or standing on the 18 yard line and trying to hit the crossbar as many times as I could. It paid off because I was in the youth team by my second year in Manchester, which was a big step up from the B team. It was a first taste of the big time, if you like. Because of the reputation of the Busby Babes, producing young players had become crucial to United and still is today. So all the training staff would come to the youth games, which were watched by some pretty big crowds, and you travelled on the same team coach that the first team used and had lunch at five-star hotels before games. You were on your way. It was great for me, too, as I was playing with all my mates.

In those days, I was an inside forward, which today you would describe as a midfield playmaker. I would play inside left and Fitzy would play inside right, or the other way round. It didn't make any difference to us. We were playing every week, we were winning most of the time and I was scoring lots of goals. I used to try all sorts of tricks, trying to score direct from corners or straight from kick-off.

One day I did manage to score after receiving the ball from the kick-off. I think it was against Blackburn at The Cliff. It was a freezing cold day and the pitch was just about playable.

'Let's get this game over with,' said Fitzy as we lined up for the second half. 'I'll give you the ball from kick-off and you just run through and score.' He tapped the ball to me and that's exactly what I did, shimmying past two or three defenders and rifling the ball in.

Would that it were always that simple.

Busby was apparently getting good reports about my progress and word must have filtered home since I got a call up from the Northern Ireland youth squad. My dad, who had been so angry over that schoolboys team snub, was particularly chuffed.

Being in the youth team also brought my first trip abroad. United sent a team to compete in an annual tournament in Switzerland, which was a good way of seeing how their youth team measured up against those of other European clubs. It also made us feel pretty big time, flying abroad and staying in a swanky hotel. I was still pretty much a Coke man at the time but now that I was a Jack the Lad international footballer, albeit at Under-16 level, I tagged along when some of the players suggested going to a bar.

The mistake Fitzy and I made was going out with two big, Manchester-born lads called Eddie Harrop and David Farrar, who had probably been drinking since they were about eight.

They went straight up to the bar and began knocking back pints like there was no tomorrow – and by the time I had had three, I was beginning to think that there wouldn't be!

Apart from anything, the first time you drink beer it tastes horrible but Fitzy and I couldn't be seen to be a couple of wimps so we forced it down. I was starting to feel queasy and once the fresh air hit us on the walk back to the hotel, I could hardly stand up. As I staggered towards the glass-fronted doors of the hotel, the other lads spotted Busby sitting at a little café opposite, along with his senior coaching staff, Jack Crompton, Joe Armstrong and John Aston senior. Being caught in this state would have meant big trouble. So the lads got either side of me and helped me through the door, even though Fitzy was probably as bad as me.

They got me up to my room and I tried to crash out but I was feeling too sick and every time I opened my eyes, the room was spinning. That was the first and only time I've had that experience and it might be the reason I have never been a pints man. I did start to drink more regularly after that but it was only halves of shandy or lager and limes after games on Saturday. That was mainly to give me Dutch courage because I found it very hard to walk up to girls and start chatting them up. I preferred to stand around hoping a girl would notice me but after a couple of shandies, I'd get up the courage to go and talk to someone, particularly if she and I were both with mates. The old safety in numbers thing. I certainly didn't drink before games and it made me laugh to hear stories from people like Malcolm Allison, who would recount tales of knocking back several bottles of champagne on a Friday night and then running out the next day to score a couple of goals. I would never go out on the night before a game. And only rarely on a Thursday.

I had been writing home regularly to Dad – the normal sort of stuff about how the football was going and what the digs were like, though I only gave him the footballing details from that Switzerland trip! Yet he and I were completely in the dark about whether I had a future at Manchester United. Nobody at the club had given me any indication. Maybe they had just taken it for granted that at the end of two years, I would sign professional forms on my 17th birthday. And you could hardly go knocking on Busby's door to ask whether he was going to sign you.

I was playing well and Paddy Crerand, who signed from Celtic in February 1963, told me years later that he had watched me in one youth game and was amazed by my talent. Yet I'd seen plenty of other kids with amazing talent come and go during those two years. In any case, it seemed that David Sadler was the one who was being groomed for the top and there were plenty of other candidates in our team. Barry Fry had so much skill and Eamonn Dunphy was tipped for greatness, too. Then there were Albert Kinsey, Jimmy Ryan and Ian

Moir. And so many players wanted to play in my position, inside forward, because that was the glamour role. Between the A and B teams, the youth team and the reserves, the club must have had thirty inside forwards.

So no matter how good you were, you certainly couldn't take it for granted that you would get the call from the management on your 17th birthday and be offered that precious piece of paper – the professional contract. I didn't have any idea what my fate would be.

The second half of the 1962–63 season was exciting enough for everyone at Old Trafford. The club had reached the FA Cup Final in successive seasons in 1957 and 1958 but lost both times. Now they were closing in on another Wembley appearance, although the club's League form was really poor. They finished 19th in Division One but clinched another Cup Final place against Leicester. This was fantastic news for everyone because it was the tradition for the club to take all the staff to Wembley.

The Final was late that year, on 25 May rather than the customary first Saturday in May. So my 17th birthday was three days earlier and that was the magical age, the day when a club can sign you as a professional.

In most cases, of course, they put an arm round your shoulder and say, 'Sorry, son, we're letting you go.' I'd seen that happen to a lot of talented kids so I was still nervous when

I was summoned to see The Boss. But he was all smiles when I walked into his office.

'Congratulations, son,' he said, 'we're offering you a professional contract.'

I didn't even look at the wages, which turned out to be £17 a week, a fortune to me. It was all over in a few minutes and as soon as I got out of Matt's office, I dashed off a note to Dad, the shortest letter I'd ever sent because I wanted to catch the post.

'Your son is now a pro. I've signed!' I wrote.

He got it the next morning and though he was delighted with the news, he was not best pleased that the club hadn't invited him over to be there when I signed and discuss terms. It wasn't that he thought they would diddle me. He's just always believed in doing things the right way, my dad, and I believe he had a word with Matt about it when he came over that weekend for the Final. Being Dad, he had also feared the worst when he didn't hear from me on my birthday and was still trying to keep a place open for me in the printing trade, just in case.

You would have thought he and Mum would have had enough on their minds because two months later my twin sisters Julia and Grace were born.

I know it sounds funny, but I had only ever seen Wembley in black and white on the telly and when you walk into the stadium when it's bursting with colour on Cup Final Day, the difference is mind-blowing. Perhaps because of those days on the Orange Lodge marches, I love tradition and ceremony and when the conductor in the white suit struck up the traditional Cup Final anthem, 'Abide With Me', everyone in the whole ground sang along. It was an unforgettable experience and the noise was absolutely deafening when the players came up the tunnel. I couldn't even imagine what it must have been like walking out on to that pitch, though I hoped I would get a chance one day. The best moment of all arrived after the match when our captain, Noel Cantwell, walked up those famous steps to the Royal Box to collect the Cup, with the red and white ribbons fluttering from it.

United had started the day as underdogs but David Herd scored twice in a 3–1 win, with Denis Law, who was later to become one of my great friends, getting the other. I had another unforgettable moment the following day. The team was given the usual civic reception but, before that, they paraded the cup around Manchester in an open-top bus. There wasn't room for all of us, so Fitzy and I were allocated a little terrace to stand on at the town hall. When the bus arrived and Noel stepped off it with the cup, all the crowd were cheering and there was Fitzy and I standing and waving as though *we'd* won the cup. We felt like royalty.

CHAPTER THREE
'YOU'RE IN TODAY, SON.'

I had a wonderfully relaxed summer break back in Belfast in 1963. After that false start with Eric McMordie two years earlier, I had returned home as a professional footballer and with my twin sisters, Julia and Grace, coming along, our house was bubbling with good news. I only saw them briefly because pre-season training started in July, the month they were born, but it was great to be with my family and to see all my old school friends again and catch up with their news. One of my best mates was Tommy Irwin, who lived just round the corner from us and who went to Lisnasharragh school with me. So did Robin McCabe, my other best mate, and they were straight round to my house when they heard I was back.

They couldn't believe I'd been to the Cup Final and

wanted to know all about it. 'Did you get to touch the Cup?' they asked, and 'Did you meet the Queen?' And, naturally, they wanted to know how much I was getting paid and what Bobby Charlton and Denis Law and the other players were like, whom they'd only read about in the papers.

It was great that they were so excited and pleased for me because after two years away, I didn't know how they would react. When we'd kicked a ball around the streets of the Cregagh, I had been just another dreamer, like them. I certainly didn't feel like I was especially gifted or remarkable in any way. Although I was a better player than most of them, we'd never really believed any of us would become professional footballers, and certainly not with Manchester United. Being back with the lads, my football career seemed like a dream to me and it was just like old times as we did a tour of our old haunts, the cinema, Eddie Spencer's chippy and even the fair at Dallywinkers Lane.

I don't know whether Tommy and Robin felt a twinge of jealousy when it was time for me to go back but while I was with them, they seemed genuinely pleased for me. I suppose, too, that they shared a bit of the reflected glory. After being signed I didn't really feel any different. A bit of paper didn't make that much difference to me and I don't think Carol or my mum thought much about it. I just felt that it meant I would be staying with Manchester United a bit longer and maybe that's what they thought as well, so they didn't make a big fuss.

Turning pro did mean a big increase in my salary and to celebrate it, I treated myself to my first car – an Austin 1100. Not quite in the Ferrari league of today's United players, though I paid £400 in cash for it, which was an enormous sum for anyone, let alone a teenager. I'd actually failed my driving test twice in Manchester, not exactly helping my cause on the first occasion by turning up with no L plates, which I'd tied on with string and which had somehow blown off between home and the testing centre.

So getting fed up with English examiners, I went to a testing centre in Belfast. The examiner did a double take when he saw me and seemed more nervous than me when we got into the car. I wasn't exactly a big star but someone from the Cregagh signing for Manchester United was big news round our way. He just instructed me to go round the block and when I found myself back at the centre after five minutes or so, he said, 'Congratulations, you've passed.' What a nice man!

I didn't think it would be so easy to get into United's first team. In fact, I thought it would be some time before I made it. Despite United's poor League showing the season before, they had played some great stuff to win the Cup and with forwards like Denis Law and Bobby Charlton in the side, I didn't see an immediate opening for me or even a medium-term one.

In any case, as I have said, David Sadler was the youth team player who appeared to have been singled out for an early first team place. He was a big, strapping lad, six feet tall and able to play almost anywhere on the park. He'd also already had experience with Isthmian League club Maidstone United, so he had built up a reputation even before he joined United and was much more confident than the rest of us, known as someone who was unruffled in the best of company. Having said that, even he was gobsmacked when the team sheet went up for the opening game of the 1963–64 season against Sheffield Wednesday and he found his name at centre forward.

I was absolutely delighted for him, if also green with envy. Everyone knew that Johnny Giles, who had played in the previous season's Cup Final, was on the way out when he gave Matt some backchat after being dropped a few weeks prior to that, so it was no surprise that he was not in the team. But Matt also dropped Albert Quixall and David Herd, who was an Old Trafford legend, replacing Giles and that pair with Sadler and two other youth team products, Ian Moir and Phil Chisnall, who had both been in and out of the side for a couple of years. It seemed that Matt was already in the advanced stages of producing another team of Babes.

I was still playing in the youth team or the A or B teams, with the odd reserve team game thrown in, so I was more than surprised to get a call up to the first team squad for the home game against West Brom on September 14, seven games into the season. As thrilled as I was to be in the squad, I didn't expect to play because I was told that I was 12th man, which didn't even involve getting your kit on in those days because there were no such things as substitutes.

Unbeknown to me, however, Ian Moir had picked up an injury and Matt knew I would be playing before we had the normal pre-match meal at the local golf club. He didn't say anything, perhaps thinking that it would put me off my food, but Paddy Crerand told me before we got on the bus. He wasn't one for keeping secrets, was Paddy. I still wasn't convinced though, until Matt wandered down the aisle on the way to the ground.

'You're in today, son,' he said casually.

Matt didn't give me any instructions, that wasn't really his way. He wouldn't have wanted to put any pressure on a new player. I didn't feel particularly nervous in the dressing room. In fact, I popped out for a cup of tea at a refreshment bar with some mates and didn't get back until fifteen minutes before kick-off. All players develop their own routines before a game, based on habit and the state of their nerves. Alan Gowling would prowl around the room, looking whiter and whiter and then he'd disappear into the toilet and you'd hear him throwing up. I was to meet lots of players like that over the years, though they were fine once they were out on the pitch and got their first touch of the ball.

Nobby Stiles showed his nerves in a different way. After taking out his teeth and putting in his contact lenses, he would check his kit over and over again, as if anyone would have tampered with it since the last time he had ensured it was all there. Bobby Charlton, surprisingly, was another of the nervous ones and would take a nip of scotch before he ran out.

A bit of drink was quite natural in any dressing room then, particularly on cold days, but Bobby's habit was quite ironic seeing that I was to become the one most associated with drink and he was always the clean-living one. We used to keep a bottle of scotch in the skip, along with the kit and our boots, and Jimmy Murphy, Matt's number two, would have a swig before the game, too. I even think The Boss sank a scotch in his office before coming down. As for me, I always had half a bar of chocolate in my pocket, which I would eat before going out. Other than that, the only routine I followed was to change into my kit and sit under my peg in the dressing room and read the programme.

The most fantastic thing about that first day as a first team player was walking down the tunnel and hearing the noise from over 50,000 fans, which just grew louder and louder and louder as we got nearer the pitch. The tunnel was on the halfway line in those days, and the hairs on the back of my neck really did stand up. I was up against Graham Williams, a Welsh international who had a reputation for not taking prisoners. Ironically, I had made my reserve team debut against him in the Central League twelve months earlier. I also made my international debut against him in Swansea.

He was the Stuart Pearce of his day and by way of welcoming me to Division One football, he gave me a fierce whack early on in the game, as wily old pros were prone to do to newcomers.

I recovered from that and began giving him a bit of a run round. I was a right little so-and-so! When you're the new kid in the team playing with a man of Bobby Charlton's stature, you're supposed to show a bit of deference and give him the ball occasionally. But once I got it, I didn't want to give it to anybody because I was so used to almost owning it in the youth team. So while my team mates were screaming for it, I was trying to beat three or four opponents and doing all the tricks I was used to performing for my B-team pals. If my team mates had had enough of me before the end of the first half, Williams certainly had, giving me another clattering to try to keep me in line.

At half time, Matt told me to move to the other wing, which probably saved me from a decapitation, though overall, for all my Fancy Dan stuff, I don't think I played that well. For one of the first and only times on a football field, I was in awe of it all. It wasn't nerves, it was just that I hadn't quite been prepared for what it would be like and I spent most of the 90 minutes getting acclimatised. The next day's newspapers were kind enough, saying that I'd showed glimpses of talent, that sort of thing.

'BOY BEST FLASHES IN RED ATTACK' was the headline

in the *Manchester Evening News*, though I've no idea whether that was meant to be good or bad.

I knew from the reaction of the other lads, however, that I hadn't been brilliant. They all came over and made a fuss of me in the dressing room afterwards, as they always did to a young lad who'd just made his debut. The Boss also came up and said, 'You did fine, son.' But I felt the other players were just being nice, it didn't seem absolutely genuine and they were hardly going to say, 'You were crap, son.' The nicest thing about it was that we won 1–0 and my mate, David Sadler, got the goal.

Anyway, my name didn't appear on the team sheet for the next game, so it was back to the A and youth teams. I wasn't that disappointed because I wasn't sure I was good enough. So I continued to work as hard as I could on my game, determined to give a better performance if I got in again. I also consoled myself with the thought that I had made it into the first team much quicker than I had anticipated. At the start of that season, having been given no intimation that I might be close to a first team spot, I had set myself the goal only of earning a regular spot in the reserves for a year or two. The only sad thing about my unexpected call up was that there was no time to tell my dad, who was mortified to miss my debut. And some more unusual circumstances meant him missing my second match as well.

I had got into a routine of going home most weekends to see the family and the new arrivals. Mum was especially delighted to see me. She would ask the normal motherly things like, 'Are you eating properly?' and 'Are you behaving yourself over there?'

Manchester was as much a mystery to her as it had been for me when I first arrived and with the four girls to look after, she didn't really have time to come over and see for herself how I was getting on.

Carol, who was 16, had started to play her role as surrogate mother for the twins, which gave Mum a break. Carol was pleased that I seemed to be doing well but she was not much of a football fan and I think it all seemed a bit strange to her. As I was not a first team player, I was allowed to go home for Christmas and was looking forward to lounging around for a few days. Then on the morning after Boxing Day, there was a commotion outside our house as the telegram boy made his way down Burren Way.

The telegram he delivered was from Old Trafford, instructing me to contact the club immediately. United had been thrashed 6–1 at Burnley the day before and Matt had obviously decided to shuffle his side again for the return match in Manchester on 28 December. Before they started messing about with the fixture list, all clubs played back-to-back local derbies at Christmas to keep travelling to a minimum. When I phoned the club, they told me to jump on the first flight but I didn't think I was going to play, I just thought that they wanted me as cover.

'Look, if I come over,' I told them, 'you'll have to get me on a flight home from Manchester after the game.'

When they agreed, I started to believe my dad, who said, 'You must be playing if they're in such a hurry to get you back.' As proud as he was, there was a bit of sadness in his voice, too, knowing it was too late for him to arrange time off work to travel to the game.

When I got to Old Trafford, I discovered not only that I was playing on the right wing, but also that Willie Anderson, who was still only 16, was playing on the other flank. He was another dashing young winger and for both of us to be in the first team at our ages suggested that Matt was rebuilding his team faster than we had imagined. I can't remember how Willie played but I was much more pleased with my performance and with my first senior goal – a right-footed shot from the edge of the penalty box which flew into the corner. I gave the run around to Alex Elder, who was already an established Northern Ireland international and who was to go on to win 40 caps. We ran out 5–1 winners.

I hardly needed the plane on the trip home and I was up early the following morning to see what the *Belfast Telegraph* had to say about my performance. To my astonishment, they had a picture of my goal on the back page, which just seemed so unreal to me and to all my mates. Kicking a ball around in the streets, we had all pretended to be playing for some big club in England and now I had scored for Manchester United and there was the picture in the *Belfast Telegraph* to prove it! There was a sense of disbelief among Tommy and Robin and the others and I found it hard to take it in myself.

When I was with my team mates in Manchester, it was a different world, one in which scoring goals was second nature, it was our business. But in Belfast, I was still wee Georgy from the Cregagh Estate and when I was back in that environment, it seemed that I was reading about someone else, too. That *Belfast Telegraph* must have passed through a hundred sets of hands and my goal was a big talking point on the estate. And it was as if I'd scored for them, too, which made me a bit weepy.

This time, when I got back to Old Trafford, I expected to keep my first team place and to the surprise of many people, Anderson also stayed in for the following match, a 3–2 third round FA Cup win at Southampton. I didn't know how long it would last but I got better and better in a 13 match League spell, in which I scored another six goals. I also got my first taste of European football in the Cup Winners' Cup and I grew to love those big European nights. There seemed to be such a different atmosphere to League matches, you were aware they were something special. And of course, they were always under floodlights, creating that sense of theatre which I had felt watching Wolves against those Russian aliens on Mr Harrison's TV in Belfast.

Even when we drew the holders Tottenham in the second round, it had a different feel to a normal domestic match and after seeing them off and beating Sporting Lisbon 4–1 at home in the first leg of the next round, we had hopes of going all the way. But unbelievably, we got stuffed out of sight in the return leg, beaten 5–0. We were absolutely terrible, it was our worst-ever performance in Europe. Matt, who never usually said much after a game, whatever the result, was fuming that night and tore into everyone. Europe, remember, was always special to him and after seeing so many of his team killed in Munich in the cause of European glory, he didn't take kindly to our spineless efforts.

Liverpool beat us 3–0 on their way to the Championship, though we were hopeful of retaining the FA Cup. We were drawn against Sunderland in the third round and looked to be out when we trailed 3–1 with five minutes to go. Amazingly, we came back with me scoring the equaliser with virtually the final kick of the game. In the replay at Roker Park, Bobby Charlton scored one of his long range thunderbolts for a 2–2 draw and in the second replay, it was one-way traffic as we beat them 5–1, with Denis Law scoring a hat trick. But our luck ran out against West Ham in the semi-final. They had Bobby Moore, Geoff Hurst and Martin Peters, who were to become World Cup heroes for England in 1966 and ran out comfortable 3–1 winners.

After sampling the excitement of Wembley on FA Cup

Final day the previous year, I had been looking forward to experiencing it as a player. And I might have set a record by doing so. Preston beat Swansea in the other semi-final, which caused great interest in the press because, at 17, Howard Kendall became the youngest player to appear in a Final. Well, he was born on the same day as me, so if United had also made the Final, we'd have had to look up our birth certificates to determine which of us had been born last. It was disappointing not to get to the Final but I didn't dwell on it too much. I had got to the semi-final in my first professional season. I felt good about that and I reckoned there would be plenty more Finals to come.

Now that I could count on playing regularly, my dad was able to plan trips in advance to come and watch me, and my mum would also come when she could. She wasn't that keen on flying but she loved putting on her Sunday best and wearing the red and white. Supporters dressed more smartly in those days and Mum was always keen to look her best for her son. Sadly, I didn't get much chance to talk to them before or after games because they would travel over late on Friday nights after my dad finished work and head back straight after the game.

Despite my first team status, I was still turning out for the youth team, as was David Sadler, which you could never imagine happening today. But the FA Youth Cup had become the

Holy Grail for the class of 1963–64 since United had not even reached the Final for six years and we were all aware that the Busby Babes had won the competition five years in succession. So every set of youngsters that came along afterwards was measured against them. We weren't really expected to win it that year but because we were all trying to make our mark, we played above ourselves. And as we played together as a team, we had a great spirit.

At that time, Chelsea had taken over as the best youth side in the country, but in 1963–64, Manchester City were reckoned to have the cream of the crop. They breezed through to the semi-finals, which were played over two legs, and when they drew us, they began crowing about how they were going to humiliate us. It was always going to be a fierce encounter, not just because of the rivalry between the two clubs but because there were so many local players in each side who understood what these games meant, even at youth team level.

A crowd of just under 25,000 turned up for the first leg at Old Trafford and as we came out of the tunnel, I remember City's Mike Doyle, who was a real United hater, screaming across at us and some of his team mates joining in, shouting things like, 'We're going to stuff you.' There were some terrific players in both teams – we had Jimmy Rimmer, who went on to become England goalkeeper, Willie Anderson, David Sadler and Fitzy and me. As well as Doyle, City had Glyn Pardoe, who was to become a first team regular for years, and Bobby

McAlinden, a lovely player who was later to become my best buddy in the States. The hero that night, though, was Albert Kinsey – who later went to Wrexham – who scored a hat-trick.

Doyle was even more outspoken before the second leg at Maine Road twelve days later, which brought out a crowd of 21,000. Against all the odds, we won again, this time 3–2 and it produced one of my favourite photographs. Doyle and I set off together to chase a ball into the City box and, United-hater that he was, he was desperate to beat me to it. The veins were standing out in his neck as he closed in on the ball but he didn't notice the goalkeeper coming out and knocked it past him into the net. There was a great picture in the *Manchester Evening News* the following day of Doyle in a heap and me leaning nonchalantly against the post, laughing at him. If I'd kept a scrapbook at the time, that would have taken pride of place.

We were hot favourites to beat Swindon Town in the Final. Don Rogers scored for them in the first leg but my goal made it 1–1 and, before 25,000 fans at Old Trafford, we won 4–1 with Sadler scoring a hat-trick. Our captain was Bobby Noble, an England youth international who was a brilliant left back.

Yet three years later, after winning a League championship medal, he was to suffer head and chest injuries in a car crash on his way home from a game at Roker Park. Though he bravely battled back to full fitness and played a couple of games for the A team, he was still suffering from double vision and was forced to quit on medical advice. It was a shocking reminder that your career could end unexpectedly at any moment and not necessarily through anything that happens on the field.

Between the two semi-final legs against City, I had made my Northern Ireland debut in a 3–2 win against Wales in Swansea, making me the youngest player to wear the green. Goalkeeper Pat Jennings also made his debut that day, the first of a record 119 caps. Big Pat was to become an Irish legend and we became great mates over the years. Sadly, though, his debut came at the expense of Harry Gregg, who was dropped after the 8–3 defeat by England in the previous game. For some reason, I don't remember much about the game, although I know Jimmy McLaughlin did most of the damage for us. And I do remember that, once again, I came up against Graham Williams. Maybe it didn't register with me because we were playing away at a place like Swansea, which was small beer compared to Old Trafford. But I remember my dad being upset when the local paper was less than flattering, saying they didn't know why everyone was making such a fuss about me. They changed their tune after my next match against Uruguay a fortnight later.

That was my home debut, of course, so everyone was expecting a lot of me and I was determined to put on a show. It probably helped that the Uruguayan left back seemed equally determined to kick me into the front row of the stands because that sort of behaviour has always spurred me on. I'm a bit like that off the field, too. If people try to stop me doing something or tell me I'm incapable of doing it, I will bust a gut to prove them wrong. Anyway, I gave this guy a real torrid evening and though I didn't manage to score, I like to think I inspired my team mates to a 3–0 win!

That was an extraordinary week because I had already played against Nottingham Forest in a First Division match on the Saturday and in the first leg against Swindon on Monday. The Uruguay game was on Wednesday and the following day, I flew back to Manchester to play in the second leg against Swindon. That's four games in six days at three different levels of football, which must be a record. And I can't see anyone beating it because no coach in his right mind would allow a player to do that these days.

Me? I would have played seven days a week if they had let me. All I had ever wanted to do in Belfast was kick a ball around and now I was doing it for real, for one of the biggest clubs in England. And once I was on that pitch, I never wanted the final whistle to go. If I was playing well, I didn't want the game to end and if I was having a quiet game, I wanted it to carry on until I had a chance to do something. I remember having a stinker against West Brom in a game we were losing 1–0 until the final minutes. Then I got a couple of chances and took them both and we won 2–1. When the whistle went, the West Brom players were looking at each other in amazement, as if to say, 'How did that happen?'

I was on cloud nine.

It was around this time that I was really starting to get noticed by the national press. I suppose I stood out because I was different. Footballers didn't have long hair in those days and were not supposed to play with their shirt outside their shorts. And you were told never to take out your shin guards. But rules are meant to be broken and I broke all of them, not because I was a rebel or was trying to make some sort of statement. It was just the way I was. I was just being me. Long hair had become fashionable and like a lot of other young men at my age, I just decided to let mine grow. The club didn't seem to care, the only thing they insisted upon was that you travelled to games in your club suit and tie and that was no problem at all. I was proud to wear them, like every other player.

I was the odd one out when it came to the pre-match meal, too, and as it turns out, I was ahead of my time on the nutritional front. All the United players used to order steak before a game, which we now know is about the worst thing you can eat, because it takes so long for your body to digest meat. I would prefer cornflakes and sliced banana, much better for providing some instant energy, as was the half a bar of chocolate I took into the dressing room, though I wasn't aware of that at the time. Not surprisingly, after my upbringing, I still liked my toast (toasted both sides by this stage!) smeared with honey as well as butter. That would have been sheer luxury back in Belfast. Only occasionally, if I actually had an appetite before a match, would I eat a bit of chicken or a poached egg.

And it must have been around that time that Dad finally told the printing firm in Belfast that I wouldn't be needing a job! He and Mum were delighted by how quickly my career had taken off, though Mum told me not to let it go to my head. I doubt that she approved of my hairstyle either, though she didn't say anything.

Off the field, in 1964 something odd was happening. All the old values in life were changing as the Sixties began to take hold, led by pop groups like The Beatles and The Rolling Stones. It wasn't just the music they played, it was the way they dressed. Looking back, it makes me laugh to think that The Beatles were considered so outrageous at the start when they wore ties and jackets on stage. But it was the start of an amazing time, all peace and free love, and I was certainly starting to get my share of the latter.

Drugs were not something I grew up with. I didn't know anyone who took them as kids and I was never offered any as a young player, let alone feel tempted by them. I was still drinking in moderation after matches, mostly beer, but I didn't particularly enjoy the taste of booze. I drank because it helped me to relax and talk to girls. Although I was a regular in the first team, I didn't mix with the other first team players socially, partly because they were older and many of them were married. I was part of this new generation and I wanted to go to clubs and parties with my mates from the youth team, even though my two closest pals, Fitzy and Dave Sadler, were getting occasional runs in the first team by then. Dave had also moved into digs with me at Mrs Fullaway's, which made us even closer mates.

If I'd scored on Saturday, I'd be flying high by night time and with the adrenalin flowing, I wouldn't need much of a drink. There was no professional Sunday football then, so there didn't seem any harm in staying out late. But neither drink nor girls were a distraction then. I lived for playing. When you walked up that tunnel in your kit at three o'clock on Saturday afternoons, it was like stepping into another world. And I never worried about the game, never thought about who we were playing and who might be marking me, I just went out and did it.

Every game was like a new adventure, another dream.

CHAPTER FOUR
FIFTH BEATLE

When Leeds regained their place in the old First Division in 1964 under Don Revie, they were a club with real attitude. They had flitted between Divisions One and Two for all their professional lives but under Revie, they were determined not just to stay in the top flight but to challenge for honours against the country's leading clubs. They had changed their strip to all white in honour of Real Madrid, the most outstanding side in Europe in the late Fifties and early Sixties, and as time went on, Leeds often played football that was worthy of Real.

I remember them winning one League game 7–0 and playing so superbly that the other team could hardly get the ball off them. Sadly, however, some of them were also the masters of football's black arts, going over the top of the ball in a deliberate attempt to injure an opponent and pulling shirts or tread-

ing on a player's foot behind the referee's back. They had so
many talented players that they didn't need to do half of it but
they seemed always to want to steal an edge. So they would
moan all game at the referee, and if they got a weak one, he
was likely to give decisions their way just to shut them up.
They were also the first British team to introduce diving, which
we thought of as a continental trait.

Leeds certainly started as they meant to go on when they
came to our place in December 1964, the first of many tough
games against them. It was a brutal encounter and a fairly dull
one, as they defended for long periods and then stole victory
1–0 through a Bobby Collins goal after our goalkeeper, Pat
Dunne, dropped a cross. I was marked by Paul Reaney, who
was one of the best full backs I've played against and he
hardly gave me a kick. By that, I mean he hardly allowed me
a kick at the ball, though he delivered plenty of his own to my
legs. I had never worn shin pads until that day, they had
always felt awkward to me and I could never remember how
to keep them in place. But after that, I always wore them
against Leeds and, if I hadn't, my career might have been over
much earlier.

Johnny Giles, who was always wound up for games
against us because he was a former Manchester United player,
once went over the top and caught me so fiercely that the
impact tore open the tie-up holding the pad at the top of my
sock and his boot went right through everything and into the

bone of my leg. If I hadn't been wearing pads, my leg would have been shattered.

Gilesy would literally add insult to injury as well.

'Why can't you be more like Bobby?' he snarled at me when he kicked me in another game.

I didn't even know what he meant by that. He could have been referring to Bobby Charlton's reputation as an ambassador for the game, though it was more likely that he was expressing anger that I didn't react like Bobby, who was renowned for his complaining. Instead I would either kick him back or try to make a fool of him when I got the ball. I was thinking, he's kicking lumps out of me, I'm not just going to take it! He was perhaps upset that I didn't allow him to put me off my game and kept coming back for more, but what did he expect me to do, just let him trample all over me? Tough luck, mate.

Giles was a good footballer and so was Collins but I've always found them tough off the ball as well. Billy Bremner used to put it about, too, though he was another player with terrific football skills. And Leeds also had Peter Lorimer who, like Bobby Charlton, could hit rockets from 30 yards or more. He was reckoned to have the hardest shot in football. Then there was Eddie Gray, a great wing player, with whom I became friendly and still keep in touch with today.

I had produced one of my best performances at the start of the 1964–65 season when we beat Chelsea 2–0 at Stamford

Bridge. I loved playing at Chelsea because they were the glamour side of London with some excellent players. And, of course, it was a night game, which for me, was always an extra buzz. It was another of those occasions when everything we tried came off and I gave full back Ken Shellito such a roasting that both teams applauded me off at the end, which is not something that happens too often.

The press, who are always looking for new young stars, also picked me out for the first time and my dad was so chuffed that he still has the cuttings from that match. They were a bit flowery compared to today's writing, *The Times* reporting:

> *The company saw as fine an exhibition of wing play as they are likely to enjoy for a long time. It came from Best. He even had the Chelsea crowd, it seemed, longing for him to have the ball and float his way past man after man. Shellito, in particular, must have felt that he was trying to push back a genie into his bottle.*

That win was part of a sequence of 13 wins and a draw. Leeds put an end to that in December 1964 and, as the season wore on, they became our main rivals for the championship. We were also drawn against them in the semi-finals of the FA Cup in April the following year. This time, I knew what to expect and not only wore shin pads, I packed an extra pair. The game at Hillsborough was one long punch-up which ended 0–0 and the replay, at Nottingham Forest's ground four days later, looked like being another goalless draw until Billy Bremner headed the winner.

I was upset at losing another chance to play in the Final but a 3–1 win over Arsenal at Old Trafford made us the 1964–65 champions. I was delighted not only to score one of the goals in that game but also with the fact that I'd played in all but one of our League games. It proved not only that I had become an important player in the side but that I was able to stand up to the rigours of regular football at the highest level.

We had a chance of a second trophy in the Inter Cities Fairs Cup, since renamed the UEFA Cup. But we were all knackered, physically and mentally, and after beating the Hungarian side Ferencvaros 3–2 at home in the first leg, we lost to a penalty at their place. Unfortunately, Matt lost the toss for venue in the play-off and we went back to Hungary on 16 June and lost 2–1. I can't say we were happy but I was relieved that the season was finally over and that I could enjoy my summer holiday.

I was enjoying my football and seeing the world, both with United and Northern Ireland, though the old saying about travel broadening the mind did not apply to my trip to Albania with the Irish in November, 1965 for a World Cup qualifying game. It was the final game in the group and we needed a win to qualify for the 1966 World Cup Finals.

I'm told Tirana is not exactly a bundle of laughs today but it must be paradise compared to when we were there. There were no direct flights in and out and we had to stay for four days and they were the longest four days of my life. The hotel, which defied any normal definition of the word, was disgusting, the food was inedible and at the ground, they were cutting the grass with hand clippers. The grass was so long that there might have been a couple of tigers hiding under it for all we knew.

It also poured with rain all the time we were there and when we complained that we were bored and that there was nothing to do, they found some rusty old bus and took us on a sightseeing tour of a mental hospital. By then, some of the lads were almost ready to be admitted. We cheered up when we discovered there was a cinema and things were so dull there that we sat through a whole film in Russian, with Albanian subtitles. We couldn't even avoid the rain in the cinema because there was a hole in the roof and, by the time the credits rolled, our shoes were resting in puddles.

When match day finally came around, we were not what you would call motivated. It was still goalless at half time after some real scrappy football and though we managed to get one in the second half, it ended up 1–1. Northern Ireland have never been giants of football themselves but this was a humiliation. You didn't mind being knocked out by Italy, or Spain or Germany, but Albania!

It meant we would miss the most famous of World Cups for British fans in 1966. My United team mates like Nobby Stiles and Bobby Charlton had been talking about it for months, England having been given automatic qualification as the hosts. It would have been fantastic for me to have known that I was going to take part in it as well, but it was not to be. As we waited at the airport to leave Tirana, I actually prayed that our flight wouldn't be late because I couldn't wait to get out of there. And I didn't understand why they had armed guards at the airport because all they had to protect was a shack – and there was no way anyone in their right mind was going to try to smuggle themselves into the country. Perhaps that was why the mental hospital was so full.

The next season, 1965–66, did not start well. We won only one of our first five games and I was dropped after one of those one-sided conversations with Matt, which anyone who played under him would be familiar with.

On Friday mornings, we trained at Old Trafford, instead of The Cliff and Matt used the referee's room, just off the tunnel, as a temporary office. We all had to walk past it on the way back to the dressing room and if you were called in, it normally only meant one thing. You were going to be left out of the team.

I was walking off the pitch one Friday when I heard Matt call out from his room, 'Could I have a word, George?'

I went in and he told me to sit down. Then he looked up and asked, as he had done to dozens of players before, 'How do you think you're playing, son?'

This was his way of telling you that he didn't think you were doing it on the pitch.

'OK, Boss,' I said.

'Aye,' said Matt, 'but do you think you could play any better?'

'Yes, Boss.'

'Well, I think you're right. So I'm leaving you out this week.'

'OK, Boss.'

I didn't think I had been playing particularly poorly but it's natural for young players to have dips in form and though I was devastated to be left out, I wasn't completely surprised. There was no point arguing, in any case, so I stood up ready to walk out when Matt said, 'Just one other thing, son.'

'What's that, Boss?'

'I don't like some of the things I've been hearing about your social life. Don't start getting into the wrong company and bad habits. Keep your mind on your football and you'll be back in the side soon enough.'

Matt was fairly kind to me in the press, too, saying, 'George has been running into trouble but people forget he's only 19. I'm sure the lapse is only temporary.'

I had been going out a bit to clubs like the Twisted Wheel, which opened as a nightclub in 1963. Before that, it had been a café popular with students and the beatnik crowd, but when it was turned into a club, it became one of the hottest places in town. It became a great place for soul music, though at that time they also had live rhythm and blues bands like Long John Baldry and Alexis Korner who I bumped into many times over the years.

For all that I hadn't been getting drunk on my nights out and you couldn't drink in the Twisted Wheel in any case. I was more interested in the music and the girls than the booze.

My dad phoned up when he read the papers.

'What's going on?' he said, knowing that I'd been dropped.

'Nothing, Dad. The boss just says I need a rest. Honestly, there's nothing for you to worry about.'

Matt liked a drink himself but he had seen plenty of players ruin their career through booze and I imagine he thought he would nip it in the bud by shocking me. In fact, it was the pursuit of women rather than booze that was keeping me from my bed. So to speak.

Matt did shock me because I'd become used to playing in every game and it was punishment enough not to be able to play in the opening match of our European Cup campaign, the first leg against HJK Helsinki in Finland. So, for once, I was delighted at the opportunity to play for Northern Ireland against Scotland in a Home International match at Windsor Park.

After the Albania debacle, I had begun missing quite a few internationals that I probably could have played in. It was the old 'club versus country' debate and if The Boss told the Irish officials I was injured, there was not much I could do about it. But there was no reason not to play against Scotland. In fact there was every reason *to* play, to show Matt that I was in good form and after I turned on one of my better performances we won 3–2. The Boss must have been impressed, because he recalled me for the return against Helsinki four days later in which I banged in a couple of goals. We ran out 6–0 winners for an aggregate score of 9–2.

In the League, we continued to be inconsistent but everyone felt that it could be our year in the European Cup when we reached the quarter final and beat Benfica 3–2 at home in the first leg.

Because of what was to follow, Matt's pre-match instructions in Lisbon to keep it tight for the first 20 minutes have entered football folklore. His insistence that we do so, however, was only sensible advice. British teams struggled in Europe for a long time because they refused to adapt their tactics, believing that playing at the same frenetic pace as in domestic football was the way to frighten and beat the continentals. In most cases, those tactics were suicidal against cultured teams that could hold possession for long periods.

On top of that, Benfica, who won the cup in 1961 and 1962 and were the losing finalists in 1964–65, had never lost a

European game in their magnificent Stadium of Light and when you felt that atmosphere, you could understand why. The stadium held almost twice as many people as Old Trafford and the Portuguese fans were fanatical. Compared to the noise they made, Wembley on FA Cup Final days seemed almost sedate. There were firecrackers and flares and chanting from fans who fully expected their team to crush us.

Most neutral observers didn't give us a prayer of drawing, let alone winning the tie, particularly as, in Eusebio, Benfica had one of the world's greatest players. Matt, probably like the rest of us, must have also been thinking about our 5–0 humiliation by Lisbon's other club, Sporting, two years earlier. Beautiful as Lisbon was, it was not a city which held happy memories for us.

Benfica warmed up the 75,000 fans by presenting Eusebio with his European Footballer Of The Year trophy before kick-off, just to let us know what we were up against. As I walked up the tunnel and heard the noise, I had the same hair standing up on the back of the neck experience as I'd had before my debut against West Brom.

But I didn't feel any fear. I wasn't in awe. I didn't have any premonitions about how I was going to play, that's something you never knew, but I did know that I was ready. That, whatever the outcome of the game, this was the sort of stage I was meant to play on. The ground, the playing surface, everything was perfect.

It was perfect theatre.

We followed Matt's instructions to keep it tight. Well, for the first six minutes anyway. We tackled hard and when we got the ball, we just played it across the back line. Then Bobby was brought down as we tried to counter-attack and it was a good opportunity for Tony Dunne, our full back, to deliver the ball into the box from the free kick. We poured men into the penalty area and I took up a position on the edge of the box and as I went up for the ball, two defenders jumped with me.

I sensed the goalkeeper starting to come out to try to punch clear, too, but I seemed to find an extra spring as I pushed upwards and got to the ball first. As I headed it, I knew I had made really good contact on it but I couldn't see where it was going and it was only as I hit the deck and twisted my head round that I saw it in the back of the net. It was a fantastic feeling, not just the exhilaration of seeing the ball in the net and knowing that I had scored in front of a crowd like that – but also because it gave us some breathing space in the tie. We were now in with a real chance of getting the result we wanted.

So six minutes later, when I received the ball just inside their half, I saw no reason to be negative. I dipped a shoulder and swerved inside a defender and I just knew from that point that I was going to score. A second defender came at me but I knocked it past him and it was as if I was watching a move unravel on video, all the while knowing the final outcome. As I left the second defender trailing behind me, I looked up to see the 'keeper coming towards me and normally, in a situation like that, I liked to wait until he gave me an indication of which way he was going before making my own move. A slight movement of the body can normally indicate what they are going to do but this time, I caught the look of uncertainty in his eye and instead of waiting, I knocked it past him before he could make up his mind.

On television re-runs, all they ever show is me in the moment that I'm sliding the ball in, as if someone had laid the ball on for me and that was all I had to do. But there was so much more to it than that and given the situation and the circumstances and the enormity of the game, it has to be one of my favourite ever goals.

I put the ball in the net again soon afterwards as the game continued almost in silence but it was disallowed for off-side. Then I went off on another long run. I got the ball on the left wing and knocked it past the first defender, then another and another, four or five in all.

'George, over here, George!' I remember Bobby screaming, wanting me to pass to him, but I was in no mood to give the ball away.

As each defender came at me, he must have looked favourite to get the ball and I felt as though I was struggling to get any pace in my legs, the way you feel in a dream when you're trying to run away from someone. But each time, I just got there first, knocked it a yard or two past him and collected the ball and then went through the same process again and again and again.

Eventually, a defender did manage to force the ball away from me but still I knew the run was amazing. It was like an out-of-body experience, a dream sequence, as if I were hovering over the pitch, watching someone else do it and when I replay it in my mind, it is always in slow motion.

It was like when you lie awake at night before a game imagining yourself on the pitch doing brilliant things. Even professional players have those dreams and, like everyone else, the way you imagine playing in your dreams rarely becomes reality on the pitch. But this night, everything we did came off. We were actually doing those things and on nights like that, everyone grows as a performer.

Good players become great players and great players become gods. It just spread through the whole team. Bill Foulkes, our big centre half, was usually required only to hoof the ball clear from the danger lines; he wasn't someone who could pass the ball. Yet here he was laying it off like Franz Beckenbauer and even trying to take players on.

It was surreal stuff. I've seen other great teams play like that but to be a part of such an experience was unreal.

Strangely, although I can replay almost the whole 90 minutes of that match in my head, I can't remember a single thing after the final whistle went. I can't remember the dressing room, or the hotel we stayed at or what sort of reception we got from the Portuguese fans afterwards. I've no idea why that should be so because I have perfect recollection of much of our travels. What my rooms were like, what we ate, even the names of the waiters.

But in Lisbon, perhaps because I was so wrapped up in my performance, those details are a blank to me. I barely remember half time, except for the fact that we were celebrating and Matt was trying to tell us that we had to be careful, that it wasn't over. To make sure it was, I laid one on for John Connelly in the second half and, after Shay Brennan had knocked in an own goal, Pat Crerand and Bobby Charlton both scored too.

We had an unbelievable 5–1 win.

It was hailed by the press as the greatest ever performance by a British side on foreign soil and we weren't going to offer them any argument on that one. Geoffrey Green of *The Times* said, 'Best seemed quite suddenly to be in love with the ball and the whole side followed his lead' and of my second goal, he said, 'The goalkeeper cleared straight down the middle of the field, Herd headed backwards and downwards and there was Best, gliding like a dark ghost past three men to break clear and slide the ball home – a beautiful goal.'

The British press were great, although it was the Portuguese paper *Bola* that christened me El Beatle, because I was a Brit with long hair, and the name stuck from then on.

At the airport the following day, for some reason, I bought a huge sombrero, the biggest one they had in the shop. It was out of character for me as I was never the flashy sort, but I was on such a high that I got carried away with it all. I was wearing a black leather overcoat and of course, I made sure I had the hat on when we arrived back in Manchester. There was so much excitement in the country about our win that the picture appeared on the front pages of many newspapers. It was the first time I'd appeared on the front pages and it was a strange experience. It added to the surreal nature of the previous few days, though it was a reality I was now going to have to live with.

The press had started following me after that game against Chelsea but the Benfica win was another notch up. Following that, everything went nuts. I even got my own column in the *Daily Express* and people wanted to know everything about me. Not just my football views but what clothes and music I liked and what clubs I went to. Suddenly everything I did was hip or cool.

Everything was going mad off the pitch. Beatlemania was at its height and for the first time young people had their own stars, musicians around the same age as themselves. Things were becoming so much more relaxed after the straitlaced Fifties. Kids wanted to show their emotions and once the British press amended my nickname to the Fifth Beatle, I became an instant target for them. I became an icon, I suppose, though it's difficult to see yourself as one.

I had a foretaste of the madness that was to come six days after the Benfica match. A friend of mine in the rag trade, Malcolm Mooney, had already persuaded me to become a partner in a male boutique in Sale which we called Edwardia and, as luck would have it, the grand opening was just after my greatest game. We knew it was going to be a lot bigger than we had initially thought after all the fuss over the Lisbon match but even we couldn't have imagined how big. Two hours before I was due to open the shop, there were four hundred schoolgirls banging on the windows. It was more surreal than it was on the Stadium of Light pitch – if that's possible.

By this time I was becoming swamped with commercial demands.

'George, you're going to need help with this,' Denis Law said to me. 'Why don't you use my agent, Ken Stanley.'

'Get an agent? Me?' I said. Actors might have had agents in those days but players didn't – except for Denis, of course, though as one of the first British players to play in Italy, he couldn't have negotiated his move without one.

Well, I fancied a trip to London, where I assumed Ken Stanley had his suite of offices, so I agreed to make an appointment to see him. Unfortunately the hub of Ken's empire turned out to be in Huddersfield – home to Denis's first club – a couple of rooms in an office just off Huddersfield town square, with two girls to sort out the mail and take care of any secretarial duties.

Ken gave me a warm welcome and sat me down in his office to give me his little speech about life, which I was to hear many times over.

'George,' he said, 'life is like a chocolate cake and being successful depends on how you divide up the slices. There's a slice for your football, a slice for commercial work ...' and so on.

It was a bit like Forrest Gump's speech about life being like a box of chocolates, except that Ken reckoned it was more like a cake!

Ken would have been a great subject for a movie because when he and I had meetings with potential clients, it was like a scene from *Charlie Bubbles* starring Albert Finney, which is one of my favourite films.

I'd be sitting right there with Ken and whoever the potential clients were.

'Will George be happy to sign autographs for an hour afterwards?' they'd say.

'It depends on what the deal is and how committed he is that day,' Ken would reply, talking about me as if I wasn't there.

Talk about 'Does he take sugar?' – I might as well not have been there because neither side asked me anything directly. It was as though I was invisible and sometimes I felt like putting my hand up and saying, 'I *am* here, you know!'

The other thing that amused me about the whole situation

was that here I was, supposedly the Fifth Beatle and the biggest name in football, and my agent's office was in Huddersfield.

I've nothing against Huddersfield but it has never struck me as the epicentre of the commercial world.

The jobs Ken got me didn't reflect that, either – not that it was his fault because advertising was pretty basic and a long way from the slick machine that it has become. My first big TV advert was for Irish sausages and featured not just me but my mum, Carol and my twin sisters, Julie and Grace, all of three years of age. Carol wasn't that keen but my mum took the most persuading because none of my family are what you would call showbiz types. They like to keep themselves to themselves.

'I'm not appearing in front of any TV camera,' said Mum when it was first put to her.

'You don't have to act, Mum,' I said. 'You don't even have to say anything. Just sit down and make out we're all having a normal breakfast together.'

'How can it be normal,' she said, 'with all the cameras and the other TV people watching us?'

But I convinced her it was only pretend and eventually she agreed. At least the twins were too young to protest.

I barely had a speaking part. The advert showing us all sitting around the breakfast table eating bangers and after biting into one, I had to look up and deliver the immortal line:

'Cookstown are the Best family sausages.'

Catchy or what? My mates never stopped taking the mickey out of me over that one. Of course, like all TV people, they had to do about a hundred takes, which didn't improve my mum's mood.

Of course, having the name Best meant the advertisers got even more excited. They could have all sorts of fun with that one.

Being a sportsman who obviously needed the right kind of diet, I was approached by a lot of food companies. I did an advert for Spanish oranges and another for the Egg Marketing Board, which contained another line Kenneth Branagh would have killed for. It went, 'E for b and be your B', which stood for 'Egg for breakfast and be your Best.'

As you can tell, advertising sophistication was in its infancy. When Ken informed me that he'd set up a modelling contract, I at least looked forward to getting some free, trendy gear from Carnaby Street.

'Who is it with?' I asked him.

'Well, not exactly Carnaby Street,' he replied. 'It's for the Great Universal Stores catalogue.' So much for being a style icon!

Some bright spark at a record company also cottoned on to the Fifth Beatle idea and decided that it would be a great hoot if I released a record. This was the first of many such requests over the years.

'I would be delighted to do so,' was my reply – which

never varied over the years either – 'but for one tiny problem. I can't sing.'

'What on earth has that got to do with it?' was their puzzled, and equally unvaried, response. They reckoned they could use all kinds of electrical wizardry to make me sound like Frank Sinatra, but I wasn't interested.

It was inevitable that the commercial world would latch on to a footballer eventually and I just happened to be the first. But I think Mum found it hard to take and not because I had pressganged her into appearing in the Cookstown sausage advert with me, she just felt that everything was happening too fast and was worried that things would go wrong for me, that I might go downhill as quickly as I went up.

She never said anything to me but I sensed that she felt uneasy about so many people putting me on a pedestal, as though it was an invitation to others to knock me off.

It was almost as if she knew that things might not always be this rosy.

I didn't have time for such thoughts. I was too busy lapping it up. It all seemed a bit unreal but I was determined to enjoy it. I was young, not bad looking and had one of the best jobs in the world. I couldn't see how anything could go wrong really.

I had already been earning good money – over £1,000 a week, when you added all the win bonuses and crowd bonuses and championship bonuses together. That's almost three times the national average wage today. In 1966, it was a fortune, so I didn't really need the commercial stuff, but you would have had to have been crazy to turn it down.

When that started kicking in, I seemed to have money to burn. That was about the only thing I didn't do with it, though some might say that spending it on a series of expensive cars wasn't much different. I had already given my Austin 1100 to my dad when I moved up to a Sunbeam Alpine and now I bought myself a Lotus, which was the prestige car of the time.

The players all got their cars from the same dealer, a guy called Hymie Wernick who in those days, operated from underneath the arches near Victoria Station, so it was easy just to phone Hymie and tell him what I wanted. I changed cars as often as most people change their shoes, buying a succession of Jaguar E-types, all different colours, which are collectors' items today – my first Jag being a saloon with a VTC 777B licence plate – although the way I drove them, I'm sure none of mine made it to vintage status.

A flash car gave you real pulling power in terms of the girls, not that I needed any help in that department. But a nice car came in handy, because the girls, who were coming out of the woodwork, were mostly young, like me, and still lived at home. So until I got a place of my own, we did what every other young couple did and made the most of the back seat. Mine was just a bit more luxurious than most.

I was also getting sackfuls of fan mail. Ken's girls were working almost full-time on it for a while. The great thing was that the other players didn't treat me any differently and Matt didn't say anything about all the attention I was getting. The other players did rib me a bit about The Beatles comparison, though they realised, as I did, that the key to it all was the football. I knew, too, that if I hadn't been a star footballer, none of the other work would have come in.

On the home front, United came down with a bump after that great night in Lisbon. Our first game back was against Chelsea at Stamford Bridge, and for once, a game in the bright lights of London failed to inspire me. We lost 2–0, which as good as ended our hopes of retaining our title.

Worst still, from a personal point of view, I took a knock on my already damaged right knee in our sixth-round FA Cup tie at Preston, which we drew 1–1, winning the replay 3–1. I had been having cartilage problems since the previous season. It would lock up in the middle of games, though I had to limp through the match as the substitute law allowing one injured player to be replaced had not been brought in then. Matt and our trainer Jack Crompton knew all about my knee and Jack would give me a fitness test on the pitch before some games. But I would lie and say everything was all right because I knew that once the game kicked off and the adrenalin started to flow, it wouldn't feel so bad. Now, though, it was clear that the operation I needed could not be put off for much longer. Matt spoke to me about it and we agreed that I would go in for an operation once we were out of the European Cup.

Effectively, we thought this would mean the end of the season because we did not expect to lose to Partizan Belgrade in the semi-finals. But Denis also had a bad knee and in the first leg in Belgrade, he missed a couple of easy chances as we lost 0–2. I played reasonably well but the knee started to swell and hurt again and there was no chance of me playing in the second leg. With Denis out as well, United struggled to break down Partizan's defence and only won through an own goal. Our last hope disappeared when Paddy Crerand was sent off for retaliation. Everyone was devastated but particularly Matt.

'We'll never win the European Cup now,' he apparently told Paddy. He wasn't in the best of health and apparently spoke about quitting but there was no doubt in my mind that Matt would carry on. Despite all the doom and gloom merchants, I felt that we were a young enough team to come back stronger if we qualified again.

For the third successive season, United lost in the semi-finals of the FA Cup, beaten 1–0 by Everton at Burnden Park. Even if we had won, I would have struggled to be fit to sit for 90 minutes at Wembley, let alone play. These days, with keyhole surgery, a cartilage operation is routine but then they had to slit your knee open, take out the cartilage and sew you up again, which meant a minimum of six weeks' recuperation.

And that was if nothing went wrong. A bad operation could spell the end of a player's career.

When I came out of hospital, I was under the care of the club physio Ted Dalton, a lovely old boy but not really at the forefront of modern medicine. He would give me ultrasonic treatment twice a day.

'It's looking a lot better this morning, son,' he pronounced one day, when I jumped up on the treatment table.

'Yes, Ted,' I replied, 'that's because you're looking at the wrong leg.'

My dad had been trying to persuade me to see Bobby McGregor, the Northern Ireland physio, who had no qualifications but was regarded as a legend, a bit of a miracle worker. With the ultrasound not producing results, I was worried that I might never play again. I had been told that everything was OK and that I'd make a complete recovery but when you rely on your body for your living, you can't help having that little nagging doubt in the back of your mind. I wouldn't have been the first or last player to discover that an operation like this had gone horribly wrong.

So I asked United for permission to see Bobby but their view, as you can understand, was that they had access to the best qualified medical people and didn't want to put one of their star players in the care of some quack in Ireland.

I suppose some people thought Bobby *was* a bit of a quack but after that experience with Ted, I figured it couldn't do any harm to see him. He had his own little practice above a sweet shop, and though I don't think he was a Marxist, he operated the communist policy of 'from each according to their means'. He had patients from all walks of lives – bank managers, accountants, window cleaners and pensioners, and he would charge what he thought they could afford. If a little old lady went to see him, he would accept an apple pie from her in lieu of payment, whereas the bank manager would most likely find himself paying £100. As for me, I would have happily paid him twice that amount but because he knew me so well, he wouldn't hear of me paying.

Bobby was a quiet man, about my height but a bit stockier, with thinning hair and he was, I suppose you would say, a bit quirky. But like his other patients, all the Northern Ireland players loved him. If we were staying in a hotel, he would come round just before we were going to bed and ask us all how we were. Then he would give us all massages, insisting they would take the tension anyway.

'No, we're not tense, Bobby, honest,' we'd say, but he wouldn't listen and sometimes it was the early hours of the morning before the last player got his massage.

'Come and see me at The Oval,' he said when I phoned him to make an appointment.

Bobby was the Glentoran trainer and even had a spell as their manager, but after spending so much time on the terraces of the ground as a kid, I felt strange walking down through the dressing room area and into the treatment room. Naturally, it was far from United standards. It was a poky little place with bits of equipment scattered everywhere and this strong smell of liniment. Bobby didn't bother too much with small talk.

'So the leg's still giving you trouble is it?' he said. 'Well, hop on to the table and let's have a look.'

I laid down on the table and Bobby started prodding around the knee, saying 'Does it hurt here?' and going 'Ahem … ahem' as he examined it. But he probably already knew what the problem was because he was one of those people who you felt only had to look at you to know what was wrong.

After a few minutes' prodding, he walked away without saying anything.

'What do you think?' I said, but he didn't answer, just came back with a piece of wood, which he handed to me.

'What's this for?' I asked.

'To bite on. What I'm going to do now might hurt a bit.'

A bit! As soon as I bit on the wood, he quickly grabbed around the back of my knee – the right one, I'm pleased to say, stuck his fingers in and waggled my ligaments around. For a few seconds, the pain was so unbearable that I thought I would bite right through the wood.

'How does it feel now?' he said when he'd finished, standing back. And though it was sore, the pain didn't last very long.

'It feels a lot better,' I said, feeling the knee.

He brought out a jar of sweet-smelling cream which he smeared all round the knee.

'What's that for, Bobby?' I said.

'It will help the healing process,' he replied.

'Yes, but what's in it?'

'Can't tell you that. But it will do you good.'

I later learned that this was a cure-all cream, which he administered to every patient, no matter what they were suffering from. You could have had a bad back or a broken leg and Bobby would have given you his cream, though the ingredients were his secret. I don't know whether it was psychosomatic or what but Bobby's treatment did the trick and a week later I was kicking a ball again.

United may have ended the season with nothing, but our efforts were recognised in the footballing honours. Bobby, who joined up with England's World Cup side as soon as the domestic season was over, was both Footballer of the Year and European Footballer of the Year for 1966, the latter a prestigious award which Denis had won in 1964. I was third in the poll for Footballer of the Year, which made me feel a little less sorry for myself as I sat at home, nursing my damaged knee.

Not that I spent all summer at home. Danny Bursk suggested going away on holiday somewhere sunny, so we booked a two-week package holiday in Palma Nova, Majorca, having been assured by mates who had been there that it would be a shagging paradise.

Well, it was, but only for Danny, who was at it like a rabbit from the first night to the last, while I didn't manage to get my leg over on the whole trip. Danny and I both pulled the first night but while he took his girl to bed, mine didn't want to know and I spent the rest of the trip desperately trying to pick someone else up. I was getting desperate towards the end of the holiday and going for uglier and uglier birds.

But I hadn't reached the height of my fame then and, perhaps, I hadn't quite perfected my chat-up lines.

CHAPTER FIVE
FORBIDDEN
FRUIT

I have never been a great fan of the England football team.

They have always turned out teams that are strong and well organised – well at least they did until Kevin Keegan became manager. But I've always felt that their teams tend to lack that spark which most great sides have, something to make them that little bit different, that little bit special. I have always believed that a truly great side needs 10 good players and a genius. Brazil had one in Pele, and a few more who were not far off it. Holland had Johan Cruyff, Argentina had Maradona and France have got Zinedine Zidane. Paul Gascoigne had a good spell for England for a while but he was never in that class.

Teams can sometimes succeed by making the best of what they've got, however, and that was definitely the case in the summer of 1966, when England hosted the World Cup. They weren't the best team but had the enormous advantage of playing at home, and at Wembley, at that, which was a stadium where they did not lose often. But like all home nations, they were under enormous pressure from the press and fans who expected them to win it. Sir Alf Ramsey, the England manager, fuelled that fever twelve months before a ball was kicked in the competition by saying, 'England will win the World Cup.'

They didn't start like potential winners, drawing 0–0 with Uruguay in the opening match of the competition. But the first game is a massive showpiece occasion and people were expecting so much of England that the result was almost a blessing in disguise in that it took a lot of pressure off. The English press always over-react to victory or defeat. If England lose, they're written off as hopeless and when they win a game, they're suddenly potential world champions. They were writing glowing reports again after Bobby Charlton scored a brilliant effort against Mexico in the second game, which England won 2–0 and suddenly, everyone was up for it again. England then beat France in their final group game to clinch their place in the quarter-finals and World Cup fever took over the whole country.

Ramsey was forced to leave out an injured Jimmy Greaves for the quarter final game against Argentina and it turned out to be a dull, defensive, negative game, partly because of Argentina's spoiling tactics and partly because England were playing without their top striker and without wingers to provide chances. England got lucky, though, when the Argentinian captain, Antonio Rattin, who was a fantastic player, was sent off after arguing with the referee and Geoff Hurst, who had replaced Greaves, headed the winner in the 77th minute.

England came up against Portugal and Eusebio in the semi-final but, as in the Stadium of Light a few months earlier, my pal Nobby kept him quiet for most of the game and restricted him to a goal from the penalty spot in the last ten minutes. By then England were already two up, Bobby Charlton scoring both goals, and hung on to victory.

England started as favourites against West Germany in the Final, which was only natural as they were the host nation and even when they fell behind in the twelfth minute, they sensed an inevitability about their victory. But they were lucky when the Russian linesman awarded a goal after Hurst's shot rebounded off the crossbar and, according to the official, bounced over the line for the third goal in extra time.

Like all World Cups, it was a fantastic carnival and watching it only heightened my regret at the cock-up in Albania the previous year which had prevented me and the Northern Ireland team from being a part of it. Instead, I could only watch in envy as my United team mates Bobby and Nobby picked up the trophy.

I was particularly delighted for Nobby, who had never got

the credit for his footballing ability because of his reputation as a hard man. He also looked a bit of a moody so-and-so when he wore those Mr Magoo glasses off the field, but in the United dressing room he was known as Mr Happy because he was such a bubbly character who was always ready with a laugh. The World Cup allowed the nation to see that side of him because as England progressed, even non-football fans got wrapped up in it and the media made sure they got to know everything about players they had hardly heard of at the beginning of the tournament. But if there was a picture that summed up Nobby, it was the one showing him doing that little jig at Wembley as the team celebrated their final triumph, with the lid of the Jules Rimet trophy on his head.

Not everyone in our dressing room felt as happy for their English team mates. Paddy Crerand, about as anti-English a Scot as you could wish to meet, was enraged at England's good fortune when Hurst scored that controversial goal against the Germans in extra time. And I wouldn't have been surprised to hear that Denis Law was dressed in lederhosen and standing at the German end on the big day. The Scots always support two teams – Scotland and anyone playing against England. But I thought it was great, not just for England but for British football generally. It gave a fantastic buzz to our domestic football, which at the time was full of Irish and Scots, as well, so they got a bit of reflected glory. And it improved our standing in the world. If you loved football, or were lucky enough to play it at a professional level, you couldn't have chosen a more exciting decade to live in.

You also couldn't have chosen a more dangerous one if you were a potential alcoholic.

Anything went in the Sixties and anything seemed possible. We were the first generation not to go to war, we didn't even have to do national service. So we saw no reason not to party to our hearts content, whatever that entailed. For many, it was taking drugs, though fortunately, given my addictive personality, I never had any inclination to try them.

For me, it was drink and women and I had made a great new friend to share these pursuits in Mike Summerbee, who had signed for Manchester City the previous season. I used to keep bumping into Mike at Time and Place, which had become the new trendy nightclub in town. It was one of those new multi-purpose clubs, which had a dance area, a bar upstairs and a casino, and it quickly became the in-place. If you could get in there, you had cracked it and as young, professional footballers, we had no trouble getting in. Most of the single players at the two Manchester clubs went there, and Mike and I soon became friends and started knocking about together. He was a perfect foil for me because I was still a bit shy and he was far more outgoing and streetwise.

There was a whole gang of us who used to do the rounds of the clubs together, including Kenny Lynch, whom I first met in Le Phonographe, which was to become Blinkers; Waggy – Malcolm Wagner – who ran a hairdressing shop; Danny Bursk, a fur trader; Malcolm Mooney, my pal in the rag trade; and a lad called Tony Marsh who used to be an MC for The Beatles.

We wouldn't just go out in Manchester, however. We felt the world was our oyster.

At weekends, Mike and I and some of the others would jump in our flashy motors and drive down to Birmingham or London for a change of scene. Birmingham was buzzing then and Mike had become friendly with boxer Johnny Prescott, who came from there, and a pal of his called Chalky White. So after a weekend game, Mike and I and any of the other Manchester crowd who fancied it would drive down on Saturday night. We'd meet the others in a place called the Elbow Room, a bar-cum-disco which was always full of girls. And then we'd move on to the Rum Runner, a similar sort of place and again crawling with women. If we got lucky, we would stay over in Birmingham and go back to Manchester on Sunday night.

And other times, a crowd of us would jump on a late train from Manchester to London on Saturday night and do a crawl of the clubs in the West End. Tramp was already the big place and was always full of faces and that became my favourite on one of my early trips. I liked the fact that you didn't get bothered in there, it's a private club and you were not on offer to the general public. I also got to know a back way out to avoid the press.

Alex Harvey, the bandleader, used to hang around with us and there was another lad in our gang whom I only ever knew as Lobster Lenny, because he went as red as one after five minutes in the sun. We were all out for a good time and, despite the disastrous time I'd experienced in Spain with Danny Bursk the previous summer, I thought it was a great idea when someone suggested that all of us should spend the summer of 1966 in Majorca – Mike and I and all our pals from Manchester, Birmingham and London.

About thirty of us went, renting out a couple of large villas with six or seven bedrooms in them – you'd sleep wherever you could. We also got friendly with a couple of American lads called Craig and Radar, who would join us for our nightly trawl of the clubs looking for women and knocking back beer and champagne. We didn't normally have to look far for either. I was still shy when it came to chatting up women but with the fame that had come with the Lisbon win and the El Beatle tag, they were coming up to me in droves and it was a question of me taking my pick.

We didn't yet have to worry about newspaper photographers hiding behind palm trees with long lenses as they do today. And we didn't have to worry about girls having second thoughts the following morning and going running to the papers, making all sorts of accusations. Could you imagine it now? If I were up to those tricks these days, I would have been hounded to death by now.

Another of the regular characters in Majorca was David Sirocco, who used to do yoga on the beach and made a living giving people massages. He was the local eccentric. All week he used to dress from head to toe in white, including a white bandanna which David Beckham would have died for. Then, when he went out to party on Saturday night, he would be dressed from head to toe in black.

We all had such a great time in Majorca that it became our haunt for the next few years, as long as I didn't have to go on tour with the club. As soon as the football season ended, we'd fly out and I would make sure I was one of the early arrivals so that I could bag a room. Then it was every man for himself and if other mates flew in during the holiday, we would find some room for them somewhere. The places were absolute tips by the end because they were typical singles holidays. We'd lie in bed late and then wander out for breakfast and a sunbathe on the beach. Then it would be a few beers during the day and maybe an afternoon siesta before we went out for the serious partying in the evening. We'd never get back until the early hours, starting all over again the following day.

Sometimes, I wouldn't get back to England until a week before pre-season training, which could be a total of almost three months. And I'd be absolutely knackered by then. I even used to get a mate of mine, Tony Griffin, to drive my car over. I took a few of my Jaguar E-types and one year, a Rolls Royce, which was a big help in the pulling stakes. But I don't know how I didn't kill myself because the roads were very primitive in those days and highly dangerous. Every morning, you'd see cars that had gone over the edge of the cliff. The roads were bad enough in the daytime, yet I'd be driving back in the early hours of the morning after drinking since early evening. Given my driving record over the years, I was lucky to survive those Majorca trips.

Once I discovered Majorca, my trips home to Belfast became less frequent. Before, I used to spend a lot of time there in the summer and made a point of going over at Christmas. I even used to write frequently and point out nice reports on my performances in the papers which the family might have missed. But gradually, I drifted further and further from the family. I was enjoying the sort of life that I could only have dreamed of a few years earlier and suddenly it was Belfast, not Manchester, which seemed like an alien world to me.

I suppose I was like someone who leaves home for the first time to go to university and discovers an exciting new world which makes their old one appear a little dull. And with a lot more money in my pocket than a student, I was starting to have a great time at the university of life.

Even so, I did manage to make a brief visit home at the end of the summer of 1966. The jungle drums must have been working from the moment I landed at Belfast Airport because soon after I got home, the street outside our house was swarming with people.

I hadn't realised what an effect that Benfica game had had in Belfast. When I went home, I just expected to be treated like one of the locals – I was Mrs Best's boy from the Cregagh again. But this time it was pandemonium in Burren Way. People were actually pressing their faces to our windows, hoping to get a glimpse of me.

'You don't know what it's like for us, George,' Carol said to me as we sat in the relative safety of our kitchen. 'We get this in the street all the time, people just staring at us because we're your family. Just pull the blinds down.'

'No,' I said, 'I'd better go out there or we'll never get any peace.' I was quite touched by the turnout, even though I knew visits home would never be the same again. So I went outside and signed some autographs and thanked everyone for coming.

'I hope you'll let me have a quiet day with my family now,' I told them.

I thought that was the end of it but later in the day, we heard some noise outside and my mum eased up the blind to look out of the window.

'What on earth are those two up to?' she said.

I looked out to see a couple of reporters, who must have climbed into the garden at the end of our street and trampled through all the others to get to our house. We gave them short shrift but it was the end of a normal life, not just for me, but also for my family. It was sad to think that my visits home were now going to be an ordeal for my family as much as for me. This is one of the things about learning to cope with fame. It gets you from all sides. I'm sure it had an effect on the number of times I went back to see my family too.

'We always loved to see you at home, George,' Carol told me a lot later, 'but it was also a relief sometimes when you left and we could get back to a normal life.'

When Mum had a sixth child, my brother Ian, in July 1966, she was finding it difficult enough to cope as it was. I was sending home money each month to help them out but Mum and Dad were both proud, self-sufficient people and didn't want to be living off someone else, not even their own son. So Mum continued to work, even with five children to look after.

Given their circumstances, it was a bit surprising that they had a sixth child and I always remember my dad phoning to tell me that Mum was pregnant.

'I've got something important to tell you, son,' he said, stuttering over the words.

'What is it? What is it?' I said.

'Well, your mum is having a baby.'

'That's great, Dad'

'So, you don't mind, then?' he said, sounding relieved.

I was delighted for them, though with three-year-old twins, and two teenagers in the house, the new baby didn't make life easy for Mum, especially as she had begun worrying about me. Luckily, Carol was 19 by then and had become quite adept at coping with babies. And Barbara, who was 14, had started helping out as well. Yet there is no denying that it was a lot of work for my parents, and while I know they were proud of my success, I can't help thinking that coping with their son's fame can't have made things any easier.

While there was now much mickey-taking from the rest of us if any English international player in the United team missed a tackle or a scoring chance, the feelgood factor generated by England's World Cup win created a great buzz in the football world at the start of the 1966–67 season.

Bobby and Nobby, who should have been exhausted after their efforts, seemed positively inspired as we began the season with four wins from the opening five games. Everyone at Old Trafford was desperate to regain the Championship and get another crack at the European Cup, knowing that was the Holy Grail for Matt and aware that he didn't have that many years left to achieve it because his health wasn't great.

His mind was sharp enough, though, and when our form started to dip a little, he went out and paid £55,000 to Chelsea for goalkeeper Alex Stepney. He also freshened up the side by bringing in John Aston Junior and Bobby Noble. That gave us a new impetus, until our old friends from Leeds took another point off us at Old Trafford. They were becoming my personal bogey team. I rarely played well against them and rarely scored.

Although I was pretty happy with my overall form, I got into hot water with Matt again when news reached him that I was going out with a married woman called Dahlia Simmons. I later earned a reputation for dating two Miss Worlds, Marjorie Wallace and Mary Stavin, but I went out with a lot of normal, working-class girls who were *absolutely* stunning – far more stunning than either of the beauty queens.

But of all of them, Dahlia was probably the most beautiful.

And of course, when everyone started warning me to stay away from her, that was the worst thing they could have done.

We met in Colin Burne's nightclub, Reubens, and I was just knocked out by her looks. She told me she was married but I persuaded her to give me her number anyway and we started seeing each other in what we thought was a discreet way. We'd go out for dinner at one of the more out of the way restaurants, away from the centre of Manchester, and as we couldn't go back to her place and I didn't think Mrs Fullaway would be impressed, we would stay over at one of her girlfriend's houses. It's impossible, however – as I found out – to be discreet or keep a secret for long in Manchester, because it's a village compared to London and everyone knows everyone else's business.

I managed to keep it away from Matt for quite some time. In fact he was probably the last person to find out. But when he did, he was furious. He was a strait-laced sort of person and would have been appalled at me dating a married woman and would also have been worried about its effect on the image of the club. So I wasn't surprised when I was told that he wanted to see me in his office. It was like being summoned to the headmaster's study because, despite all the nonsense that has been written about Matt being a father figure to me, he was very much The Boss and even the senior players were nervous when they were summoned to see him. I don't know whether it was deliberately arranged that way to make it more intimidating, but Matt's office was at the end of a long corridor and for any player going to see him, it was the longest walk of their lives.

They should have called it The Green Mile.

I had a pretty shrewd idea what Matt wanted when I walked The Mile and he was not one to beat about the bush.

'Son,' he said, 'it's not for me to interfere in your private life but why this girl? Why someone who is married?' He looked genuinely baffled. 'There are hundreds of nice girls out there who are single and might even make you a nice wife. Why can't you go out with one of them?'

'I don't know, Boss,' I mumbled. 'I just like her and I didn't realise she was married when I met her.' That was a bit of a white lie, of course.

If Matt had really understood me, he would have known why Dahlia – as forbidden fruit – was irresistible to me, quite apart from her fabulous looks. In the early days, because of my Belfast accent and my shy ways, I had struggled to pull girls because I wasn't very good at chatting them up.

But now that I was famous, it didn't matter that I was shy and didn't always have that much to say for myself because they were throwing themselves at me. So I would deliberately go for the ones who were supposedly unattainable as a sort of challenge. In a way, it was the same sort of approach that made me a successful sportsman. Pulling girls had become a sport for me and so I wanted to be the best at it.

I couldn't really have explained that to Matt, who called me into his office again a couple of more times when there were further stories about Dahlia. I didn't know what to say to him, so I'd sit there and say what he wanted to hear.

'Yes, Boss, you're right, Boss, it won't happen again, Boss.'

And then, of course, as soon as I left his office, I would be on the phone arranging to meet Dahlia. I didn't really think it was any of his business. I thought I could do what I wanted.

Matt also spoke about the situation to my dad, who no doubt kept it from my mum. Dad had words with me, too, but he knew well enough not to try to interfere, though he appreciated that Matt was trying to act in my best interests, that he wasn't simply trying to pry into my affairs or be a busybody. It was the same when he approached Dad about my drinking. Dad understood that Matt simply wanted me to be in the proper state to play football.

Inevitably, Dahlia's husband got to know about what was going on and he came looking for me one night in Time and Place. I had started to gamble a bit then - though not in great amounts, maybe a few quid - and I was sitting playing blackjack when he walked in. He came and stood right behind me.

I tried to stay calm and kept playing as though everything was normal but he started telling me what he was going to do to me.

This went on for a few minutes, when, luckily, one of my pals walked in.

'Are any of the lads upstairs?' I asked, knowing that the gang used to meet in the bar up there.

He cottoned on to the situation right away and disappeared upstairs. Soon, one by one, my mates wandered down, each making a point of strolling over to me.

'Everything all right, George?' they each asked.

'Yes, yes,' I replied. 'I'll let you know if I need anything.'

Simmons finally got the message and moved off. He and Dahlia split up and I kept on seeing her for a few years, as we could be a lot more open about our relationship. We were both mad about each other, even though I had the feeling inside that it would fizzle out sooner or later.

I was still too young to think about settling down, especially with so many stunning and willing young women around. The problem was that I found it impossible to be faithful to anyone and I didn't want to be with one person.

I wanted to be able to come and go as I pleased.

If Matt was exasperated about my choice of sexual partners, he started tearing his hair out when he heard about my new late-night drinking haunt, the Brown Bull, which also doubled as a small hotel. I say 'late-night' but it was more like all night and they should have called it the Hotel California because people checked in but never checked out.

At first I used to drink in a place called The Grapes where my team mate Shay Brennan hung out. In fact, Shay had a couple of hangouts, the other one being the Circus, which was a good little meeting place in the centre of town but one of the smallest pubs you'll ever see. If they got twenty people in there it was crowded and if one of them was Shay, four had to leave for it to be comfortable.

I didn't really like the place so I would catch him in The Grapes instead. Then they pulled The Grapes down so I was looking for a new local. I had passed the Brown Bull a million times and never felt any inclination to go in. It was the worst location in the world, underneath the arches of a railway station and right on a crossroads - a real rough area and noisy too. It had absolutely nothing going for it at all. So, naturally, one night when I was out with Waggy, we decided to drop in for a drink.

If the place looked bad from the outside, it was nothing to what it looked like inside but then I've always liked scruffy boozers. Not that we would have gone back after that first night if we hadn't bumped into the owner, an American guy called Billy Barr, who had just taken over the place after leaving the forces. He was one of those people you just took to straight away.

Apart from Waggy and I, there were only a couple of guys in there, who were sitting on what I thought was a bench but on closer inspection turned out to be two orange boxes. But the décor didn't matter because Bill was such a great host.

'Are you lads hungry?' said Billy, halfway through the evening, once we got chatting. 'Do you fancy something to eat?'

The next thing we knew, his wife Leila was bringing out a couple of T-bone steaks.

A few nights later we went back with a couple of mates and word must have got round because almost overnight this little back-street pub became one of Manchester's in-places. It helped that the Granada TV studios were close by because all the young actresses in town and the young hopefuls began staying there, which brightened the place up and offered me the chance of some new conquests.

'There's a nice young lady in number four,' Billy would say to me - he had about six rooms upstairs. 'Why don't you knock on her door and see if she fancies coming down for a drink?'

Billy didn't even have to tart the place up. It was still a complete dive but a dive with the right people in it. Everyone just used to flock to it – all the footballers and showbiz crowd, who probably liked it better than the more glitzy places because it was such an authentic corner of Manchester.

Jimmy Tarbuck, whom I'd met a few times through Kenny Lynch, would use the Bull if he was in town and so would Michael Parkinson, whom I've known since he was a young reporter in Barnsley. The place became a mad house and Billy was doing such great business it would have been rude to close at the normal chucking out time.

So every now and then the police would raid the place. Tarby was in there during one raid and a young woman copper came up to him.

'What's that you're drinking there?' she said, pointing at his glass.

'Ta very much,' replied Tarby, handing over the glass with a big smile, 'I'll have a large gin and tonic please.'

Some nights Billy just couldn't get any more people in the place. A local guy took over the pub next door and started getting the leftovers. Had it not been for the fella who owned it, Billy might have thought of asking for a share of the profits because they'd all been generated by the Brown Bull.

Matt *hated* the Brown Bull. If he could have had his way, he would have had the place pulled down, though for some reason, he could never remember the name of it.

So when he asked me, 'Have you been in that Green Pig again?' – at other times, he called it the Black Cow or the

Brown Horse – I could look him straight in the eye and answer truthfully, 'No Boss.'

Poor old Matt was caught between the pit and the pendulum. He wanted to get me to toe the line but he also knew that I was his greatest asset, who could be his leading player for another 15 years. I was also the one who could deliver his European dream so he never really came down on me like a ton of bricks. We had seen how ruthlessly he had dealt with Johnny Giles and there were many other players who were shown the door for minor offences. The only sense in which you could describe him as a father figure was that, like my dad, he didn't really hand out any discipline. If I hadn't been who I was and doing the business for Matt, I would have been well and truly kicked out. Matt also wanted to keep any bad stuff away from the public domain, to preserve the image of the club, which is probably another reason why he didn't want to be seen dropping me every five minutes.

If I had poured my heart out to anyone at Old Trafford it would have been Matt's number two, Jimmy Murphy. He was a dour Welshman but with a heart as big as a house. He and Matt were of similar ilk, they had been brought up rough and ready and seen it all, been through everything together. And, of course, Jimmy did a magnificent job as stand-in manager when Matt was recovering after Munich.

Matt and Jimmy played the good cop, bad cop routine. They were both good cops really, but someone had to play the hard man and that was Matt, while Jimmy would soften the blow after you'd been punished. Sometimes, after Matt had given me a dressing-down, Jimmy would call me into his room and say, 'You don't want to listen to that old bugger.' That was how they worked it and though I don't know whether it was deliberate or not, it made for a perfect partnership. Everyone knew and understood the situation.

You rarely saw Jimmy on the training ground, though, which was strange. You would have thought it would have been the other way round, but the Boss always took training and Jimmy would sit back a little, spending time in the office making phone calls to sort out young players from other clubs. He probably did more than Joe Armstrong when it came to the youngsters.

Jimmy's bark was definitely worse than his bite and I found him easy to talk to. Sometimes, after I'd done one of my disappearing acts, he would have a quiet word and if I had a problem I wanted to talk about, I would have gone to Jimmy and not to Matt. But I never did because I just wasn't the sort to open up to people.

It's easy for me to say now but it might have been better if Matt had been harder on me. I had been getting away with things since I was a kid, only small things. But as I got away with more and more, it encouraged me to believe that I could do anything I wanted. The normal laws of the club didn't seem to apply to me.

Matt couldn't do anything to hush things up though when I was involved in a car accident which could have left me on a manslaughter charge. Not that I considered it my fault as, luckily, it happened early in the evening, when I hadn't had a drink. I was just pulling away from some lights, it was pouring with rain and this girl ran out in front of me, presumably without realising that the lights had changed. Also, she had an umbrella up so she wouldn't have seen my car. I was probably only doing about ten miles per hour when I hit her but the impact on her body made a sickening noise and she broke her pelvis in the fall. Danny Bursk was with me and there were plenty of other witnesses, but when the case came to court, I was found guilty of careless driving and fined £10. I also had my licence endorsed.

I felt awful about it but it was fortunate that it hadn't happened later that night. For starters, I would have had a good few drinks inside me by that stage. I was starting to stay out later and later – and I was also drinking more because I was beginning to enjoy it. I hadn't liked the taste of booze that much at first – it had just been something to give me a bit of confidence – but now I really had the taste for it.

I didn't feel any particular pressure on the pitch, everything seemed easy for me on the football field and I was so fit that I was easily able to run out the booze in training. Or so I thought. Drink certainly wasn't a crutch for me at that time. I was just like any other young person who works hard all week and goes a bit crazy at the weekend. I was just going a bit crazier than most, but I was always back in work on Monday morning, willing and eager to perform. As a professional athlete, I was able to cope.

The other reason that it was lucky my accident happened early in the evening was that I was not in the habit of driving within the speed limit, particularly after I'd had a drink. Let's face it, you can't get behind the wheel of an E-type and not put your foot down and I had a nightly battle of wits with the police. They would park up in little cul-de-sacs in Chorlton, waiting to catch speeding or drunken motorists but there were a lot of different routes from the town centre to Mrs Fullaway's and I mostly managed to elude them.

Also, at weekends, I would sometimes stay in the flat in Crumpsall, which Mike Summerbee and I had begun renting together to entertain the ladies. That was our little hideaway, a place we could escape all the madness and where Kenny Lynch used to come and stay. It was just a one-bedroom flat in one of those big, old, Victorian houses in Manchester. But it was enough for our needs because it also had a big lounge which doubled as a bedroom if necessary. And if we slept there on a Saturday night, the following afternoon we would wander over to Didsbury, where a bookie pal, Selwyn Demmy, had a bachelor flat that put ours to shame. It was always immaculate and Selwyn would put on a Sunday afternoon tea that my mum would have been proud of. Except that he also

My first dribble — and not a defender in sight. Aged 13 months.

Carol and I pose (reluctantly) outside Burren Way.

They say the camera doesn't lie, so that really must be a quiff developing on my head in this photo booth shot.

With uncle George Withers, my sparring partner, in 1963.

Playing big brother with Ian on the beach in Northern Ireland.

Alone with my thoughts on a trip to Crossgar.

Come On You Reds. Mum and Dad are greeted by Mrs Fullaway as they arrive for a game at Old Trafford, 1965, Mum immaculate as usual.

Suited and booted for a match day away trip.

With Mrs Fullaway's daughter and her dog Kim.

*One of my favourite
pictures. My tormentor,
Mike Doyle, has just scored
an own goal in the 1964
FA Youth Cup semi-final.*

*Opposite:
No standing on ceremony
at The Cliff training
ground after another
hard day at the office.*

*Clean shaven, clean living,
hopeful young professional
at Manchester United.*

*Checking my look is
just right before another
post-match night on
the town, 1964.*

*Opposite:
And people wondered
why I was called The
Fifth Beatle, even though
I'm holding a snooker
cue rather than a guitar!*

*Showing off my perfect
technique. Notice how
the police inspector in
the front row has been
sent the wrong way by
my body swerve.*

Trying my hand as a DJ at Mrs Fullaway's house.

With Dad before the 1968 European Cup semi-final against Real Madrid in Spain.

Bobby watches me take on the Benfica defence and (right) an emotional moment as we celebrate his goal in the 1968 European Cup Final. A magical time that I still treasure.

*The moment I won
the European Cup!
Only joking lads.
But we knew after
my goal in the first
minute of extra time
that the Cup would
finally be ours.*

*With the Footballer
Of The Year trophy,
presented to me by
the Football Writers'
Association in 1968.*

Receiving my award as European Footballer of the Year in 1968.

Matt Busby and the European Cup winning squad with the trophy before the 1968–69 season.

Acting the fool with actress Juliet Mills, daughter of Sir John. I think I later left that jacket in a French restaurant.

It's a tough job but someone has to do it. Coaching the Blinkers football team with the help of David Sadler (left) and Alan Ball.

Classic pose at a pre-season photo session at Old Trafford.

*Head to head with another sporting giant,
British heavyweight champion Brian London.*

*Celebrating buying my 'dream home', Que Sera. It was the
last time I was to be pictured there without being mobbed by fans.*

Two cheeky young fans take their opportunity to get my autograph.

Living the dream — posing by my white Jaguar with 'staff', driver Bill White, secretary Pearl Goodman and business manager Malcolm Mooney.

© EMPICS/TOPHAM PICTURE POINT

© POPPERFOTO

*Leaving my second home – the FA headquarters –
after another disciplinary hearing, 1971. I'd obviously
stopped at Carnaby Street en route.*

laid on beer and wine and half a dozen gorgeous girls. All my favourite things in one place.

Some people were surprised that Mike and I remained friends, seeing that we played for two of football's biggest rivals, especially as both City and United had many local lads in their sides then and the United supporters were mostly from Manchester. Today, that's true of only about a third of them. The derbies then were total warfare and if your team lost, it was complete humiliation. You would go into hiding for a couple of days. Nevertheless Mike and I never let it affect our relationship and to get everyone going we'd even choreograph a couple of moves before matches.

'When we kick off,' he would say, 'you run over as if you're going to tackle me and I'll put the ball through your legs.'

'OK,' I'd reply, 'then a few minutes later, you come in for the tackle and I'll do it back to you.'

We knew that would make both sets of fans happy, though I am glad I was Mike's friend because he could put it about a bit on the field. I suppose with players like Nobby trying to kick them into the stands, forwards had to be able to look after themselves.

I spent a lot of time on the Green Mile that season but the strange thing was that Matt never protested about all the outside work I was doing, the modelling and the boutique stuff, which meant I didn't get as much rest as most foot-ballers should have. It must have been a concern for him, but he never said a word about it. I can't imagine that happening today.

I even did an advert for Playtex bras, but not modelling one I hasten to add. It was another commercial that would seem corny on today's television. I had to walk into a bar – bit of typecasting there – sit down at a table, then look up and catch sight of this beautiful girl. Naturally – and we're still in the realms of normal life here – I send over a note asking if I can buy her a drink. And here it loses the plot a bit – because she had to refuse.

The message was that if you were wearing a bra that uplifted you like a Playtex, you could even say no to George Best. From my own experience with women at that time, I can only assume that Playtex was not the best-selling bra company!

I hated the modelling because you'd have three- or four-hour photo sessions, which I found completely boring. But my agent was pushing all this stuff my way and the money was great, so I felt I had to do it. It was all immaterial, even the boutiques I opened. They were just somewhere to hang around in the afternoons. What mattered to me was the football. Even the girls and the drinking didn't affect my career at that point. Football came first and I trained as hard as anyone at the club to improve my game. And though I had now moved on to drinking vodka, and at times quite a lot of it, that was mostly after the Saturday match. Being supremely fit, I could easily recover from that. I didn't have hangovers and never had any more of those spinning room experiences.

When I think back, they were probably the happiest days of my life, in 1966 and '67. Talk about fulfilling a dream – those days were just pure perfection, pure theatre, the whole thing. I was playing with and against great players, the grounds were packed to capacity every week and I was travelling the world doing something I loved. I didn't have to lift a finger. All the travel arrangements were made for me and I didn't even have to pack because my landlady or whatever girlfriend I had at the time would do it for me.

And I was still only 20. Just a few years earlier I had been kicking a ball about in the streets of Belfast. Now I was being paid fortunes to do it. It would have been difficult for anyone to have kept their feet completely on the ground under such circumstances. It felt like I was living in a fantasy world and could act accordingly.

When we played Nottingham Forest, our closest rivals for the title, in February 1967, there were over 62,000 people inside Old Trafford and our average attendance for the season was 54,000. Forest were a bit of a surprise package but with two games of the season left, we needed just a point to win the title. The first was against West Ham at Upton Park, which wasn't an easy place to win, especially with their three World Cup winning players. So, not surprisingly, Matt was full of caution beforehand, telling us to keep it tight, but we murdered them 6–1.

That was the sort of side we were, brimming with confidence and capable of doing that to anybody. My goal against West Ham was my 10th of the season, which may not seem a lot after I'd played in all 42 League games. But I probably made twice as many for Denis and the other players.

Thanks to the Brown Bull, I became more friendly with team mate Shay Brennan during that season and it would be difficult for anyone to meet Shay and not become an instant friend because he is one of those people who gets on with everybody and never has a bad word to say about anyone. I also got a lot closer to Paddy Crerand, Noel Cantwell and Denis Law. Denis fell in love with Italian food during his spell at Torino so it was probably at his bidding that the three of them developed a routine of going to an Italian restaurant with their wives on Saturday nights. I don't know why, maybe because I was now one of the established players, but I began popping in to see them. I wouldn't eat with them, I would just stay for half an hour on my way out to a club or wherever. But it helped our friendships and Denis is a bit like Shay. You can't be miserable in his company.

Despite having so many different personalities in the dressing room, we became a tight knit group, not that you would have believed it if you'd seen us in training. We used to kick lumps out of each other every day and it would often end up in punch ups. Outsiders are surprised to hear things like that and there was a great kerfuffle a few years ago when John Hartson kicked his West Ham team mate Eyal Berkovic in training. But when you get a bunch of fit, strong, competitive young men all competing for a few places in a football team, that's exactly what you are going to get – fighting.

The players used to organise six and seven-a-side games between ourselves at the Stretford End, where they had concrete pillars to stop the fans getting on to the pitch and we would smash each other into the pillars. I remember one day when big Bill Foulkes knocked Denis Law to the ground and Denis just got up and punched him. Bill hit him back and the next thing, everyone was piling in.

Harry Gregg was always liable to give you a clip round the ear as well, if he thought you were out of order with a challenge. But it was all left behind at the end of the day and on the pitch on match day we would fight alongside each other. It was a special team and after the way we won the championship in 1967, we felt we might be on the verge of even more spectacular feats.

At the end of the 1966–67 season, we went off on a post-season tour to Australia and New Zealand, stopping off in California to play in a tournament in San Francisco against Celtic and Italian side Bari. It coincided with my 21st birthday, so Dave Sadler said, 'We've got to go out and celebrate, George.'

I asked permission from the Boss and Dave and I went out to a nearby English pub called the Edinburgh Castle. San

Francisco was the centre of the hippy universe at the time, the place where it was all happening, where everyone was freaking out and doing their own thing. But still a Cregagh boy at heart, I spent my 21st birthday at the pub with Dave, sinking a couple of beers and eating fish and chips.

Life couldn't get much better than that.

CHAPTER SIX
LIVING
THE DREAM

I had made my reputation as an entertainer and a provider of goals. But in 1967–68, I took over as the team's main goalscorer, though I am sure the likes of Denis and Bobby will tell you that that was because I became greedier and wouldn't give them the ball even when they were better placed to score than me.

I have to admit that that was true at times. I might have been shy off the field but I'd always been full of confidence on it. That was the place where I truly came alive. You will find that is true of a lot of sportsmen, who express themselves when they are competing but are totally different when they are on civvy street.

I remember a game against Chelsea when I dribbled past a couple of players on the touchline and Denis was screaming for the ball in the middle and I decided that, having done the hard work, I wasn't going to let him get the glory. So although I was at an acute angle, I smashed the ball into the net. It wasn't what you would call percentage football but the way I figured it, the ends justified the means. If I'd missed, Denis would have been justified in having a go at me. But if I scored, I didn't see why he should have any complaints.

I never really thought of myself as just a winger, anyway. I had a bit of a free role and in that season I also played a few games at inside forward, my old position, when Denis was out injured. So I would roam all over the field, which was great, and over the years I played in every position up front except centre forward. And I wouldn't have minded a go at that.

The goals were flying in for me from the start of the season and by January, we were five points clear at the top of the League. But we lost to Spurs in the third round of the FA Cup, so bang went my dreams of Wembley for another year, even if it wasn't quite as painful as losing in the semi-final.

We had the customary easy draw in the preliminary round of the European Cup against Hibernian of Malta, which has always had one of the most thriving United supporters' clubs outside of this country. So it wasn't a particularly hostile atmosphere over there in the second leg and we returned their hospitality by playing out a 0–0 draw. We had won the first leg 4–0 and Denis had no complaints about my service on that occasion, scoring two goals, with David Sadler getting the others.

After that, I played my best ever game for Northern Ireland against Scotland at Windsor Park in the Home Internationals championship in October 1967. I just felt the buzz that day, felt it was one of those occasions when I could try almost anything and expect to get away with it. It's a feeling you only get perhaps once or twice in a season but I felt it that day and every time I got the ball, I ran straight at their defence.

And after the first few times I took them on, I could hear the anticipation in the crowd every time the ball came towards me. Scotland were a good side and were cock-a-hoop after beating England 3–2, claiming that their win at Wembley against the 1966 World Cup winners meant they were the true world champions. We were helped by the fact that neither Denis nor the great Jimmy Baxter was available to them but it was still a special day for us.

Any victory for us was special and the only mystery is how we only won 1–0. On another day, I might have scored three or four myself but their goalkeeper Ronnie Simpson, who was only winning his third cap, played a blinder. He was unbelievable. I was hitting shots that were flying towards the top corner and he was suddenly appearing from nowhere to tip them over. At least I had the satisfaction of making the winner for Dave Clements. And people in Ireland still talk about that game, including my dad.

In the first round proper of the European Cup, we came up

against Sarajevo, which had the potential to be one of those tricky ties and it certainly looked like turning out that way when we only managed a goalless draw over there. But we had a fairly comfortable 2–1 win at Old Trafford, their goal not coming until the dying minutes.

I got the second goal against Sarajevo and we had a 2–0 success against Gornik Zabrze, whose name I wouldn't like to attempt to pronounce, in the quarter final. We lost by a single goal in the second leg at their place, which gave us a second semi-final place in three seasons. Despite the disappointment of 1966 and the feeling of some people that we'd blown our chance of winning the European Cup under Matt, we were now beginning to feel that we were destined to win it and were almost as obsessed as him about doing so. Matt wasn't pleased, though, when we drew Real Madrid, who he felt were the best team left. But considering that the other sides were Benfica and Juventus, it didn't really bother us. They were all great clubs with incredible records in European competition.

As against Benfica, we had to play the first leg at home and, once again, it looked like we were up against it when we could only win 1–0 at Old Trafford. I scored with a left-foot shot of which I was particularly proud. So once again, we had to try to make the Final the hard way.

Some sides would have gone out to defend, to try to hold on to what they had. But that was never the Matt way or the United way. We knew that if we were to make the Final, we would have to outplay them in Madrid. There were 125,000 fans in the Bernabeu Stadium, very few of them wearing red and white, and though I would like to say that I was confident of repeating our efforts in Lisbon, I knew, like everyone else, that this was our biggest test yet.

It became even bigger when they quickly went 2–0 ahead with goals from Pirri and the brilliant Gento. We got lucky when Zoco put the ball into his own net but Amancio made it 3–1 at half time and, let's face it, it looked bleak. Anyone watching would have thought it was all over but Matt wasn't giving up that easily. Moments like those sort the men from the boys. And on this night Matt showed that, as a manager, he was one of the greats. He was brilliant in the half-time team talk. We trooped in, all feeling a bit down but once we'd settled down with our tea, Matt set about restoring our confidence.

'It's only 3–2 on aggregate,' he said, 'so that's how we've got to look at the game, that we're only a goal down and if we equalise, it could be a completely different game.'

He then sprung his master plan on us by saying, 'Let's give them something to think about in the second half, as well.' He pointed at David Sadler. 'David, you move up front.'

People like to say that Matt didn't talk tactics but he knew when to make a switch and it paid off when David scored.

We were still only level overall but Matt had been right. The goal changed the game and now it was us with our tails up and sensing that we might pull off another sensational result.

About fifteen minutes from the end, I got the ball on the right wing and I remember they had this little full back called Sanchez, who was a good player. We had been having a tussle all through the game but, with time running out, I knew that I had to try to make it count whenever I got possession. I drew him towards the tackle but he was too clever to lunge in, jockeying for position and trying to nudge me towards the line and out of the danger zone. I feinted to go inside but then took the ball past him on the outside, relying on my speed to get a yard or two of space to make the cross.

I had my head down in sprinting mode but as I gained the extra ground, I looked up out of the corner of my eye and spotted a red United shirt in the penalty box. Instinctively, I smashed the ball towards it, with Sanchez still trying to catch me to make the covering tackle. I made the cross just before he got to me, the force of his impact causing me to stumble. As I tried to regain my balance, I looked up and saw that the red shirt in the box belonged to centre half Bill Foulkes.

I couldn't believe it. At a time like that, you're hoping to see Bobby or Denis or David running on to the ball. But Bill!

He'd hardly been dominating the goal-scoring in Europe before and in the next moment, I expected to see him blasting it wide or over the bar as he usually did in such a situation. But to my astonishment, as I stood watching for what seemed like two or three minutes, he sidefooted the ball into the net as cool as you like. It was another of those slow-motion moments which only reverted to real time as we ran over to congratulate Bill and tell him well done!, but that now he'd done his bit, not to cross the halfway line again.

We then kept the rest of the game in slo-mo, knocking the ball about and making them run all over the place.

It was a great result, not just because we had beaten such a good side but because we had all been down in the mouth after losing the League title to Manchester City. We had played our final three Division One games between the two Real matches and we lost two of them to finish two points behind City. So defeat in Madrid would have left us with nothing from a season in which, for much of the time, we had played brilliantly. I scored 28 goals in my 41 League games, which was only matched by Ron Davies and was only four less than Dennis Viollet scored for United in 1959-60, which is still a club record.

It felt awful not having a winners' medal to show for all my goals. But we had set our hearts on the European Cup that season and with Wembley already chosen for the Final against Benfica, it really did seem to be our destiny.

Of course, there was also enormous pressure on us as the first English side to reach the Final and the build-up seemed to begin as soon as the final whistle blew in the semi-final. And although we had beaten Benfica 5–1 on their own ground two years earlier, we knew they would put up a much better show. We also had to go into the match without Denis Law, who'd been suffering from a knee injury.

We were very nervy in the first half and I didn't get too much room as the Benfica players were determined that I would-n't make mugs of them again and were always doubling up cover on me. The first half seemed to go by so quickly and we were a bit down at half time. We didn't feel like we had played anywhere near our best, though we'd played the ball around and looked comfortable enough. Matt, who was always telling us not to fly at teams from the start, was reasonably pleased. He said, 'Let's keep playing it around but let's get at them a bit more in the second half. Let's frighten them a bit more.'

In fact, they frightened us when Eusebio let one fly from 20 yards and the ball cracked against the bar and, fortunately for us, rebounded back into play for the defence to clear. But then David got away down the left and sent in a cross which Bobby Charlton, of all people, met with his head. And it wasn't a thumping header, it was one of those glancing, delicate efforts that Denis was the master of. For Bobby to score a goal like that, it did seem that someone up there was pulling for us. It was almost too much of a fairy story. Bobby, one of the survivors of the Munich disaster, scoring the goal that wins the European Cup, and many headlines must already have been written when Jaime Graca spoiled them by equalising ten minutes from the end. And but for a brilliant save by our goal-keeper Alex Stepney at the feet of Eusebio three minutes from the end, Benfica would have won.

It was a hot night and, as usual, Wembley's lush grass was

tough on the legs and all our coaching staff ran on to the pitch before the start of extra time to give us all a rub. It's funny the little things that stand out in your mind because I remember John Aston and my old pal, Ted Dalton, bumping heads as they jumped up from the dugout. Paddy and Nobby were walking between all of us, clenching their fists at us and saying, 'Come on lads, let's finish them off.'

Matt was probably the calmest man on the pitch and the most relieved after seeing us almost lose it in that final ten minutes.

'We've been giving them too much of the ball,' he said, 'but if we can stop doing that, we'll win this. They're getting tired, they're not used to this pitch. Let's go back to what we were doing before. Let's stop giving the ball away. Let's get hold of it and keep it and make them do all the running.'

I took his advice to heart when I got the ball in the first minute of extra time. Stepney punted out a long clearance which Brian Kidd kicked to me. As the centre half charged at me, it was like that dream sequence from 1966 again as he looked favourite to win the tackle until I just knocked it through his legs and collected the ball the other side of him. Then, as the goalkeeper Henrique came out, I whipped round him and rolled the ball in, just as I'd done in Lisbon. He must have been more than fed up with me. Like the goal in Lisbon, it really annoys me that TV re-runs only show me tapping the ball into the net, as if that was all I had to do.

Another funny thing about that goal is that Shay Brennan always claimed that he 'made' it for me as he was the player who knocked the ball back to Stepney. Kiddo did a great job controlling the kick from Stepney and I went past the centre half and 'keeper. But Shay reckons he should have had an official 'assist' for playing the back pass!

We knew it was over after that and so did they, Kiddo and Bobby scoring again to leave us 4–1 ahead before the end of the first half of extra time. Even Matt didn't have to tell us to take it easy for the final 15 minutes. The game was won, we were all knackered and we just played out time using as little effort as possible.

Then the final whistle blew and all the emotion boiled over as never before.

To this day I can still see Matt's face as the referee blew for time. It was a picture of elation but pain and relief as well. Playing in Europe had been his personal dream and he had to fight the football authorities to get United in. Even when he managed that, people said that it was a waste of time, that European football would never work.

Matt didn't mind taking on the authorities but he must have felt a lot of guilt over Munich – if it wasn't for his dream those players wouldn't have died. I'm sure that was going through his mind at the end of the game and I'm sure he felt that only by winning the trophy could he make up for that. Bobby and Bill, who had lost pals in the crash, must have had mixed emotions as well. It's something I was to understand more and more myself from personal experiences in the years ahead; guilt is a terrible thing, and there is none worse than when you hold yourself responsible for the death of somebody else.

It would have been fitting, given all of Matt's efforts, if we had also been the first British club to win the European Cup but after our slip-up in 1966, Celtic beat us to it in '67. Even so, that night at Wembley is still remembered as one of the great nights of English football and it seems that punters can't get enough of the reunion dinners. I thought the spell might have been broken when United finally won the competition again in 1999 but our 1967–68 team is still just as popular. When we had the 25th reunion dinner in Manchester in 1993, we sat through the whole game again and that was interesting because I had forgotten how well we played, how we knocked the ball around.

I was also puzzled about how we took up the positions we did for the goals in extra time. I don't remember changing position for my goal but when you look at the tape, you can see that I had come in from the wing and taken up the centre forward's position. And for the killer goal, the third, there was Brian Kidd in my position on the right wing, taking the ball past a defender and knocking it in for Bobby to score. It seemed as though I was watching a different game because, for most of the match, Kiddo hadn't moved from centre forward and I had been out on the wing. Then, without me remembering it happening, we had reversed it and scored two goals.

I also noticed that I was the only one who changed shirts with one of the Benfica players. All the way through the celebrations, you can see me there with a white shirt on, while all my team mates are still in blue, which we wore just for that occasion. I remember parading in that white shirt and feeling on top of the world.

Sadly, it is the last thing I remember of that night.

It's a shocking thing to admit, I know. But I had been getting a taste for the drink more and more and I ended up getting so drunk that after the greatest day of my footballing life, everything is a complete blank. I don't remember leaving the stadium and I don't even remember going to the official dinner at the Russell Hotel, though I'm told I was there.

But I do recall coming back to Manchester with the trophy and the victory parade. There must have been almost half a million people on the streets of the city and riding on the bus through all the cheering crowd, waving banners and flags was fantastic. I'd dreamed of making a bus ride like that when the team came back with the FA Cup in 1963, just after I'd signed professional, and this one was even noisier, even more colourful. I felt like part of a returning army.

I was voted the 1968 Footballer of the Year and European Footballer of the Year, the third man from United to win it in five years. And I was the youngest ever to win the European poll. I was just 22, I was one of the most famous footballers in the world, I was earning a fortune and, within reason, could have almost anything I wanted. I was on top of the world and it seemed like just the beginning of a long and glorious career.

CHAPTER SEVEN
ESCAPING
THE MADNESS

The lads and I had a boozier time than ever in Majorca. The European Cup triumph had raised my profile even higher and everyone we met wanted to buy me a drink, plus the lads wanted to celebrate in style with me. Things couldn't have looked rosier. But when I got back to Old Trafford, the whole team seemed to be suffering a collective hangover from the triumph over Benfica.

Maybe it was because we had finally achieved the ultimate goal that left us a bit flat. But we made a poor start to the season and questions started to be asked about whether Sir Matt, as he now was, was right to carry on. Everyone had assumed that he would retire as soon as he had won the European Cup and he did hum and hah a bit.

But when something has been a big part of your life for so long, it is difficult just to walk away. When you spend your whole life trying to achieve something and then manage to do so, it is very difficult just to disappear. In hindsight, maybe he should have made a clean break or moved upstairs. But if he had done the latter, he would still have had a massive influence on the club and on who was to be the next manager.

Sir Matt certainly wasn't 100 per cent physically and he seemed completely drained after 1968. Otherwise, he might have done more to bring in new players and freshen up the team. Naturally, a hell of a lot of players wanted to join us. Mike England, a big centre half at Blackburn, was mentioned as a possible signing and I knew that Alan Ball, one of the stars of England's 1966 World Cup side, would have loved to have come to us because he told me so. Those two would have been a good start to the rebuilding – the best centre half in the country and the best midfield player. But Sir Matt didn't make a move, so Mike England joined Tottenham, where he proved a fantastic success, and Bally went to Everton.

Some conspiracy theorists reckon that Sir Matt, knowing he would soon retire, did not want to build up another great side for his successor to inherit. But I don't think he was that cunning. It was probably just a natural running down as a manager and if he had built up another side, maybe he would have carried on much longer.

We'd become so star-struck by Europe that we couldn't

seem to do it in the League any more. But we were up for the two-legged tie in the world club championship against Estudiantes of Argentina. This annual competition between the European Cup winners and the South American champions – or should I say annual kicking match? – had begun in 1960.

We should have known what to expect because Celtic had had three brutal games against Estudiantes the previous season. In the second leg in Buenos Aires, Celtic goalkeeper Ronnie Simpson was struck by a missile before the kick-off and had to be replaced, but that was kid's stuff compared to the play off in Montevideo, which Celtic lost 1–0. The police had to keep running on to the pitch to break up the fights between the players, which resulted in the referee sending off six men, four of them from Celtic.

Our two meetings weren't games, they were sword fights. And although we were warned beforehand not to get drawn into any violence, it was clear from the kick-off in the first match in Buenos Aires that they had no intention of playing football. They were kicking lumps out of us, were diving all over the place and when I tried to make a run down the wing, there were firecrackers landing on my boots.

Some of their tackles fell just short of murder though, unbelievably, it was Nobby who got sent off for a bit of retaliation after Carlos Bilardo had split open Nobby's eyebrow with a back header. Bobby also had his shin cut open with a tackle so fierce that it went right though his pad. They somehow beat us 1–0 and we looked forward to a better game at Old Trafford, thinking they wouldn't dare play with such violence at our place. But on the return game they were just as dirty and I was growing more and more frustrated that the referee was letting one of their players kick me from pillar to post.

Finally, near the end, he decided to book him but I thought he had waited far too long. I chinned the guy as he was being booked and got sent off and it was the most satisfying red card I've ever had. It was also a relief that we only drew 1–1 to lose on aggregate because Sir Matt would have had a problem getting 11 players willing to turn out for a play-off.

We at least couldn't fail to beat Waterford in the first round of the European Cup. In fact, we could have sent Denis out on his own to play them since he scored seven of our goals in a 10–2 aggregate win. Our League form, though, was horrendous at times and, in January 1969, Sir Matt announced that he would retire at the end of the season to join the United board and become general manager.

Naturally, he wasn't going to leave while we still had a chance of retaining the European Cup and after seeing off Anderlecht and Rapid Vienna, we were back in the semi-finals, where we faced AC Milan. They played really well in the San Siro to beat us 2–0 but we suffered a disgraceful piece of refereeing at Old Trafford. After Bobby had pulled the aggregate score back to 2–1, Denis hit a shot which was a yard over the line before a defender cleared it. But the referee didn't give it and that was it – we went out.

I finished top scorer again in 1968–69, with 19 goals from 41 League games, which also meant that I had only missed two League games in three seasons. But after all the success we'd had, I didn't enjoy losing and I felt that there was more and more pressure on me to score. The team was changing, Sir Matt was on the point of leaving and that lovely atmosphere we'd had in the dressing room at Manchester United had just disappeared.

My mates Dave Sadler and Mike Summerbee had got married in 1968, which was great for them, but which naturally had left me without two of my best social companions. Not that it had any effect on my habits. I partied all night just the same.

Personally I had no interest in getting married, never gave it a second thought. If I had still been living in Belfast, I would probably have been married by the time I was 19. But in Manchester, where things had probably changed more in ten years than Belfast had in a hundred, anything went. It was an era when you could do your own thing and when we were on a night out, I always stayed longer than everybody else.

It was a bit like a quote I once read from former Leicester player Frank Worthington, that he always wanted to feel that he was the last man in the world going to bed. My mates still insist that they used to drink as much as me. But they didn't. If we were in a nightclub that closed at two in the morning, they'd go home. I would go on to a club that stayed opened until six and if I went home and couldn't sleep, I knew where to go at nine in the morning and get a drink.

By this time, Billy Barr had given me a key for the Brown Bull so that I literally had booze on tap. Considering the amount of business I brought him, it was the least he could do and if I'd drunk the place dry for a fortnight, he would still have been well ahead of the game. Sometimes, it seemed as though I *had* been there a fortnight. I was always the last non-resident out of there and more and more often I would then drift off to Phyllis's in Whalley Range.

Phyllis's was a drinking den run by the mother of Phil Lynott from Thin Lizzy. It was used by all the late-night workers when they finished their shifts. For me, it was the final stop from the night before and a lovely little place, with nice carpets and a little bar, more like someone's front room than a public bar. Sometimes, when you went in at six in the morning, Phyllis had an Irish stew on, which had been bubbling for three days. So you would have Irish stew for breakfast with a large vodka.

I became friendly with Phil — he was a great guy — but he and the lads in the group were into the heavy stuff, the drugs, and it killed him in the end. He was just 34. I never saw them taking drugs — they knew I wasn't interested and I don't think they would have done that in front of me. But I certainly saw

Phil under the influence enough times – although he could have said the same about me.

The worst that happened to me around this time was that I began to get blackouts, though only over the course of a couple of days' drinking. It was the sort of thing I laughed about at the time, not remembering where I'd been the night before or who I'd spoken to and, if I was too drunk to drive, where I had left the car.

Like most people, I didn't understand what blackouts were, I didn't realise that they were a sign that my drinking had gone beyond the normal social thing. It was just a case of 'I can't remember a thing after we left so-and-so club' and no one considered it a big deal. Sadly, on nights when I *could* remember where my car was after a session, I was not always sensible enough to abandon it. At the start of that 1968–69 season, I had finally lost my game of dare with the police after crashing my car following a boozy night out. I was banned for six months and fined £25.

If I'm honest, looking back, I was already beginning to develop a drink problem. In one way, it was a natural progression, staying out later and putting more and more away. But I also felt that things were not the same any more. They couldn't be because 1968 was such a watershed for United. Having won the European Cup, the team was on the verge of breaking up, Sir Matt was on his way out and a new manager would naturally have his own ideas about how the team were to play.

As much as I enjoyed all the changes that were happening in the outside world, on the pitch, I wanted everything to stay just as they'd always been. And I couldn't handle the fact that they were changing so rapidly.

I had now also been a first team player for five years, although still only 22, so a lot more was expected of me than your average young player. I was no longer a promising youngster for whom people could make allowances. I was the top player in Europe, I'd scored in the European Cup Final and I was expected to produce performances like that, week in, week out. The stakes had been raised and off the field, the pressure became intolerable.

Every man and his dog wanted a piece of me, I was getting swamped with commercial offers, TV and radio were making demands on me and it was all too much. When that stuff had first come along, it was great and I enjoyed both the fame and the money it brought in. But I was only 22 and the novelty had already long worn off. I would simply fail to turn up for events and go off on a bender instead. In the past I'd always run away in times of crises but now I turned to booze, which was much the same thing. I didn't run away physically, but mentally I escaped in the bottom of a glass.

Outsiders didn't understand the pressure I was under and I got lots of stick in the press from people saying that I was throwing away a glittering career. In their eyes, my life was one long round of parties and glamour, with a bit of football thrown in. But they didn't have to live with the realities of being George Best twenty-four hours a day, unable to walk down the street to get a newspaper without a dozen people following me, and all the other tedious things that go with superstardom. Because that's exactly what I'd become, a superstar and it didn't feel anywhere near as good as I would have imagined. And the only occasions when I could escape the madness and feel like a normal person was when I sat drinking with friends in a quiet bar.

I felt restless, I felt unhappy with the expectations put upon me but they weren't things I felt I could talk to Sir Matt about, even if I'd wanted to. And he was on the verge of leaving, in any case. When things have gone wrong in my life, I've never found it easy to talk to anybody about my problems, though I accept that you're probably better off if you do. If I'd been living at home, it would have been a bit different because I can talk to my dad about anything, but he wasn't there, and couldn't have been there with a big family to look after at home. OK, I could always get him on the end of a phone but that's not quite the same thing and when you are apart for so long, families can drift further and further apart.

Around this time I had got a little interested in horse racing and I kept bumping into a Newmarket trainer called Ian Walker who was a regular at Old Trafford.

'Why don't we form a three-man syndicate and buy a

horse?' he said one day, the third man being Alan Ball with whom he and I were both friendly.

'Great', I said, thinking it would be a nice hobby, something that could help me get away from the hurly burly. Bally, who was a racing nut, was more than up for it.

Naturally, we left Ian to buy the horse since we wanted to make sure it had a leg at each corner and he came up with this two-year-old which we called Slim Gypsy. It ran quite promisingly first time out in the summer of 1969 and I had visions of swanning around Royal Ascot in my top hat as it carried off one of the big juvenile prizes.

But a United Dairies cap might have been more appropriate because after a couple of more runs, I felt that a milk round was about all Slim Gypsy was good for. The only result that I had was never having to pay out a penny in training fees. Ian never sent me a bill.

Sir Matt and United had been looking everywhere for a new manager, which you would have thought would have been an easy task. But the big-name managers were probably frightened off by the thought of Sir Matt looking over their shoulder and just before the end of the 1968–69 season, it was announced that reserve team coach Wilf McGuinness would take over in the summer. I don't know who was more surprised, the players or Wilf.

I liked Wilf, he'd been with the club all his life and when he had to stop playing at 22 after breaking his leg, he stayed on as a coach. He was unbelievably passionate about the game and a popular guy. But taking over the first team was a task he was never going to win and one of his first problems was that, at age 32, he was younger than some of the players he would be picking. That would make it hard for him to win the players' respect, although I, for one, was willing to give him a chance.

I did my best for him on the field as well by scoring 13 goals in as many games. But I was finding it increasingly difficult to get motivated because the team was so poor. Billy Foulkes and Shay Brennan were coming to the end of their careers and the people who were replacing them were not up to it. You hate to be cruel but we had players like Steve James, who went on to play for Kidderminster Harriers and Tipton Town and Anglo-Italian Carlo Sartori. He was a nice lad, Carlo, but not much of a footballer. He's now making a successful living as a knife sharpener in Manchester and I'd say as a footballer, he was a pretty good knife sharpener. There was also the likes of Paul Edwards, Frank Kopel and Tommy O'Neil. After playing with Denis and Bobby and Billy at their peak, the declining standards were hard to take.

It would have been OK if it had been the other way round, if I had started in a poor team and then progressed to a better one. But I was losing interest and for the first time, started skipping training, a bit of adult mitching. Although I had always loved training, I had seen it as a means to an end, the end being the game on Saturday. Now that the game was likely to be more a punishment than a reward, I didn't see the point in being 100 per cent fit for it. The game was the icing on the cake for me but when there was no more icing, I couldn't be bothered with the cake.

My frustrations were starting to come out on the pitch too, causing me to do some silly things on the spur of the moment. And every time I did something wrong, the FA came down on me like a ton of bricks. I was booked by referee Jack Taylor in a League Cup semi-final against Manchester City and at the end of the game, as we walked off, I flipped the ball out of Taylor's hands. I was angry at the booking but the gesture was more playful than anything. Taylor obviously didn't think so because he mentioned the incident in his official report and, of course, TV were there and kept re-running the incident. The result was a four-week suspension and a £100 fine, which was certainly not a punishment to fit the crime.

I took my anger out on Northampton, who are fittingly known as the Cobblers, when I returned to the team for a fifth-round FA Cup tie which we won 8–2, yours truly getting six of the goals, to equal the Cup record. It was one of my most satisfying days in a long time. I scored one with my head, dribbled round the 'keeper for another and generally took the mickey. It also allowed me to poke fun at my mate Denis, who had scored six in a Cup tie for Manchester City at Luton in 1961 before the game was abandoned and the goals struck off. And City lost

the rescheduled game in which Denis also scored! It was interesting that the press, who'd always been gushing about my
feats before, now put a negative slant even on my outstanding
football feats. One paper carried the headline 'SIX OF THE
BEST ON BAD BOY'S RETURN'.

After that effort, I felt I might finally earn the consolation
of an FA Cup Final, though we got the worst possible semi-
final draw when we were pulled out of the hat against Leeds.
So the shin pads came out of mothballs again and, true to form,
the game at Hillsborough was another punching and kicking
match which finished 0–0. The replay was at Villa Park, so we
stayed in a hotel in Birmingham. Feeling a bit bored, I began
chatting to a girl, as you do, on the night before the match and
while I was talking to her, I looked up and saw that Wilf had
clocked me.

The following day, not long before we were due to leave
for the ground, I bumped into the girl again and we sat down
for a longer chat. She told me that she was married but that her
husband spent a lot of time away from home. So I said, 'Well,
maybe I can pop down and keep you company', and she said
she would like that. We were getting on well but I was called
away by Wilf for something or other and when I had finished
talking to him, she was gone.

About twenty minutes before we were due to leave for the
match, knowing that we wouldn't be coming back to the hotel
afterwards, I went up to the girl's room to get her phone

number. All the players had been told to meet downstairs to get on the coach and when Wilf saw that I wasn't there, he put two and two together and made five. I was just talking to the girl in her bedroom when Wilf stormed in, screaming and shouting, so angry that the veins on his face were standing out.

'Get your arse back downstairs!' he yelled. 'We're leaving in fifteen minutes.'

'I'm only chatting, Wilf,' I said.

'I don't care,' he replied. 'In case you've forgotten, we've got an FA Cup semi-final in a couple of hours.'

I made my apologies to the girl and went downstairs but then I just thought 'Screw you, mate, I might play football for you but that doesn't mean I have to be treated like a schoolboy.'

So I went back to the girl's room and this time, we both reckoned we'd done enough chatting and we had a quickie before I left. Realising what must have happened, Wilf just turned his back on me when I came down.

'I'm sending him home,' he told Sir Matt.

Sir Matt stood up for me as usual and told Wilf we'd sort it out when we got back to Manchester. But he should have saved his breath because I had my normal nightmare against Leeds. Their players had also got wind of what had gone on in the hotel and Johnny Giles had a go at me on the field about it. You would have thought he'd have been delighted but he seemed to consider my behaviour a slight not just against United but against all professional footballers. I should have made him pay when I had a chance to score the winner but I fell over the ball and it ended 0–0 again.

Leeds won the third match at Bolton 1–0 and I'd literally screwed up what turned out to be my last ever chance to reach the FA Cup Final.

It was a horrible season, 1969–70, which also brought me a lot of stick from the Northern Ireland fans. Once again, we had played above ourselves in qualifying matches for the 1970 World Cup and needed a draw against Russia in Moscow in the final game to go through on goal difference. But I played for United on the Monday, got a bit of a knock and had to pull out. Irish officials were furious that I'd been allowed to play a club match so close to an important international, which they lost 2–0, and they were even more angry when I played for United the following weekend.

I can't remember what the injury was, though I know I wasn't all that keen to go to Moscow after my Albania experiences. I knew it would cause uproar because whenever I missed games for Ireland, I got stick from the fans and a lot of bad publicity back home. Some people would blame the club, some would blame me and it made for some nasty reading for my family, who were getting increasingly worried by some of the things written about me. It can't have been easy for them at all.

In fact, it was starting to have a disastrous effect on my mother.

CHAPTER EIGHT
GOING
MISSING

I couldn't wait to get away to Spain in the summer of 1970. But first, I had to go home to Belfast for Mum and Dad's 25th wedding anniversary. I had been missing more and more family celebrations over the years, sometimes because of football commitments and sometimes because I was too busy enjoying myself elsewhere but this was one event I had promised I would attend. I also thought it would give me a little dose of normality in what was becoming a crazy existence. It would do me some good.

I had been warned by Carol that Mum had started drinking, although I took that to mean that she was having the odd glass or two. Mum had never gone out very much but once Ian was toddling around, Carol would take charge of him and the twins and Mum and Dad were able to go out together for the first time in years. She had always been quiet, had Mum, but she became more outgoing as she started mixing with other people. She'd had a hard life, too, holding down a couple of jobs while bringing up six children, and maybe when she finally got time to enjoy herself, she grabbed it with both hands.

Anyway, they threw a big family party at Burren Way and naturally the drinks were flowing. It was strange, because I'd never seen Mum drink before, though she always smoked, and there was an obvious tension between her and my dad. She'd be sipping a glass of wine and my dad would be watching her and then she'd make an excuse to leave the room and come back a lot tipsier – clearly having had a drink or two on her own – a classic alcoholic's trick which I was to learn in later years. But if my dad challenged her, she would deny it. They went on with this charade all the time I was there.

So it was an uncomfortable weekend, but I didn't think she had a drink problem at that time, any more than I saw myself as having one. As far as I was concerned, if you weren't falling over or feeling ill, then the drink couldn't be doing you any harm.

What I did realise was that my parents were both finding it difficult and, in my mum's case, near impossible, to deal with my fame or, as it was now becoming, notoriety. I was such a hot item that all sorts of nonsense was appearing in the newspapers and although most of it was not true, Mum and Dad, like any other member of the general public, believed what they read in the papers.

You could talk till you were blue in the face but if they had seen a story in black and white, they thought there must be some truth in it. Some of the stories were horrendous and even if Mum and Dad hadn't seen them, you could be sure that some kind soul would phone and tell them. They got a phone call once saying that I had been killed in a car crash which, given my driving record, could well have had a ring of truth about it. So they were sitting around worrying for hours until they finally got in touch with me. I was always phoning to put them straight on some of the more fanciful stories, but they worried just the same.

Once the news got around that I was home, our house was mobbed for days. It was worse than any of the other times I'd been back to Belfast. And, of course, the streets were no longer full of kids kicking a ball about but of British soldiers and tanks. I'd seen pictures of them on TV and in the papers but seeing it with my own eyes for the first time, it really came home to me what my family were now living with on a daily basis, constantly having to look over their shoulders. Carol was in the church choir and she sometimes had to run through the tear gas to get to the church.

I asked Mum and Dad if they had considered moving to England, which they had, but they didn't want to be driven out by the Troubles. So I thought I could at least help make their lives easier by buying them a fish and chip shop. One had just come on to the market so I walked into the estate agent's and said, 'I'll have it.' Just like that.

Mum had worked in a chippy for years, like a lot of the family. I saw it as a way for them to have an easier time, running their own business at the hours that suited them. Carol and Barbara went to work there as well but, typically of Mum and Dad, they wanted everything just right in the shop. So they got fresh fish in every morning and insisted on the potatoes being peeled by hand and then they'd spend hours cleaning up before they locked up. Before long they were working 14 hours a day.

So instead of them going into semi-retirement, they were working harder than when they were working, so to speak. This wasn't what I'd had in mind for them.

As I've said, there seemed to be stories about me in the papers every day, but heaven knows what Mum thought a few months later when she read that I had become engaged. And this time, the story was true, though the announcement was as much a shock to me as to my mum. I had met this stunning blonde girl on United's pre-season tour to Copenhagen but sadly she had had a boyfriend in tow who didn't seem to appreciate my interest in her and I didn't even manage to get a phone number. So in a moment of weakness, or madness, or both when I got back to Manchester, I told this to some of the press lads, who got their counterparts in Denmark to run an appeal on behalf of a Lonely from Chorlton. I received a sackful of mail and among them was the object of my lust – Eva Haraldsted.

I invited her over and took her back to Mrs Fullaway's, whose face was a picture when this long-haired Viking girl walked in.

The press were having a field day and before I knew it, Eva had announced that we were getting married. This was news to me but the idea grew on me after a while and I thought fine – it was going to happen. But meeting someone in a hotel lobby, fancying them like mad and inviting them over for a dirty weekend is not quite the same as courting them for a year or two and deciding to walk down the aisle. It was all a bit of a mistake and, within a few months, we were falling out in a big way.

When we finally split, Eva sued me for breach of promise and was awarded £500, which I believe was the last case of its kind. The only satisfactory thing about the whole ridiculous affair was the chance it gave me to get one over on Sir Matt. He called me in as soon as he heard about my 'engagement'.

'What on earth are you playing at?' he stormed.

I sat there straight faced and said, 'Well, Boss, you told me to get married and settle down. I was just following your advice.'

He was red in the face by this time. 'I didn't mean right

away,' he said. 'And I didn't mean for you to marry the next girl you met!'

Wilf was made team manager at the start of the 1970–71 season but it didn't give him any more authority in the dressing room and there were a lot of players bickering behind his back. It was only a matter of time before he went and the axe fell after another poor performance against Derby on Boxing Day.

I don't suppose I helped his cause by failing to turn up for training on Christmas Day, deciding to sleep off a hangover. When I turned up for the game the following day, Wilf wanted to send me home but Busby overruled him again, instead imposing a £50 fine. I stayed in the team and scored in a 4–4 draw, but that wasn't good enough to save the manager's job and I felt very sorry for Wilf. He was absolutely shattered when they told him he was sacked. Can you imagine getting the job that you've dreamed about all your life and then 18 months later, being told you're not wanted?

Wilf was such a nice man and loved the club so much that he didn't even dish the dirt after he left, but the way he was treated by Sir Matt, one could hardly have blamed him if he had.

I was starting to miss training more and more. When you've played at the highest level and won the biggest honours, it's hard when you start getting beaten every week. So I didn't see the point of working my butt off in training because it had reached the point where, even if I played a blinder, it was unlikely to save us from another defeat. It had become a bit like playing for Northern Ireland, although this viewpoint brought me into conflict with Bobby Charlton.

Bobby and I had never been the greatest of mates, on or off the field. I think he thought I was a greedy little so-and- so who wouldn't give him the ball, but then I thought he was a bit of a glory hunter as well, looking for the chance to unleash one of those long-range shots rather than giving the ball to me. He was always a bit dour, as well, and a real moaner on the pitch, but a United man through and through. So while I didn't think it was worth giving my all in such a poor team, Bobby didn't see it like that. He felt that it was up to the senior players – and I was now one of them – to work even harder to pull the club up. He was such an establishment man that Denis began calling him Sir Bobby long before he was knighted.

When I started going missing, Bobby was pretty disgusted and felt I was letting the side down. He didn't say anything to my face but he was very frosty towards me and I felt his disapproval. I also knew that he voiced it to the management, telling them that it wasn't right for me to be treated differently to everyone else and that it wasn't helping team morale at a time when we all needed to pull together.

He was right, of course, but he didn't realise what my problem was and at the time, neither did I. I didn't deliberately set out to go drinking all night and let my career go to pot. It is no excuse but I was drinking because I was depressed about the team and if I played badly myself, I would get even more depressed and go back to the drink.

It became a vicious circle but I couldn't see that my drinking and my failure to turn up for training was a factor in the team's downward spiral. I probably felt that I could stop if I wanted to – and maybe I could have done if the team had improved. But I would have laughed if you'd said I had a drink problem, and I don't think Bobby thought that, either. He just thought I was being selfish.

I wasn't worried about Bobby having a go or about the coldness between us. You don't have to be bosom buddies with all your team mates and a football club is no different to any other workplace. If you're employed in an office of 40 or 50 people, there are bound to be some that you don't get on with but you still work with them because you've all got a common cause. Football is the same. Look at Andy Cole and Teddy Sheringham when they played in the United side. They didn't give the appearance of being close. Yet to see them play, you would have thought they were best pals.

You probably wouldn't have got that impression seeing Bobby and me on the pitch and I also upset him with an off-the-cuff remark during a TV interview. Bobby and his brother Jackie both idolised their mother, Sissie, who was the sister of the great Newcastle forward, Jackie Milburn – the Bestie of his day in the late Forties and Fifties, though he didn't have to face the media pressure that I had. Sissie obviously had football in her genes and unusually for a woman in those days actually took kids for coaching.

So when I was asked by the interviewer who'd been the biggest influence on my footballing career, I replied, 'Sissie Charlton.'

It was a deliberate dig and a bit of a cruel one, having a go at Bobby's mother. Again, Bobby didn't say anything about it to me but I'm sure he would have heard about the remark and it didn't do anything to improve our relationship such as it was. Maybe because he has experienced personal problems of his own, Bobby has matured and mellowed a bit and we get on fine now. I enjoy his company and he will come up to me and say, 'Look after yourself, kid', by which I know he means to stay off the drink. He even seems to have lost that sombreness he had when he was a young man.

Of course, the Munich crash, and the guilt he must have carried around from being a survivor, must have had a huge effect on him. Jackie once said that his kid brother stopped smiling after the crash. In later life, I'm pleased to say, he's learning to smile again. But back then, it was almost impossible for us to be friends.

With no immediate replacement for Wilf, Sir Matt returned as manager, but none of us believed that it could ever be the same as before. The team was too much in decline and we all just hoped that the club could get a big-name man in before too long.

I never thought of leaving because I'd had such great times at United and couldn't imagine playing for anyone else. But when Jimmy Murphy was pushed into a scouting role in 1971, it really did seem like the end of an era.

On the pitch I was becoming out of control and facing a ban after collecting three bookings. As results continued to go against us, I found it harder and harder to cope with the frustrations and was lashing out at other players or officials. The last booking was for a foul on Glyn Pardoe in the Manchester derby. Although I could tackle with the best of them, I was never regarded as a dirty player but the tackle on Pardoe probably looked worse than it was because I'd chased across the field to get to him and took him out with a sliding tackle. Unfortunately, it was a damp pitch and I slid in much faster than I had expected. There was a terrible cracking noise and I knew instantly that he'd broken his leg. In fact it was a double fracture which ended his career and straight away, my old adversary, Mike Doyle was screaming in my face, calling me this and that and threatening to do me.

It was totally accidental and I felt awful. When something like that happens, you don't want to play on, you just want to walk off.

Joe Mercer, the Manchester City manager, made me feel a bit better when he sidled up after the game.

'Don't worry about it, son,' he said, 'it was just an accident.'

And later, Pardoe said much the same. Let's face it, if you deliberately wanted to break an opponent's leg, you would go over the top, not slide in. And the damp pitch contributed to the momentum I'd built up when I made contact with him.

The booking meant a trip down to London in January 1971, to stand in front of the FA's disciplinary commission, like some naughty schoolboy, and promise never to misbehave again. At least Sir Matt was also going to plead on my behalf, but unfortunately, the hearing was in the morning, which meant getting an early train from Manchester and I was increasingly finding it hard to get up early in those days, especially after a heavy night.

As a result, poor old Matt ended up travelling down on his own, though I did eventually get to FA headquarters at Lancaster Gate. Once I struggled out of bed, I caught the first train I could and arrived two or three hours after Matt, who had made some excuse about my absence to the FA.

Given that they had to delay the hearing, it was amazing that they showed such leniency, giving me a suspended six-week ban. The fine was much steeper, £250, but with the money I was earning, I didn't give it a second thought.

I never used to get hangovers as such but on this particular day I was feeling absolutely dreadful, and spending time in a stuffy atmosphere didn't improve matters. As Sir Matt and I went up in the lift in our hotel afterwards, I threw up, which in any normal situation would have been horribly embarrassing. But clearly I wasn't normal then because I didn't care. It was almost as if I was a baby with his dad and Sir Matt was going to say, 'Don't worry about it. I'll clean it up. Everything will be all right.'

To be honest, I had reached the stage where I didn't care if they suspended me for two or three months or a year. I'd just lost interest in playing and when you start going through the motions, it's time to pack it in, which was an idea that grew more and more in my mind.

Sir Matt no doubt expected me to knuckle down now that he was back in charge but I wasn't thinking straight, wasn't capable of thinking straight most of the time. In the early days, I had rarely gone out on Thursday nights but I did the follow-ing week and once again, was in no state to go into training the next day. Sir Matt didn't bother trying to contact me, he just hoped that I would turn up at the station on Saturday for the trip to London to play Chelsea.

Some hope.

Chelsea was the fixture I normally loved playing in more than any other. Big club, big players, packed ground. But that week it didn't interest me at all – although I did fancy a weekend in London. So having missed the train with the lads, I caught another later on to go and visit Irish actress Sinead Cusack, whom I'd just met.

It was utter madness. Here I was, one of the world's most famous footballers and I just decided not to play in an important game and instead went out on a date. It's hard for me even to explain what state of mind I was in to do such a thing. I just felt the whole world was on top of me and when I woke up that mid-morning and realised that I'd missed the train, I didn't think that it was worth bothering. If I'd been thinking clearly, I might have been able to catch a later train to get me there in time but I convinced myself I wouldn't make it and told myself that even if I got down there, I'd only get a rollicking from the Boss, who probably wouldn't play me anyway.

I had phoned Sinead earlier in the week to arrange to see her after the match so I saw no reason not to go through with that part of my plans. I didn't think it would be such a big deal. But once the press found out I wasn't playing and realised that I was with Sinead, a quiet weekend in North London became more like the siege of Sydney Street.

Sinead's flat was in Noel Street, Islington, and one of her neighbours either tipped off the press or we were spotted when we went out for dinner on the Saturday night. So when we woke up to a commotion outside on Sunday morning, Sinead looked out of the window to see what all the fuss was about – and her jaw dropped open.

'What on earth have you been up to, George?' she said as

I jumped up to join her and saw scores of pressmen and TV crews on the pavement.

'I've missed a football match, that's all,' I said.

Sinead – who later, of course, married Jeremy Irons – was a lovely girl and I felt that she was someone I could talk to. As another star from Ireland who was learning to cope with fame, we had things in common, even if she wasn't under the spotlight to anywhere near the extent that I was. She just happened to be around at the time and I felt sorry for her because she got caught up in something that was nothing to do with her. She had been expecting a quiet weekend but, thanks to me, spent four days with me as a prisoner in her own home.

Things were really getting on top of me now. To me, my life seemed to be in crisis. But to everyone else, it was just a bit of fun, something to give the nation a laugh. So after TV pictures outside the flat were aired on the news, people started turning up outside, chanting my name. And when we drew the curtains and turned on the TV to take our minds off it, we were forced to watch updates of our situation on the news!

It was surreal and utterly unbelievable that, with all the things going on in the world, the story of two single people shacked up in a flat in Islington was topping all the bulletins and filling the front and back pages of the newspapers. The news columnists were writing all these pompous opinion pieces about a pampered footballer going off the rails and the back pages were speculating as to whether Sir Matt should sell me or kick me out.

The sheer scale of the story only added to my confusion and depression over how my life was going. And poor old Sinead couldn't understand it. She must have felt as though she was harbouring a mass murderer.

Some people might say incidents like that were a cry for help – and they probably were – but I didn't particularly see it like that at the time. I just acted out of instinct, *drunken* instinct. And the interesting thing, looking back, is that Manchester United never got me out of those situations. It was always my friends, my friends outside football.

Waggy was one of the best at sniffing me out when I went to ground. He missed his vocation as a gumshoe, although it was Malcolm Mooney who came and rescued me from Sinead's flat after four days of hell.

To most people Matt was portrayed as the great father figure, but to me he was more like a headmaster. A symbol of authority. Yes, he'd given me the odd pep talk and tried to keep me on the straight and narrow but that was more in the interests of the club and how he perceived its image. He certainly would have thought it undignified to make any direct contact with me or to appeal to me through TV. He would no doubt have seen that as a sign of weakness, both on a personal level and as the head of a club like Manchester United.

Sir Matt just let the situation blow over and waited for me

to return in my own good time, as he always had. And when I got back to Manchester, he didn't sit me down for a chat and ask why I was behaving the way I was. He just called me in and told me he was suspending me for two weeks. I don't know whether he had given up on me or just couldn't understand me. I could hardly make sense of my own actions at times so it would have been impossible for him. Sir Matt was very much the old school type, while I was the Fifth Beatle. United had never had to deal with a star football player before and Sir Matt had little idea of how to handle me or what was happening around me. Willingly or not, I represented a generation that was alien to him. In that sense, he would have been more like a grandfather figure than a parental one.

From my point of view, I was trying to cope with the sort of fame and media attention that no other player had ever had to put up with. And I was only young and having to work things out by myself as I went along. So naturally, I made a lot of mistakes – but then so did the club.

I would hope, though, that United learned from their experiences with me and when you see how Alex Ferguson has protected people like David Beckham and Ryan Giggs, you have to say that they are more aware of the problems of fame these days. I certainly wouldn't like to think what might have happened to Beckham if he had played in my era. Ferguson dropped him when he missed training because, according to him, he had been looking after his ill son, Brooklyn, but Fergie has still managed to keep him happy behind the scenes. If that had happened in the Sixties, quite a few managers might have said 'Screw him' and shown him the door.

I think at the end of the day, if a player is doing the business for the club, then the club should make an effort when things go wrong. No one could ever have accused me of not doing it for United and if someone from the club had come and found me and spoken to me when I went missing, I would have listened. Although the fact that I was suffering from an illness called alcoholism meant that things might still have turned out the same, perhaps.

But no one ever did come.

I was probably getting beyond help from football people but my situation was in stark contrast to the one in which Eric Cantona walked out on United in 1996. Obviously, he wanted to come back, he wanted to play for United but he was too proud to admit he had made a mistake. So Alex went to France to see him, to talk him round, and it took a big man to do that. I can't think of many other managers who would have been willing to do the same. Sir Matt certainly wouldn't have done so.

Sir Alex has often said that he wouldn't have been able to handle me but it is fascinating to wonder how he and I would have got on. If he had been in charge when I was playing, maybe he would have come and grabbed me when I went missing and things might not have turned out the way they did.

It might have made a difference if I'd had more responsibility at the club, too, and there was talk of my becoming captain during Busby's second spell. A lot of people mentioned it and I fancied the idea. Being captain of United is a bit special and one day I plucked up the courage to suggest to Sir Matt that I might like the job. But his reaction didn't give the impression that it was the best suggestion he'd ever heard.

After my two-week suspension, which was incredibly lenient, I cleaned my act up for a bit and only missed one more game that season, and finished top scorer for the fourth year in a row, with 18 goals from 40 games.

Not bad for someone who was spending more time in pubs and clubs than on the pitch, I thought. It was, however, becoming harder and harder to work off the excesses of the night before.

I rounded off the season on a high when I scored a hat trick for Northern Ireland against Cyprus, but managed to get involved in another controversy in the Home Internationals match against England. I have always liked to try different things on the pitch, trying to score from a corner or straight from kick-off or from the halfway line. Also, I'd always thought that if you could get your timing spot on, it might be possible to nick the ball from a goalkeeper in the split second between him throwing it out in front of him and making contact with his boot. And who better to demonstrate this against than Gordon

Banks, generally reckoned to be the best keeper in the world during that period.

As Gordon released the ball to punt it upfield, I nipped in and flicked it over his head, running round the other side of him to head it into the net. Unbelievably, the referee disallowed it.

'What was wrong with that, ref?' I protested.

'Foot up', he replied, which can be construed as dangerous play.

But goalkeepers in those days got all sorts of batterings which didn't even result in a free kick. In the 1958 Cup Final, for instance, Harry Gregg was bundled into the net with the ball by Bolton's Nat Lofthouse and a goal was given.

Ironically, it turned out that I had reacted too swiftly. Had I let the ball drop closer to the ground, the goal wouldn't have been disallowed.

Around this time, in order to get a bit of peace and quiet, I finally decided to buy a house of my own in Bramhall, Cheshire, which I called *Que Sera*, and also got myself a little red setter for company. As it turned out, I would have got more privacy if I'd bought a giant goldfish bowl and lived in that. The guy who designed the house was a bit of a gadget freak, to put it mildly, and almost everything was controlled electronically. If I sat in bed with the control panel, I could open and close the curtains at the flick of a switch, turn on the lights in the hall or open the garage doors. In the lounge, I could flick another switch and the television would disappear up the chimney and I half expected Santa Claus to appear when I reversed it.

I loved all these gadgets at first but one night, I came home around three in the morning – obviously one of my early nights – to find the garage doors open. Naturally, I thought someone had broken in so I went into the garage and picked up a wrench before gingerly walking into the house and exploring the rooms.

There was no sign of any disturbance downstairs and when I finally got to the last room, my bedroom, the dog was cowering in the corner. I assumed he must have trodden on the control panel and accidentally opened the garage so once I had calmed him down, I got into bed. Within minutes, the curtains started opening and closing, the TV in the lounge began yo-yo-ing up and down the chimney and the garage door was clang-ing open and shut. It was a nightmare.

When someone came to investigate the following day, it turned out that the mechanism was affected by planes flying overhead and as I was close to Manchester Airport, the gadgetry had to go.

I had been looking for a place of my own after Mike Summerbee and I had got rid of our little hideaway in Crumpsall. I'd kept it on for a while after Mike got married but then the landlord decided to put the rent up to a ridiculous price. We'd really done the place up nicely and he was probably hoping to make a killing with a new client, thinking we would leave all the stuff we had put in. Instead, I got a few of the boys together, drove a van round and took out all our furniture, curtains, carpets, the lot. I even took up the underlay.

On reflection, I might have been better off paying the increased rent because once fans discovered my house in Bramhall, I was a prisoner in my own home. You'd get groups of tourists standing outside and if I just walked down to the local shop to get a paper, I'd have thirty people following me and asking for autographs. It was so bad that I had to keep the curtains closed all the time – assuming, of course, that I could find the remote control.

When I think about it now, that house seemed to symbolise my life at the time. Chaotic, unpredictable, with nothing working as it was meant to.

CHAPTER NINE
OFF THE RAILS

We all knew that Sir Matt was going to end his managerial career for good at the end of the 1970–71 season and there was a lot of speculation that his influence would help United to sign Jock Stein, who had won six titles in a row with Celtic and also led them to a European Cup triumph in 1967. In Scotland, he was as big a god as Sir Matt and I would have loved him to have come to Old Trafford. With a reputation as a disciplinarian, he might even have managed to keep me in line and I might have stayed for another ten years. But obviously I have no way of knowing that for sure. It's purely hypothetical.

Sadly, so was the news that Jock was to be the new manager, since nothing ever came of it and Don Revie of Leeds was then mentioned, which was a bit strange considering the hatred between us and Leeds. After the experience with Wilf, the club seemed determined to bring in a big-name manager, but whether Sir Matt's presence frightened them off or not, I don't know.

Anyway, we ended up with Frank O'Farrell of Leicester. He was a very quiet man and a lot of the players didn't take to him but whoever we got would have been compared unfavourably to Matt. I didn't mind Frank, though I didn't get off to the most auspicious of starts when I was sent off at Chelsea in his second game of the 1971–72 season for swearing at the referee, Norman Burtenshaw.

Chelsea seemed to be an eventful place for me, but I managed to escape a ban when I told the FA that I'd been swearing at my team mate, Willie Morgan! It's true that Willie and I were never good friends and I always thought he was a bit jealous of me and tried to be like me, with the long hair and in the way he wanted to play. A lot of players who came through at that time were hailed as the 'new George Best', particularly if they also bore a physical resemblance to me. Anyway, between you and me, I *had* been swearing at Burtenshaw, not Willie, but for once, at the FA disciplinary commission, I got the benefit of the doubt.

As if I wasn't getting into enough scrapes on my own, people started making them for me. The Troubles in Belfast had moved on from the drums and cakes marches which I had known as a kid and before our game at Newcastle in October

1971, someone claiming to represent the IRA told police that I would be shot if I played.

I was under enormous pressure as it was and having enough problems just keeping my life together, without that. And it wasn't just the threat that bothered me. It was the effect I knew it would have on my family. They were living with the Troubles on a daily basis, which was hard enough for them. And although they worried about me, at least they felt that was one issue I was safe from in England. The threat was supposed to have been related to a rumour in Belfast that I had made a donation to one of the Protestant organisations, which was utter rubbish.

I phoned my dad to reassure him and tried to sound as cheery as I could.

'It's probably only a crank,' I said.

'You can't be sure of that,' he replied.

He wouldn't have been human if he hadn't worried about it. I was worried myself and so were the club, so I wasn't surprised when Frank O'Farrell called me in.

'We'll understand if you don't want to play,' he said. 'The decision has to be yours and we'll support you whatever your decision.'

I told him that I would think about it and I did give it a lot of thought. But I kept coming back to the feeling that I couldn't *not* play, otherwise, where would it all end? There could be death threats every week and I'd never play again. I might have been thinking of quitting but I wasn't letting anyone else dictate how and when. And typically of me, having let the team down so many times, when the manager offered me a Saturday off, I insisted that I wanted to play.

It was tough on my team mates, who couldn't have felt too happy getting on the team coach with me. I was escorted by a couple of detectives who refused to allow me sit in my normal window seat in case anyone took a pot shot at me. And there was a mad panic on the day of the game when they discovered that the coach, which had been parked in the hotel's underground car park overnight, had been broken into. So it had to be checked for any explosive devices and the news didn't make my team mates any less jumpy. But like most footballers would have done, they were making a joke of it, saying things like, 'I suppose this is the work of your Irish mates, Bestie.'

Newcastle's St James Park would also have been an ideal place for a marksman because the ground then was surrounded by high-rise blocks of flats so they deployed tons of police everywhere, scouring the rooftops with high-powered binoculars. It was hardly the best preparation for a game but once we kicked off, I forgot all about it and simply got on with trying to play. And thankfully, the only shot on target that day was my winning goal. Instead of an IRA terrorist, the threat had obviously just come from some plonker, but you never know do you? Sadly, John Lennon discovered that and the man who killed him, Mark Chapman, was a fan of his.

Even after the game, police were taking no chances and gave us an escort back to Manchester, though Newcastle manager Joe Harvey broke the ice at the press conference when he said, 'I wish they had shot the little bugger.'

Thanks, Joe!

I know things like that were even tougher on my family, especially as my mum's drinking was getting heavier and they were forced to sell the fish and chip shop, making only a few hundred pounds in profit. But I was also finding the whole fame thing difficult to deal with as well.

That thing about being an icon, the Fifth Beatle, I just found it so freaky. I was just a kid from the Cregagh Estate in Belfast trying to make sense of my life as a footballer and as a person but I was being held up as some enormous star who could influence other people's lives. Obviously I *was* affecting other people's lives if they were threatening to shoot me. Yet it was such a fantasy that I couldn't get to grips with it. It was as though it was all happening to someone else.

I even found it difficult to watch myself playing on TV because I couldn't identify with the person on the screen, even when I was looking at a game that had finished only a few hours earlier. It's like some actors who say that they can't watch themselves on TV. They talk about what I was experiencing, that you feel like you are two different people and it's not a healthy experience.

There were also big showbusiness names turning up to

watch me play. The previous season, 1970–71, following a goal I scored at Huddersfield, who had just come up from the Second Division, I got a note from the ex-prime minister, Harold Wilson. He was a big Huddersfield Town supporter and he wrote that he had never enjoyed a goal scored against them before my effort. He had written to me before from Number Ten to congratulate me after those six goals against Northampton in the FA Cup in January 1970. I thought, what is the prime minister doing, writing to me?

It all just added to the feeling of unreality.

Things got even more surreal a few weeks after the death threat incident when Eamonn Andrews jumped out at me with his little red book on *This Is Your Life*. I was involved with a clothing company called Lincroft, who had designed a new range of suits which I had agreed to put my name to and we were to announce the deal at a press conference.

That, of course, was where Eamonn was to make his move. And to make sure that I didn't go missing on the day in question – as if – the company arranged a party the night before at a flat in London, with endless champagne and pretty girls with endless legs. The idea was that with everything I might possibly need on tap, there was no reason for me to leave the flat. As an extra precaution, however, they stationed a couple of private detectives outside.

The best-laid plans and all that, or in this case the Best-laid plans. Around one in the morning, I decided to take one of the girls to Tramp and, wanting to look good, I put on this new cream suit, which Lincroft had made specially for me to wear at the launch and then the *This Is Your Life* programme.

When I came out of the flat, I spotted the two 'tecs in their car and thought they were press men.

'Do you think you can lose them?' I said to the girl, who was driving.

She did but lost herself as well before we eventually got to Tramp and spent a few hours there. Luckily for the detectives, I then returned to the flat, with the suit a lot the worse for wear. It wasn't the only one.

I was so knackered that I just crashed out, still wearing the suit, which was a real lightweight number that creased easily. The Lincroft people threw a fit when they saw me, wearing something that looked more like a washed-out dishcloth than a new line. Someone got busy with an iron before we got into the studio with Eamonn and, having heard about my exploits the night before, they put someone on every exit door during the recording.

Like most of those programmes, it was a pretty tame show, though I thought they should have called it *These Are Your Lives* because I felt that I'd lived through a few in the previous 25 years. My family were all there, despite vowing never to go in front of the cameras again after the Cookstown sausages advert. Like everyone else, they were on tenterhooks until I walked in and I remember at the end of the programme, as a final surprise, my little brother Ian walked on, who was just five.

I was still banging the goals in, amazingly so considering the life I was leading and my attitude towards the game. I even managed a hat trick against West Ham, which gave me great pleasure because it was against the fabulous Bobby Moore. And the way I fooled him for one of those goals is one of my warmest memories.

Not many strikers got one over on Bobby. People always went on about his lack of speed but he didn't need pace when his timing in the tackle was immaculate and his reading of the game was so good. There has never been anyone better at reading the game than him – and the year before, remember, in 1970, he'd played that fantastic game against Pele in the World Cup. Pele showed his own admiration by swapping shirts with Bobby at the end and posing alongside him for that famous picture. We all knew Bobby was good but when Pele shows his respect for you, you know you're a bit special.

Bobby was also one of the coolest customers, on or off the field and the one thing I had discovered over the years was that he would rarely commit himself, leaving the striker to make all the difficult decisions. With other defenders, I could drop a shoulder or feint to go to the right and they would dive in, leaving me the simple task of shifting to the left and getting my shot in. Bobby was too smart for that but in that game at

Old Trafford, I got the ball from a corner and cut inside, shaping to shoot. He came across to block it and as he did so, I paused for a split second and for once, he couldn't resist the opportunity and lunged for the ball. I just whipped it to the side and hit it in and I was absolutely chuffed to have made him do that.

If I could have had moments like that every week, I might have felt a lot better. But we were losing more than we were winning and if I couldn't be bothered with playing matches, I certainly couldn't be bothered with training. One week in January 1972, I didn't manage to get into The Cliff training ground once and O'Farrell fined me two weeks wages. He also ordered me to go back to Mrs Fullaway's, which was no hardship after the circus that was taking place outside my home in Bramhall. And at least she had curtains that didn't draw themselves every time a plane went overhead.

O'Farrell dropped me, too, which meant that I wasn't able to get any relief from my problems with goals like the one against Bobby Moore. Football used to be my escape from all my fame problems but now drink and women replaced it. And it became a crazy game, like being a naughty boy wanting to prove how much I could get away with. And as I got away with more and more things, I pushed the stakes ever higher.

If anyone said, 'You don't need another drink, George', that would only make me want it even more. And if someone said of a girl I fancied, 'Stay away from her, she's married', I would not rest until I had pulled her.

I was getting away with it because of who I was, or because of who my alter ego was. If I'd been a butcher or a postman, or someone in one of those normal jobs and had tried some of the things I did with other men's wives and girlfriends, I would have got a punch in the face. But I was George Best and, mostly, I got my own way. I was also flying in girls from all over the world, just to prove I could do it. I would fly in a girl from Australia who I might have met on a previous trip and after a couple of weeks, when I got bored, I would send her back.

I knew I wasn't performing to my old level on the pitch. I could do it on occasions but when you're used to turning it on 99 times out of 100, it is no use when you drop to 70. And what really hurt was getting stick from the Old Trafford fans when we lost to teams we used to murder. I never minded the taunts I got from opposition fans, it was all part and parcel of the game. Some supporters threw cans of beer on the pitch and I would pick them up and pretend to drink out of them.

At Liverpool, they used to sing 'Georgie Best, superstar, walks like a woman and he wears a bra.' So one day at Anfield, I borrowed a handbag from a tea lady and walked out of the tunnel with it on my arm. That was all knockabout stuff and their taunts were a form of respect, recognising that you were a dangerous player. But when your own fans start turning on you and mocking you, that is hurtful.

I began asking myself, 'Do I need all this?' and began answering that I didn't. But then I didn't know what else to do with my life. How could I follow a career as a world-class footballer? I still don't know the answer to that one but when the season ended, I knew that I didn't have the stomach for the Home International tournament between the British teams and I couldn't really be bothered to tell Northern Ireland. So I just hopped on a plane to Marbella.

Naturally, as soon as the press found out, they were hopping on planes there, too. Things had changed a lot from the days when I could spend three months on holiday without seeing a single newspaper lens. In the back of my mind, I was thinking that maybe I should join another club and play with them for a few years. Sometimes, just a change of environment, a change of team mates, can alter the whole context of a situation and we've seen lots of teams transformed by the arrival of a new manager or a new player. But in my heart, I didn't want to play for anyone else and that just added to my confusion.

So I'd decided to take a few months off in Marbella to think about things when Fleet Street descended on me and, before I knew it, I had announced my retirement on 20 May 1972. I was just under 26 years old.

In truth, I didn't know what the hell I was going to do but I figured that by giving the press a sensational story, they would leave me alone for a bit. I told them the decision was absolutely irreversible, but I don't think they believed me because I had threatened to quit before. But at least they did leave me alone and even if I didn't believe my retirement story either, I had given myself licence to act like an ex-professional footballer.

Funnily enough, because I was now able to drink when I wanted, I didn't knock back so much, despite the fact that it was still an enormous amount by any normal standards.

I didn't have to feel guilty about drinking, either. No one was coming up to me saying, 'You shouldn't be drinking, an athlete like you', or 'Shouldn't you be in training?' I was no longer a professional footballer, at least not for the next couple of weeks or whenever I decided to end my holiday.

I stayed at the Skol Hotel, which was to become a regular haunt, and I became friendly with the barman Juan, who'd been there for 30 years or more. I got into a daily routine, which began with me getting up mid-morning and starting the day with a couple of shandies to get rid of the crap feeling from the night before. I'd have a few more beers sitting round the pool, before switching to white wine at lunch time.

Early evening, I would have some tapas and a few beers in the little Spanish bar next to the hotel. It was a tiny place, only seating about ten people, and I used to sit with all these old Spanish guys. I must have looked out of place but it didn't bother me. I can just about get by in Spanish but as the days went by, I was chatting more and more to these old guys and convincing myself that I could speak the language.

It was complete gobbledegook but they were too polite to correct me.

After an hour or two there, I would wander into Puerto Banus and get on to the hard stuff, mostly vodka. Sometimes, ironically, I'd be driven crazy by all the drunk and stupid holidaymakers so I'd go back to the cocktail bar at the Skol, which stayed open until three or four in the morning. I'd have a few nightcaps there before wandering off to bed at closing time and the following morning, I'd get up and have a shandy or two and start all over again. It was a routine I got into and it all seems great until your liver packs up – though at that point, I never dreamed such a thing could happen.

It was a good couple of weeks, drinking what I wanted and picking up a girl here and there but, like most holidaymakers, I was feeling pretty bored by the end of it. It seemed like a good idea at the time, spending all day in the sun and doing whatever I fancied but you become like a vegetable. You're doing the same thing day in, day out, without any end result, and there is no stimulation. I was also eating out of sheer boredom. I was eating about six or seven times a day and it was basically crap. I'd stuff myself sitting round the pool, then when I was in Puerto Banus, I'd have hamburger and chips and back at the Skol, I'd order a steak sandwich from room service.

I'd thought, as usual, that a change of scenery would help me sort out my problems but it hadn't worked, yet it did convince me that I wanted to play again and give my life some purpose. Again, no one from the club had contacted me and tried to talk me round. Perhaps they knew I would go back when I was ready and if so, they were right. I went back to see O'Farrell and began training like a lunatic for the following season.

I was always like that after having a break, swapping one obsession for another, excessive drinking for excessive training. I suppose that it is another example of an obsessive personality. In any case, I had always loved training and being fit, which sounds contradictory when you consider the way I was looking after my body outside of the game. But I was always competitive and I loved that feeling of getting fit again and seeing the weight drop off.

I suppose there's a bit of guilt attached to it as well – you've let yourself get out of condition so when you come back, you train twice as hard in the belief that it will repair any damage you might have done. It doesn't work that way, of course. By now, I had already done enough damage to my body that training had become an effort. It had become like work, when before it had been more like fun, something that came entirely naturally to me.

My good intentions didn't last long. We got off to a terrible start to the 1972–73 season and didn't even win until the tenth League match of the season.

I tried to tell myself that I couldn't go on the way I had been, that I had to stay fit and turn up for training every day. And when O'Farrell took me aside he made it clear that he was running out of patience.

'I've got to think of the rest of the team,' he said. 'I can't have you affecting morale.'

'All I want to do is get back to playing and help the team to start winning,' I assured him – and I meant it at the time because football had always been the one thing in life I could rely on.

But the football was so poor that I soon drifted back into the old drinking routine, drowning my sorrows, I suppose, and it didn't occur to me that my behaviour was in any way to blame for the club's position. I put it all down to the poor quality of the players around me and the backbiting in the dressing room. Most of the players from the 1968 side had gone and Bobby Charlton was in his final season.

My life came completely off the rails in a real Black November in 1972. Poor results had worn away my determination to stay on track and twice I just couldn't be bothered to get up for training and was dropped.

At least I was still able to play for Northern Ireland but in a game against Bulgaria, I got fed up with the treatment I was getting from one of their defenders and kicked out at him. Again, it was out of sheer frustration and considering the stick I had been taking, I thought the three match ban FIFA then gave me was pretty harsh. It was certainly hard on Northern Ireland.

For some years, I had had enough of my own troubles but now, trouble had a habit of finding me. I had always tried to live as normal life as possible, despite the celebrity thing. I didn't want to hide away from the public, I wanted to be able to go out and enjoy myself in the bars and clubs I'd always frequented and I was always polite if people came up to ask for autographs. But it was becoming harder, as I was to find out one night in Reubens, a club partly owned by my pal, Colin Burne.

I went in there with another club-owning friend, Doug Welsby. It was really early, well early for a nightclub, about ten o'clock, and we sat ourselves at the bar. Apart from us, the only people in there were a group of girls on a hen night, who were at a table around the other side of the bar. They were a bit noisy but seemed in pretty good order. Then a couple of them went to the ladies, which meant walking round our side of the bar and they spotted me. I saw them pointing and giggling and when they came out of the toilet, one of them came over, or rather staggered over, and asked me to dance.

Belfast men don't dance, at least not any that I know, and she was also steaming drunk. I just politely refused. She then grabbed me and was trying to drag me off my stool.

'Look,' said Dougie trying to reason with her, 'we're trying to talk business here. Can you leave us alone?'

She had a drink in her hand, a nice ladylike pint, and she threw it over me and walked off.

It was lucky I wasn't wearing that Lincroft suit. But I decided to let it go. It didn't seem worth causing a scene, so I just got a cloth from behind the bar and wiped myself down. We thought that was the end of it but twenty minutes later, and even drunker, she staggered over again with a pint glass in her hand. I knew that an invitation to dance was now completely out of the question and as I realised she was intending to throw another drink over me, I jumped up and smacked her with the back of my hand. I didn't punch her, just clipped her to keep her off me, like you would a wasp or a fly. But just my luck, she ended up with a hairline fracture of the nose.

Whatever the circumstances or provocation, things like that never look good and I knew I could be in big trouble when she called in the police and I ended up being charged with causing actual bodily harm. There must be hundreds of cases like that before the courts every day that go unnoticed but, being me, this one was bound to bring a lot of press attention.

So I got myself a top-notch lawyer and thought we had a firm case when we retraced the girl's night. Of course, that didn't change the fact that I had hit her and, as you would expect, she turned up in court wearing pigtails and looking as though butter wouldn't melt in her mouth, even if alcohol clearly did.

I was found guilty but given a conditional discharge, though it cost me £25 damages and £75 in costs. My hotshot lawyer, by the way, was the late George Carmen, who was practising in Manchester at the time. And I think it was the only case he lost.

Worried about the hearing, which went to court in January 1973, I had been drinking even more. In December, I had skipped training to go down to London for a change of scenery and was enjoying myself so much, I didn't come back for a few days.

For once, I felt O'Farrell might have had some sympathy but he was under enough pressure for his own job and obviously didn't feel he could keep worrying about where I was. He clearly didn't think I was much use to him or the team, either, and I was making his decision to take me back look pretty silly. He went to the board and I was told that I was not only suspended for two weeks but that I was now available for transfer for £300,000. Seeing that it was to be another five years before United were to pay more than that for a player, it seemed a pretty high fee. And at the state I was in at the time, I probably wasn't worth £3,000.

Even so, my pride was hurt and I went to see Sir Matt and the chairman Louis Edwards. Even Sir Matt must have had enough of me by then and he no longer had to make allowances for me on the grounds that I was one of the club's biggest assets. The goals had started to dry up and if only I had been able to do the same, maybe things would have been different. But Sir Matt and Edwards listened to me.

'We've really got to get some new players,' I said, 'because the ones in the side at the moment aren't good enough.'

'But do you want to leave United, George?' Matt said. 'Is your heart really in it here?'

I told him I couldn't imagine playing for anyone else.

I don't know whether Sir Matt was frightened that if I made a fresh start elsewhere and got back to my best form, he and Manchester United would look silly but he agreed to take me off the transfer list just nine days after I'd gone on it.

O'Farrell was furious when he heard the news.

'You went behind my back,' he said to me in the dressing room the next morning.

What could I say? I had, so I just shrugged my shoulders. He must have also known the writing was on the wall for him if Sir Matt and the board were undermining his decisions, just as they had with Wilf. It was over for him when the side lost 5–0 at Crystal Palace in mid-December, the club's biggest defeat in four and a half years. And Palace, who had only come up to Division One in 1969, were to be relegated that year.

O'Farrell was given the push a few days later. Bill Foulkes and Paddy Crerand took over as joint caretaker bosses and if anyone could have persuaded me to stay, it would have been those two. But I knew they would soon be gone and I didn't want to wait to find out whether the new manager would want me. I also knew that it would take him some time to turn the team round and couldn't be sure it wouldn't turn out to be another fiasco. So I wrote to the board and told them that I didn't want to play for the club any more and apologised for tarnishing United's name.

In the few days that I was on the transfer list, a few interested parties had raised their heads, if not their cheque books. Malcolm Allison said that he would love to sign me for Manchester City, adding that 'all my players would welcome George in the dressing room'. Well, I knew that Mike Summerbee would have done, but Allison didn't make a bid for me after his chairman, Eric Alexander, said that Big Mal had 'been talking out of turn'. I couldn't have imagined United entertaining the idea of me joining their greatest rivals, either.

Good old Brian Clough, then turning Derby, the previous season's champions, into one of the best clubs in the country, said he was thinking of trying to buy me and John Bond said he would be delighted to have me at Bournemouth. I am sure he would have done but I didn't think I was ready for Third Division football at that stage.

The most exciting offer came from Clive Toye, general manager of the New York Cosmos, champions of the North American Soccer League. The NASL was just starting to get big and, backed by big-name businessmen, clubs were beginning to fork out millions on star name players from around the world. It also appealed to me as a clean break. If I had joined another English club, it would have been the same old circus, the same old problems. But America would be a fresh start, a place where I could walk around unrecognised. Again, I began to think that my problems might disappear with a change of scenery.

The Cosmos were owned by Warner Communications and one of their top men, Gordon Bradley, invited me to go over and have a look at the setup. So I checked into the Wessex House Hotel opposite Central Park and stayed there almost a week while they showed me round and outlined all their plans. It was all top drawer and the money they were willing to pay me was more than acceptable. But they wanted me to do a lot of promotional stuff and, not unnaturally, to live in New York full time. I didn't fancy that. I think New York is a great city and I love the madness of it for a few days. I just didn't relish the prospect of living there full time.

There was also interest from the World Indoor Soccer League in Toronto, which is about as quiet as New York is noisy. So I flew out there with Waggy in January 1973 to speak to them. Again the offer sounded good and they only wanted me for three or four months. But I wasn't sure whether I was ready for that either. I left Waggy to explain to them that I had changed my mind, arranging to meet him at New York airport for the flight home.

By the spring, I couldn't wait for my summer break so I headed off to Marbella again, this time taking a girlfriend with me, which was a bit like taking coals to Newcastle. At least, however, that made it a more normal holiday, but we had to cut the trip short after a nightmare experience.

One night, sitting in the International Bar, I felt a pain high in my right leg, just below the groin. I ignored it at first but the pain became worse and when I got back to the hotel, the leg had started to swell. I've never been one for doctors but the swelling frightened me and I asked the hotel to call one for me. The doctor turned up looking bored, used an anaesthetic spray on my leg, handed me some painkillers and told me that I'd be OK in a couple of days.

I think that even dear old Ted Dalton, the United physio, would have realised that I needed a bit more treatment than that. I was in so much pain that I couldn't sleep and when I got up to use the loo early in the morning, the leg was twice its normal size.

'I'm sorry, but I've got to get this seen to,' I said to Chris, my girlfriend. 'We're going home.'

I phoned my doctor in Manchester to arrange for him to meet me at the airport and then boarded the plane for the most agonising journey I've ever had. As everyone knows, your legs and feet can swell on planes at the best of times and my leg was now the size of a balloon. The flight, naturally, was full of British holidaymakers all wanting to chat to me and to ask for autographs. And I was sitting there with the sweat pouring out of me.

I eased my shoe off when I got on the plane and when we landed, it was impossible to get it back on again. I must have looked a right state when I hobbled through customs. Luckily, my doctor was there, who seeing how stressed I was, told me to drop my trousers.

He took one look and said, 'Fucking hell.'

He knew instantly that it was a thrombosis, which, it turned out, had started on the inside of my leg and worked its way down into my calf. Had it moved the other way, towards my heart or my brain, it could easily have killed me. My doctor, realising the seriousness of the situation from my descriptions over the phone, had already made hospital arrangements and I was in a bed within half an hour. Although it was only a short flight, it is terrifying to think, given what we now know about deep-vein thrombosis, that getting on a plane in that condition was probably the most dangerous thing I could have done.

Sir Matt came to see me in hospital and asked me how things were and whether I had been looking after myself, but I think he knew the answer to that one. Then, as he was leaving, he turned back.

'It's about time you were back playing, isn't it?' he said casually.

It was a funny time to make such a comment since I

couldn't get out of bed, let alone play for Manchester United. But I was amazed to think that he still hadn't given up on me.

Although I am not particularly religious, it did get me thinking that my lucky escape had perhaps bordered on divine intervention, as if I were meant to survive to play again. But this time I decided it would be on my own terms. When I came out, I announced that I was only willing to play football for Northern Ireland, not for Manchester United. It was a bit ironic, seeing that I had pulled out of so many games for my country but in my befuddled state, I thought it would be nice to be a part-time player!

Tommy 'The Doc' Docherty had taken over as United manager just before Christmas 1972 and steered them clear of relegation, though it was a close-run thing, the club finishing only seven points above Crystal Palace, the highest-placed club to go down. I didn't know whether Docherty knew about Sir Matt's offer but I should have taken note of him when he responded to my statement by saying, 'George Best is registered with Manchester United through FIFA and he cannot play for anyone else without our permission.'

Docherty also said that I would have to train with United before I would be allowed to go elsewhere.

Within a week, he was saying that he would listen to any reasonable offers for me and QPR, who had all but completed promotion to the first division, expressed an interest.

But nothing came of it.

Of course, my idea of playing only for Northern Ireland was ridiculous, though in reality I had been a part-time player for a number of years.

My attitude had clearly frightened off other clubs. Here I was, going for a song – and no one was willing to take me on.

CHAPTER TEN
END OF AN ERA

My thrombosis gave me the perfect excuse for a permanent retirement at 27, after two pretend ones and several other threats to give up football. But, instead, because of my stubborn nature, it became a reason to play again, to see if I could get back to match fitness and perform as well as I had before. I was still a young man and I hadn't decided what I wanted to do when I finished playing so when Paddy Crerand came round to sound me out about going back to Old Trafford in the spring of 1973, I listened to him. Paddy was working as the Doc's number two and acted as a go-between between him and me.

I had always admired Paddy, both as a person and a player with a real passion for the game and for Manchester United. And although I wasn't sure about going back, he convinced me that Docherty was a proper United man, who would bring in new players to restore the side to its glory days and most importantly, that his team would play the United way.

Eventually, I agreed to meet the Doc. He was renowned for his sharp humour and ready quips but was also serious about the game.

'Look,' he said, 'I know you've been having problems but if you miss training, nobody will know about it from me. But if you don't train, you'll have to come back on your own and make up for it. What do you say?'

'That's fine by me,' I said. 'But I'm going to need time to get fit and I don't want to be rushed.'

We shook hands on it, though I probably agreed to go back to Old Trafford more for Paddy's sake than his. But I've never done things by halves so once again I began training like a lunatic. I stopped drinking (for a bit) and began training twice a day, going back in the afternoon for sessions with Paddy and Bill Foulkes, who had taken over as the reserve team coach.

I also had a lot of weight to lose after all those months out of the game. I was more than a stone over my old playing weight of 10 stone 10 pounds. But at 27, I hadn't done so much damage to my body that I couldn't get back to my best form. Or so I thought.

Football was now taking up more of my life than at any time since I had joined as an unofficial apprentice, but I was still working on my plans for a career outside the game. Footballers were earning only a fraction of today's wages and the biggest ambition of most was to earn enough money to buy a pub. Or to marry a big-busted woman who owned one!

Well, I'd done a lot better than most and had often talked to my mates about opening a nightclub. I'd spent enough time in them to know what worked and what didn't, so when Colin Burne suggested that he, Waggy and I open one together, I told him he was on. Colin, of course, was already a successful nightclub owner and both he and Waggy were great mates.

Colin found a place called Costa Del Sol on Bootle Street in Manchester and took Waggy and I to see it one night in November. Luckily, he warned us not to expect too much because the place was terrible. I remember going into the so-called kitchen, which had maggots crawling over the stove. There was also solid grease on every surface and down the walls. How it had ever passed a health inspection I'll never know.

Everything else about it was wrong, too. For a start, all the streets outside were covered in double yellow lines, which meant it was a nightmare to park. There was a police station on the corner, which nightclubbers don't regard as a plus point, and the club was on the second floor. Perhaps because of the Cavern Club, where The Beatles started, and places like Tramp in London, all successful nightclubs were in the basement. Small point, you might think, but not when you're investing money in a business venture.

There were only a couple of people in the place on the night we went to do our recce and after our three-hour grand tour – if you could call it that – they were still the only pair in. I found it hard to envisage it as a top-class club but Colin gave an encouraging look at Waggy and me.

'What do you think?' he said.

'It's dreadful but you're the expert,' I replied. 'How much do they want for it?'

He coughed and said that for ten grand the owners would let us walk in straight away and take over.

'Ten grand for this pigsty?' I said. 'All right, I'm in.'

Three grand didn't seem like a fortune to me and I had made up my mind beforehand to be guided by Colin's advice. Waggy was always up for a laugh, too, so we coughed up a third each and set about doing the place up.

I suggested fumigating it but all it really needed was a good clean and several licks of paint. As the Yates Wine Lodge chain had been so successful, turning young people on to wine for the first time, we also decided to put in a wine bar, selling slightly more upmarket stuff than Yates.

The other big key to our success was hiring a top local disc jockey. We had to think up a new name for the place too, and went through all sorts of ideas before I suggested Slack Alice. She was an imaginary character in comedian Larry Grayson's programme, which was massively popular. The other two liked it and we thought of having a logo with Alice in

Wonderland in suspenders. I wrote to Larry Grayson asking for his permission to use the name and he sent me a telegram saying, 'I would be privileged if you named a club after us.'

Everyone at the time was also always using Larry's famous catchphrase but we could hardly have called a night-club 'Shut That Door'.

Docherty had agreed not to rush me back into the United team but after a bad start to the season, he asked me to play against Birmingham at Old Trafford in October 1973.

I didn't feel confident that I was back to form, physically, but I suppose it appealed to the old ego and I agreed to play. And when I came out of the tunnel and heard the noise from that crowd, who gave me a fantastic reception, it was almost like making my debut again. The adrenalin kept me going for a bit and I tried to do a few too many dribbles and tricks to give the crowd their money's worth.

But having only played a couple of reserve games and two or three friendlies, I wasn't able to sustain it. I was knackered by half time and was taken off, but we did win the game 1–0. Goalkeeper Alex Stepney scored with a penalty and he was our joint top scorer for a while, which tells you a lot about the team at the time.

My form did start to come back and I knocked in a couple of goals. But despite all the promises and all the new players Docherty had brought in – people like George

Graham, Jim Holton and Lou Macari – we just weren't performing as a team.

I began to wonder whether I'd made a big mistake in agreeing to come back, especially as I was now involved so heavily in preparations for the opening of Slacks at Christmas. The football was just as depressing as before and although I had not tested the Doc's promise to keep quiet if I missed training, I wasn't always in pristine shape when I turned up.

Paddy was a good lad and although we weren't mates socially he was very protective of me. He would give me bollockings at training, particularly when Docherty was watching, but privately he would try to encourage me. One morning, though, when I turned up reeking of drink, he said to me, 'You stink' and ordered me to have a shower before training.

Plans for Slacks, by contrast, were coming along nicely and we put the final piece of the jigsaw in place when we persuaded a fantastic guy called Felix Izquierdo-Moreno to come over from Spain to run it for us.

Felix worked in a restaurant in Majorca called the Gomilla Grill, which I walked in to by chance one day soon after the 1968 European Cup Final. It turned out that he was a fan of mine and he was another of those people that you took to straight away. He was the Spanish waiter from central casting, singing to customers as he rushed about from table to table and seemingly managing to do three things at once, serving drinks, preparing the food and washing up.

Naturally, I took all my mates to the Gomilla, and as time went on, most of the United players. So when we opened Slacks, he was the only man for the job. He wasn't so sure about that but the fact that his wife was a Manchester girl clinched it. Almost from opening night, the place was heaving and while my name as one of the co-owners did no harm to its popularity, Felix put the personality in the place.

As pleased as I was to be involved in the Slack Alice adventure, running a night club wasn't exactly conducive to the life of a professional sportsman. As part-owner of the club, and the most famous one, I was naturally expected to be on view most nights and, just as naturally, partake of a drink or several with customers, especially in the first few days of business after we opened at Christmas. It was fantastically exciting to see the place packed out and, after a New Year's Eve party that I managed to extend into 2 January 1974, I didn't make it into training the following day, a Thursday.

Docherty kept his part of our bargain by not saying anything to the press and I kept my part by calling Paddy and going in to train in the afternoon with him and Bill. We were playing Plymouth in the third round of the FA Cup on the Saturday, hardly the most taxing of fixtures. After helping the Doc out by playing when I wasn't properly fit, I certainly felt I was ready for this match and he didn't say anything to me about missing training when I went in on Friday, nor during the pre-match meal at midday on Saturday. Then, about an hour and a quarter before the game, he and Paddy took me into the referee's room.

'I'm not playing you today,' Docherty said.

'Why not?' I replied, shocked.

'Because you missed training on Thursday.'

I reminded him of our agreement and that I'd kept to it by training in the afternoon. But he was adamant I was out and just turned on his heel and left.

I felt utterly humiliated.

'If I'm not good enough to play against Plymouth Argyle,' I said to Paddy, 'then I ain't playing again.'

'Don't be stupid,' he said. 'Don't do anything silly. Come in on Monday morning and it will all be forgotten.'

'No, Paddy, that's it,' I insisted. 'I'm finished.'

Paddy felt a bit embarrassed leaving me there because I was already beginning to get emotional but he had to go back to the dressing room to give the players their final instructions and once he left, I just sat down on a bench and sobbed. I knew this time, it really was over.

When I'd recovered my composure, I went to the players' lounge for a cup of tea and I sat in there, listening to the crowd roaring and complaining above me. I didn't have any interest in watching the game, though afterwards Sammy McIlroy came in and told me that we'd won 1–0.

'It's not a case of "we" any more,' I said. 'I'm finished, Sammy.'

He didn't know what to say and he had no way of knowing that I meant it this time because I'd said I was quitting so many times before.

Once the crowd had gone, I went up into the stands and sat there on my own for almost an hour. I just sat and thought about all the good times I'd had and all the great occasions I'd been involved in. The stands were empty and silent but in my head, I could hear the roar of 50,000 people on that day when I first walked up the tunnel as a 17-year-old. I could see myself scoring that goal against Bobby Moore and the look of surprise on Pat Jennings's face when I put one spectacular effort past him.

I remembered those great nights in Europe under the floodlights, the pure theatre of those occasions. As I sat there, lost in my own thoughts, all those great memories flooded into my mind and the tears began streaming down my face.

There was anger mixed with my tears because I just couldn't believe it had all ended. I thought, how could it have happened, that I'm left out of a game against a side we should have beaten 7–0? And without me, they only scraped a 1–0 win. Two years earlier, when I'd gone to Spain, I had known deep down that it wasn't for good, that I'd be back at Old Trafford again. But this time, I was certain and I needed that time in the stands to say goodbye.

Eventually, a steward came up and said, 'It's time to go, George,' so I got up and walked out of the ground.

And it was a long, long time before I was able to go back.

What annoyed me most was that Docherty told the press that I had turned up for the game drunk and with a girl on my arm, which is absolute rubbish. I never turned up drunk for a United game and I've certainly never reported to the dressing room with a girl.

Paddy knows the truth and has always supported my story, even if he might have been thinking that I wasn't up to it any more. I've worked with the Doc at dinners. I think he is a funny man. But I also think he can be a bullshitter.

After such an emotional end to my Old Trafford days, I really didn't want to think about football for a while, so I threw everything into Slacks, which was already becoming one of the hottest places in town. I discovered just how hot when, a month after leaving Old Trafford, I got a phone call from the Miss World organisers. An American, Marjorie Wallace, was the title holder and she had obviously asked them what there was to do for a bit of fun in Manchester on a Sunday night, to which in those days the answer would have been 'not much'.

We were about the only club that opened on a Sunday night because of the draconian licensing laws, which meant that most other places didn't have the right licence and couldn't be bothered to get one. So being bright people, the Miss

World lot phoned me and asked if Marjorie could come to the club as a guest.

'Of course,' I said, being a generous guy.

'She will have to be paid, naturally,' they replied.

'We don't pay anybody to come in here,' I laughed. 'Normally, they pay us, but as she is Miss World, she can come as my guest and she will be very welcome.'

'No, you will have to pay her,' they said. 'It's £150 and just think of the good publicity it will bring you.'

That was a great one. I would have happily paid a lot more than £150 to escape some of the publicity I had been getting. So I laughed again and told them that she could come if she wanted and I would be happy to pose for a picture with her. But there would be no fee.

With that, I hung up but they were back on soon after, saying that Marjorie would love to come. We later posed for the picture and she had a glass of champagne while I knocked back a vodka or three. She didn't stay long, but long enough for me to get her London phone number, having told her that I was often down in the capital, which was not a lie. Now that I was a free agent as far as football was concerned, I was even able to spend weekends in London without a couple of dozen press men camped outside a girlfriend's house.

I learned from the press reports that Marjorie was supposed to be engaged to the motor racing driver, Peter Revson, and had also been linked romantically with Tom Jones and tennis star Jimmy Connors. That didn't put me off – in fact if anything, it made her a more attractive catch so I called her a couple of days later and invited myself down to London.

When I turned up on her doorstep on Friday night, she looked at my overnight bag.

'Which hotel are you staying in?' she said.

'I don't know yet,' I replied. 'I'll sort it out later.'

I didn't, of course, expect to be staying in a hotel and once nature had taken its course, she didn't mention it again either.

The following day, was a normal Best day out in London – lunch at San Lorenzo, a film in the afternoon, an evening in Tramp and a night in bed with a beautiful woman. Unfortunately, it all turned ugly when Marjorie took a phone call as we lay in bed in the early hours of the morning.

At first, I thought it was Revson, but I realised it may have been his mother when Marjorie said, 'I do miss him, you know. Tell him I miss him, I am being good and I can't wait to see him again.'

Being good! I couldn't believe it. I knew about Revson and the other boyfriends but I thought Marjorie was rubbing my nose in it. I wasn't on the point of proposing marriage but we'd only been together 24 hours and I felt that she was treating me as if I were just a bit of rough she had picked up.

When she came off the phone, I went nuts.

'How can you have a conversation like that when you're lying in bed with me?' I yelled. 'Couldn't you have made an excuse and said you'll ring back later or taken the call in another room?'

'Who the hell are you to tell me what to do?' she retorted, ironically seeing that the following morning, she told *me* what to do, saying, 'I think you had better go.'

The end of a wonderful relationship, though I told her that I had planned to leave in any case. She actually went out and left me in bed.

After I got up around midday, the doorbell rang but I didn't answer it. Out of curiosity, I did look out of the window and saw a Rolls Royce parked outside. A few hours later, the phone rang and, thinking it was Marjorie, I picked it up.

'Yes, I'm still here,' I said, 'but don't worry. I am just about to leave.'

I slammed the receiver down without waiting for a response and in hindsight, it was a daft thing to do because for all I knew, it could have been Revson or his mother again.

On Tuesday night, a couple of Manchester policemen came into Slacks and told me that two detectives were on their way from London to arrest me for theft. I told them that was ridiculous but apologetically, they took me off to Bootle nick. So despite my concerns about the closeness of the police station to the club, it turned out to be convenient after all.

Not that I was thinking that at the time. I was absolutely furious when they told me that I was being charged with stealing a fur coat, passport, cheque book and jewellery from

Marjorie's apartment. I told them it was absolutely ridiculous and I was even angrier when the police searched Mrs Fullaway's house where I was still living. Although I had walked out on United, I was still officially their player and saw no reason to change my digs. I was pretty sure they wouldn't find any fur coats or jewellery at Mrs Fullaway's house.

The local cops kept me in tea until the London boys turned up, who then drove me down to the capital without a word passing between us. In any case, I had been able to phone my solicitor, Geoffrey Miller, who instructed me not to say anything until he got there. But I didn't care because I was innocent and had nothing to hide. I was happy to be interviewed in London.

The detectives went through the sequence of the Saturday with me.

'You went to the cinema with Miss Wallace and saw such-and-such a film. Is that correct?'

'Yes,' I said.

'Then you went for a meal and then Tramp and stayed the night at her apartment?'

'Yes.'

They were pleased with this. 'And all this was on Friday the 16th?'

'No.'

They frowned. 'But you just admitted you did all those things.'

'Yes,' I said, 'but on Saturday, not Friday.'

They said that Marjorie was adamant that these events had taken place on Friday, which made me wonder what she had been on. And they also reckoned, presumably on her say so, that the theft had taken place between Sunday night and Tuesday, when I was back in Manchester.

Geoffrey, my solicitor, was a bit concerned when he discovered I'd gone ahead with the police interviews without him but I told him the same thing.

'I went to the cinema with her,' I said to him. 'I went to Tramp and I stayed at her apartment. But they've got the wrong day. For me to have done it, I would have had to have travelled back to Manchester on the Sunday and then returned to London the same night or the night after, broken into her flat and taken the stuff.'

That was assuming I had any skills as a thief because I certainly didn't have a key. And to add to the madness of it all, there was no sign of any forced entry. So whoever the thief was, he or she must have had a key to Marjorie's flat.

'I was in my club on Sunday and Monday night with about five or six hundred witnesses,' I said to the police. 'Even if I had managed to sneak out and get on a train to London, wouldn't someone have seen me? I do have a fairly well-known face.'

Their arguments were illogical but they charged me anyway and when I appeared at Marylebone Magistrates

Court in February 1974, bail was set at £6,000, which Waggy put up for me.

I was warned not to get in contact with Marjorie but I was so angry, I couldn't help myself. I phoned her a couple of times, in fact, and gave her a piece of my mind, though I felt better when she told me she had no intention of turning up for the court case.

Peter Revson was killed when his Formula One Shadow car crashed at Kyalami in practice for the South African grand prix on 22 March, five days before my trial was supposed to begin. Marjorie returned to America for the funeral, her passport and jewellery having turned up in a package sent to the *Sunday People*.

She failed to turn up again when the case was reset for 24 April and the case was dropped. The judge said that I was left without a stain on my character.

Revson's death was sad but I'd been hit by tragic news myself, just three days after my arrest.

The violence in Belfast had been getting worse and my dad got in touch to tell me that my cousin, Gary Reid, who was just 17, had been shot dead. He had become just another statistic of the Troubles, one of the thousands of innocent victims who had no interest in being involved in terrorism in any shape or form and simply found himself in the wrong place at the wrong time. He was a lovely kid whose only crime was to pop out to get a fish and chip supper for his mum and dad one night and got caught up in crossfire. The ironic thing is that it appeared that it was an army bullet that killed him, ironic because one of my family worked in the security services.

I don't think there is anyone who has lived in Belfast who hasn't been affected by the Troubles one way or another, but up until then no one in our family had been killed. We felt we had been pretty lucky. My family happened to be born Protestants but everyone – my grandads, my dad, my mum, my sisters Carol and Barbara – they were all open-minded and honest about it.

You would have to be pretty naïve to come from Belfast and believe that there is only one religion doing wrong and it is not the one you believe in. There is good and bad on both sides and it takes two to make a war, which is what we've had in Northern Ireland for all these years.

When I was a kid in the Orange Order, the anniversary of the Battle of the Boyne, on 12 July, was a day out for us. There was plenty of name-calling but you didn't join the Orange Order because you hated Catholics and you didn't join the IRA because you hated Protestants. Now, of course, that is precisely why you join those organisations. The Good Friday agreement was supposed to have brought peace but there are still beatings going on every day in Ulster and no one who lives in Belfast would be foolish enough to say that everything is all right.

Things have improved in recent years but these days it seems that some terrorists are mainly motivated by profit. There are splinter groups who are not doing it for religious principles any more, for what they or their family believe in, to right wrongs from the past or to try to build a better future. It is purely and simply for money. And drugs are increasingly playing a part in the situation now, with both sides involved in peddling them and fighting to keep control because of the vast sums involved.

In the last few years, there are no longer army tanks on the streets. Yet there are always going to be certain people who want to keep it going, who do not want peace. And that's the tragedy. Even if 90 per cent of the people want an end to the Troubles, it's not going to happen when you have got a 10 per cent hard core of people who are basically not interested in human rights.

When Gary was killed it was a difficult time for my dad and my brother and sisters because they were also trying to cope with my mum's drinking, which had become much more serious. Carol had virtually become the other children's mother now.

'George,' she told me, 'you wouldn't recognise Mummy now from the Mummy we grew up with. We really had the cream of the years with her.'

According to Carol, Mum had become very antagonistic, very moody and would make vicious comments to the children. Carol said that she dreaded going home at night and had got into a habit of creeping up to the front room window and peeking in to see what state Mum was in, so that she knew what to expect.

I felt guilty because I knew Mum worried about me and I'd given her plenty of cause over quite a few years. I was shocked, however, to hear that she actually punched a woman in a club one night. Apparently she and Dad were just having a quiet drink and when mum went to the toilet, a woman followed her in and said, 'Aren't you Mrs Best, George Best's mother?'

When my mother said that she was, this woman started slagging me off, saying I was this, that and the other. And my mum just turned round and slugged her, then went back to my dad and said, 'Come on, we've got to get out of here.'

I remembered my mum as such a quiet and considerate person that she must have been at the end of her tether to do such a thing. I felt guilty but I didn't know what I could do to help the situation and I probably wouldn't have been the best qualified person to do so in any case.

I probably drank more than she did but I didn't see it as a big problem, even if I accepted that it led to some bad behaviour. So who was I to tell her not to drink? As I wasn't there, I couldn't know just how bad her situation was and being an alcoholic myself, I knew that my dad and my sisters were much better equipped than me to deal with the situation. I felt sad but also helpless.

The difference between my dad and mum was that while he didn't mind people coming up and talking to him about football and about me, my mother hated it, particularly after that incident in the club. If people came up and asked, 'Are you Mrs Best?' she either froze or denied it. And all the stories and nonsense written about me only made matters worse for her. Sadly, it seemed Mum was far more sensitive about me than any of us realised.

I was still trying to make a life for myself outside football, but I was persuaded to put my boots back on in May 1974, when I received a fabulous offer to play in South Africa, for a club in Johannesburg called the Jewish Guild, would you believe? They offered me £11,000 to play for eight weeks but I didn't want to go on my own so I asked Waggy to come with me and after a bit of persuasion, he agreed.

It was a great couple of months and when I got home, I received a phone call from Barry Fry, who'd been on the ground staff with me at Old Trafford in the early days. Barry was then manager of non-League Dunstable Town and, always being one with an eye on a fast buck, he asked me if I would play for his club in a friendly against United reserves.

The money was good so I agreed to play, and Dunstable did brilliantly out of it because the place was packed to the rafters. We beat United 3–2 and the crowd ran on to the pitch at the end and I was mobbed.

United still held my professional registration so I had to ask the Doc's permission to play in those games, although he could hardly have refused as there was no chance of me playing for the Reds again.

Besides, Docherty had bigger things to worry about. The previous summer, he had allowed Denis Law to return to Manchester City on a free transfer, which turned out to be another of his big mistakes. At the end of the season, Denis scored with a back heel at Old Trafford to give City a 1–0 win and send United into the Second Division. The game was abandoned when the crowd invaded the pitch but as there were only eight minutes to go and it was the United fans who forced the stoppage, the League decided that the score would stand as a result.

Denis jokes about it in his after-dinner speeches today, but for the only time in his career, he didn't celebrate the goal and said afterwards that it was his most depressing moment in the game. I could understand how he felt. I didn't feel any sympathy for Docherty but I was sad that, just six years after winning the European Cup, United had sunk so low.

CHAPTER ELEVEN
THE DEMONS
RETURN

As I was now a retired footballer, at least unofficially, I had nothing to do but enjoy myself. They say the devil finds work for idle hands, although I found mine full of casino chips as, with so much spare time, I managed to discover a third vice to go with the drinking and womanising.

Gambling.

I had dabbled in it over the years but Colin Burne was a big gambler and, with nothing much to do after Slacks closed at two in the morning, we got into an almost daily habit of heading to the casino. Poor old Waggy, who didn't gamble, was left to lock up because we were like a couple of kids, anxious to get off as soon as the final bell went.

We went to a place called Soames, which was owned by

Frenchman Emile Semprèse. Slacks was doing such great business that every night, Colin and I would go to the safe, take £500 each out of the takings and head for Soames, which was one of the classier casinos. And the first thing we did was to order and pay for a couple of bottles of champagne, so that even if we lost the rest of our money, we'd have a nice drink waiting afterwards with which to celebrate or drown our sorrows.

I thought I was starting to get wild in my gambling but Colin was something else. One night, when they called last spin on the roulette wheel, he hardly had a penny left in his pocket. But he went maximum on number 22 and covered it in every possible win combination. I was holding my breath as the wheel started spinning and could hardly look, but when the ball was dropped in, it was as if this great hand came out and grabbed it and it fell straight into number 22.

Colin, who won thousands on that spin, just gave me a big grin, but it was a dangerous habit, playing with money we didn't have. A few months later, we were playing craps on tick and, half an hour after walking in, found ourselves £17,000 down. If I'd stopped to think about it, I would have been terrified. But with the adrenalin pumping, we kept on throwing and two hours later, we still had the dice in our hands, and had turned that loss into an unbelievable £26,000 profit.

It seemed fantastic at the time, like something from the movies, but when I thought about it later it frightened me to death, imagining what might have happened if things had gone the other way. Obviously, all the dealers in the casino knew us and they probably figured that because we were in every night, we must be good for the money, no matter how much we lost.

Emile also acted as if he were really pleased for us, saying, 'Well done, boys,' as we drank our champagne afterwards.

Colin was just as much a gambler in his business dealings, but fortunately he was also a genius when it came to running pubs, clubs or restaurants. He just had that knack of finding something that people would go for. I took him to Geales fish restaurant in Notting Hill Gate, telling him it was the best fish and chips in London. So, of course, he then opened an upmarket, some would say over the top, fish and chip shop in Manchester. It was all wood panelling with gorgeous girls serving behind the counter and champagne on ice. It was brilliant, absolutely brilliant.

So when he suggested to Waggy and me that we buy the old Waldorf Hotel and turn it into another club, who was I to argue? Slacks was already a fantastic success – everyone who was anyone came to it. Jimmy Tarbuck, naturally, was a regular whenever he was in town, as were Bruce Forsyth and Dave Allen. Mick Jagger came in and so did any other rock star playing in Manchester. And there were other great local characters, like Frank Evans, the Manchester bullfighter and Brian Hafferty, a local businessman who used to organise card schools. Slacks was so busy that most nights, you couldn't move in the place. So we figured that it would make sense to give people an alternative.

We opened Oscar's in November 1974 and Colin, as usual, had devised a brilliant plan to make it a multi-purpose club to cater for all tastes at all times of the day. The first floor was Oscar's itself, which did real pub grub, bangers and mash, steak and kidney pie, all that stuff. We had a big, open fire in there as well, which gave it a good feel and it became packed out with businessmen at lunchtime. On the top floor, we had a private banqueting suite called Dorian Gray and between that and the pub was a disco called Saville's which, to be honest, wasn't that successful because of Slacks.

But the real money spinner was the wine bar on the ground floor. We only opened it for two hours after the pub closed at 11 in the evening, but it's a strange thing about the mentality of drinkers. No matter how much they've had in the course of the night, if you tell them they've only got two hours left, they start knocking it back as fast as they can. They were queuing three or four deep at the bar, waving £20 notes from the moment we opened until chucking-out time.

If we had been wise, Colin, Waggy and I could have retired after four or five years with the money we were taking from the two clubs. But we reckoned there was a lot more where that came from and Colin and I were taking more and more out of the profits to gamble. And in the daytime, when there were no casinos to lose money in, we would go racing and throw our cash at the bookies. Again, we would take £500 apiece and make our own bets, though agreeing that we would split anything left in the pot at the end of the day. We also used to leave before the last race to avoid the traffic.

One afternoon at Haydock, when we'd done pretty well, we pooled our money before the last race and counted out £1,500.

'Great,' said Colin, 'you look after the money. I'm just off to the loo and then we'll go.'

He came back a few minutes later and said, 'Ready then, George?'

'No,' I said. 'I've had a bet on the last.'

It was a two-horse race involving Lester Piggott and Joe Mercer.

'Which one?' Colin asked.

'Let's watch the race and I'll tell you afterwards.'

But I didn't have to tell him because Piggott fell about 20 lengths behind at the two furlong pole.

'Let's go,' I said, pulling Colin's arm.

'How much did you put on?' he said as we sprinted to the car park.

'The lot,' I replied.

Like I said, Colin was a pretty crazy punter himself, so he didn't go mad. Instead he just laughed. 'You really are a mad bastard,' he said.

The only football I was playing at this point was a Sunday morning kick about with the waiters at the Stanneylands Hotel in Wilmslow.

We'd get a few lads together, Danny Bursk, who was a big United punter, Colin, me and whoever else we could round up, but after a few minutes, a few of our lot would be spewing up the drink from the night before. One of our players, though, was a lad called Cliff Harold. He was a real fitness fanatic, he worked out at the Midland Hotel every day and he didn't touch a drop. Yet ironically, he dropped dead of a heart attack a few months ago, poor bloke. Waggy was one of the only ones in our group who wasn't into football. But we persuaded him to play one Sunday and he broke his leg. That was his first and last game.

I hadn't been thinking of playing professionally again until I got an offer from Fourth Division Stockport County, who were willing to pay me for each game, knowing that they would more than get their money back in gate receipts. United at first refused me permission and protested to FIFA, football's world governing body, that they still held my registration. FIFA instantly announced that I was suspended from playing, although sense prevailed a few days later when United agreed to release me.

I signed for a month with Stockport to play home games only. I wasn't interested in playing for them full time but the money was fantastic and I had spent a lot of money on

Oscar's. I made my debut in a friendly against Stoke on 10 November 1975. Stockport's average gate at the time was around 3,000 but curiosity brought out over 8,000 to see if I could still do the business. I think I proved that by scoring the goal in a creditable 1–1 draw. Stoke were a good First Division side then, while Stockport were struggling and at the end of the season had to apply for re-election to the League.

I made my League debut for them against Swansea, scoring the winner in a 3–2 success. The gate was a staggering 9,000 for that match and although the crowds dipped a bit for my final two games, they were still twice the club's average.

The funny thing was that I prepared for those matches by training with Colin at the YMCA. Colin was a big lad, not fat, just heavy but he was one of those people who could run all day. There was a car park next to the YMCA which had a steep slope that must have been 100 yards long. It reminded me a bit of the slope outside my granny's summer home in Crossgar. When we had races down that, I would leave Colin way behind but over long distances, you couldn't keep up with him.

Those games for Stockport didn't mean anything to me, they were just a way of keeping myself in pocket money. But my performances alerted other clubs, particularly as I was now a free agent, when a few years earlier, any interested club would have had to pay a £300,000 transfer fee for me. It made me think about a possible comeback, so when I was asked to play in Peter Osgood's testimonial match for Chelsea, I decided I'd like to make a good impression and that those 100 yard dashes in the YMCA car park would not be enough to gain top fitness.

So I checked into a health farm for a few weeks and was rewarded with two goals in the game, even though testimonial games are obviously not as ferocious or as competitive as League or Cup matches.

Chelsea manager Eddie McCreadie was obviously impressed because he offered to sign me on a pay-as-you-play basis. That seemed fair enough, given my record of absconding and I was attracted by Chelsea. They were one of the glamour sides and I'd fond memories of some of my performances there. I was also spending a lot of time in London, so it was attractive from the social point of view, too. I figured that if Stockport could afford £300 a game, then Chelsea could certainly afford £1,000 – especially as, by saving the transfer fee, they would be getting 300 games free! But they thought it was too much money and negotiations fell through, in spite of the fact that Chelsea were the only other English side I would have signed for on a permanent basis.

Instead, when the North American Soccer League came calling again in 1976, I decided to make a clean break of it. After I turned down the New York Cosmos, they signed Pele, who was a reasonable substitute! But it still turned out to be a result for me because the Los Angeles Aztecs now wanted a big name to rival Pele and thought I'd be perfect. I went over to meet their general manager John Chaffetz and when I expressed an interest, he asked me if I knew any other British players who would be useful signings.

Not wanting to go on my own, I said I had the perfect person – Bobby McAlinden.

'Bobby Macca who?' he said. Not surprisingly, Chaffetz had never heard of him.

'You know,' I said, 'good little midfield player. Played for Manchester City?'

Chaffetz knew City, of course – well, just about – and that satisfied him. I simply neglected to say that Bobby only played once for the City first team, before being transferred to Port Vale and then Stockport. Strangely, when I had played against Bobby regularly in the Manchester derbies at A&B team level, I'd thought he was a cocky little so-and-so and I never imagined that I would one day be asking him to go to the States with me.

Our paths would probably never have crossed again but for our mutual love of gambling. After leaving Stockport, he played a few games for Glentoran, which was a bit of a coincidence seeing that they were the team I supported as a kid. And when he came back to Manchester, I started bumping into him at the casinos. He was basically acting as a driver for a big-time gambler and as such Bobby came into Slacks a lot.

As I got to know him, I really enjoyed his company and soon we became close pals. He even joined the YMCA gang, which I'm sure would have impressed Mr Chaffetz if we had put it on his CV. Bobby was pleased for me when I got the offer from LA but probably a bit envious as well.

'Why don't you come with me?' I said to him one day. 'Do you fancy it?'

'Are you kidding? I'd swim there,' he replied.

So everything was arranged with the Aztecs and to fill in the time until we were due in LA in February 1976, I played three games for Cork Celtic in the League of Ireland. Again, the games didn't mean anything to me but they helped me keep fit and Cork were more than happy with the publicity and the gate receipts.

For Bobby, the American adventure was his big break-through in the game and he was so grateful, he played fantastically from the start. Whatever his limitations as a player, no one could ever accuse Bobby of lacking heart or enthusiasm and my recommendation turned out to be an inspired one. I doubt that any of the supporters had heard of him before but because he gave 100 per cent every game, he quickly became one of their favourite players.

For me, America offered a fresh start. It took me out of the goldfish bowl at home and the drinking, gambling routine which I knew I had to stop. It also allowed me to play football without the massive pressure that had been on me when I played for United. Naturally, the standard wasn't as high and the fans hadn't got a clue what they were watching, but at first it was great because some of the best players in the world were performing there – Pele, Franz Beckenbauer, Johan Cruyff, Gordon Banks, Carlos Alberto. And Bobby McAlinden.

As with all my other comebacks, I was training like a lunatic at the beginning, working hard and playing racket ball every day as well, sometimes for three or four hours. I drastically cut down on my drinking too and for a time, at least, I kept the demons at bay.

Bobby was never much of a drinker, which probably helped, and we loved the lifestyle, sharing a house in Hermosa Beach, just south of LA central's districts and all that madness. I loved the feeling of being fit again and with the team playing well, I had no reason or desire to perform one of my disappearing acts or to start on a binge that would go on for three days. As coincidence would have it, Charlie Cooke, whom I might have paired up with at Chelsea, had also signed for the Aztecs and we formed a pretty good partnership up front, alongside Ron Davies, the former Welsh centre forward.

We went into the last game of the season needing not just to win but to score at least three goals to make the divisional playoffs. The Americans, as with all their sports, were determined to maintain the interest of every club's supporters until the final day of the season, so they had devised a complicated system in which extra points were awarded for goals. It wasn't quite a Benfica or Real Madrid occasion but I was up for a challenge like that and I scored twice in a 4–1 win over Dallas

Tornado. We then had to meet them again in the playoffs and lost 1–0 but the club were happy with the season and I was delighted with my 15 goals from 23 games.

It wasn't Manchester United, but I was playing well, and enjoying my football again.

We soon got into a nice social life there, thanks to Waggy, who knew a millionaire named Ed Peters. He had an apartment in Beverly Hills, which was next door to a house where the Manson gang performed one of their murder sprees. I say millionaire but Ed must have had a lot more than that by the look of his apartment, which was a real luxury bachelor pad. It had an open deck leading to the swimming pool, a den with pool table and fabulous furniture and fittings. And the parties he threw made dear old Selwyn Demmy's in Manchester seem very tame.

I never found out what Ed did, but he was a fantastically connected man. At the weekends, it was open house at his pad, and people like Hugh O'Brian and James Caan would drop in, which meant there was never a shortage of beautiful women, either. And if we fancied going out, Ed would get us into the most exclusive clubs and restaurants in LA, places no ordinary person would have been able to get into. He also had a guest house on his land, which Liz Taylor used when she was seeing one of her boyfriends. It was their hideaway from the press.

The craic at Ed's place was unbelievable. Talk about Bacchanalian. The scene was like the last days of the Roman Empire. There would be some of the most gorgeous creatures you'd ever seen sitting naked round the pool and talking to these famous actors as if the situation were perfectly natural. The champagne would be on tap and, apart from Bobby and me, everybody would be smoking joints.

'Glad you came now?' I said to Bobby on our first night at Ed's.

We soon became regulars there and one Friday night this beautiful blonde walked in whom I'd not seen before. She was with a friend and the expression on their faces after they looked around at the debauched scene suggested that this was not what they had expected. After about five minutes, they were turning to go.

'Why don't you come back on Sunday?' I said to the blonde. 'It's quieter then, there will only be a few of us.'

'I'll think about it,' she replied, but she did come back on the Sunday and I discovered that her name was Angela Macdonald Janes.

I was instantly attracted to her, not just because of her looks but because she was so different from the other girls I met in LA. She was English for a start, and an intelligent, independent girl, not an LA airhead just out for a good time. Her independent streak was not surprising, seeing that she had left home at 18 to work in New York as a model and was at this point employed as personal assistant to Cher. We went out on a few dates, mostly dinners, and as so often with me, it quickly developed into a serious relationship and she began splitting her time between Cher's house and the bachelor pad Bobby and I shared on Hermosa Beach. It must have been love if she was prepared to do that.

Things could hardly have been better, on or off the field. After such a long break from the game, I enjoyed that first season in America more than I could have imagined and my appetite for playing was the best it had been for a long while. So I was more than interested when Fulham offered me a contract for the 1976–77 season. Bobby Moore had inspired them to a place in the FA Cup Final the previous season, where they lost to West Ham, and manager Alec Stock, whose teams always played with style, wanted to sign me and Rodney Marsh, who was also in America with Tampa Bay Rowdies.

Rodney and I were keen to play in England in the winter months, too, and Rodney's transfer went through OK. I once again found myself in limbo. There was an overlap between the American and English seasons and the Aztecs wrote in a clause entitling them to financial compensation for every game I missed. That was still no excuse for what I felt was the pompous attitude of the Football League secretary Alan Hardaker. I had already missed signing in time for the opening game of the season when Hardaker said, 'As far as we are concerned, George Best doesn't exist in this country. When his application is received, it might go to the full Management Committee, which doesn't meet until 19 September.'

Doesn't exist indeed! Well, I soon showed them that I did, after Fulham chairman Tommy Trinder and secretary Graham Hortop persuaded the FA to accept my registration and Rodney and I made our debuts together against Bristol Rovers at Craven Cottage. I knocked in the only goal of the game after 71 seconds, although Fulham officials were probably more excited when they counted the gate receipts from an attendance of over 21,000, twice the average.

We continued to play before big crowds, with Marshy and me playing up to the fans and Bobby as immaculate as ever at the back. It was a great story for the press and, despite my previous encounters with the record industry, a company came down to talk to Rodney and me about making a record.

'I can't sing,' I protested once again, 'and as far as I know, neither can Rodney.'

'It doesn't matter,' the record company executive said. 'These days, we can make anyone sound great.'

I asked him whether he had a song in mind.

'Yes, "I'm A Pink Toothbrush, You're A Blue Toothbrush",' which was the old Max Bygraves hit.

'I've got an IQ of 158,' I said, 'and you want me to sing "I'm a Pink Toothbrush"?'

He took that as a no.

It was a very short honeymoon, on and off the field at

Craven Cottage. Fulham had made all sorts of extravagant promises to me, which included a 'luxury flat' that I felt far from lived up to the description, a car, which I never got, and a signing-on fee which, by the time it arrived, could have been a signing-off fee. Angie was decidedly unimpressed by her new living accommodation when she followed me over in late September 1976 and it put an immediate strain on our relationship, which had been great in the States.

Perhaps because of all the frustration, I got into an argument with a referee over a free kick awarded to Southampton in a match in October and was sent off for using foul and abusive language. That provided a bit of footballing history as it was the day that red and yellow cards were brought in. But I was not the first to see red – Blackburn's David Wagstaffe having that honour, or dishonour, against Leyton Orient.

The results started to go against us and when that happens, the fun tends to go out of the window, as well, particularly for me. But I had at least proved that I could play at a reasonably high level again and in October, Northern Ireland manager Danny Blanchflower invited me to play in a World Cup qualifying match against Holland in Rotterdam. I hadn't played for my country for three years but this was just my sort of occasion.

Cruyff was still the outstanding Dutch star but most of the papers reckoned that I outshone him in a 2–2 draw which thrilled Danny. On the strength of that, I was picked for the game against Belgium in Liege in November but I couldn't turn it on again. The Belgians put three defenders on me most of the time and I never got the space to do any damage. On 12 October 1977, I won my 37th cap against Holland, in a game we lost 1–0.

Back at Fulham, things were going from bad to worse. When we played Hull at home in November, the gate was under 10,000 and while attendances picked up a little, things were never the same. And once again, a visit to Chelsea, Fulham's biggest rivals, of course, turned out to be eventful for me. As we went off at the end, I had a few words with referee John Homewood and made a gesture which summed up my opinion of his qualities as an official.

He mentioned this in his report and the FA charged me with bringing the game into disrepute, which led to my getting a £75 fine. On top of all this, Angie and I had had so many spectacular fall outs that she moved out of our flat, although given the state of it I could hardly blame her. The place was so grotty that it was often a source of our problems.

She would complain about the state of it and say, 'George, you've got to tell the club that we need something better.' But I would just shrug it off. I didn't think we'd be there that long and I didn't want the aggravation. Instead, to escape Angie's nagging, I would go off on a bender and one day, after I returned from a binge session, I discovered that she had packed her bags and left. She phoned later to say that she had had enough.

I asked her what she planned to live on and she said, 'I'll manage. I'm quite capable of making a living of my own.' She was, of course, but I wasn't best pleased when I found out that she had got a job at the Playboy Club, which paid well enough for her to rent her own place.

Things had been pretty turbulent behind the scenes at Craven Cottage, which in December had resulted in Tommy Trinder moving sideways to Life President, with Guy Libby, a Surrey stockbroker, taking over as chairman. The worst news from my point of view, however, was that Alec Stock resigned as team manager and Bobby Campbell took over. Alec was one of the reasons I had joined the club. He was a lovely, bubbly character who had a romantic attitude about football and how it should be played. He was also the inspiration for the Ron Manager character in *The Fast Show* (Paul Whitehouse told me so!).

Bobby had a mass of dark curly hair and was a well set bloke with one of those bone crushing handshakes and a reputation as a bit of a disciplinarian, a sergeant major type. But despite my fears, I got on smashing with him, although it wasn't long before we were crossing swords. With the team doing so badly and Angie walking out, the good feelings of the summer had long gone and I was again seeking the answer to my problems from the bottom of a glass.

When we drew Third Division Swindon in the third round of the FA Cup, Bobby decided that, although we were at home, the team would stay at the Kingsway Hotel. It seemed daft to me to be cooped up in a hotel when I had a flat, albeit not the height of luxury, just round the corner from the ground. So I walked out and went to the Duke of Wellington in Chelsea for a drink.

I was sitting down talking to a couple of girls near closing time when Bobby walked in. He would have known that the pub was one of my favourite haunts because I used to drink there with Mooro and Marshy.

'Are you going to introduce me, then?' he said, looking at the two girls.

'Well, I would but I don't know their names,' I replied.

'Well get the drinks in then.'

Now Bobby didn't drink, so I got him a Coke or something and when he'd drunk it, he said, 'Let's go.'

I presumed he meant back to the hotel but instead we turned up at some Greek restaurant, where his family were having a party. He kept me out until four o'clock in the morning!

'You'd better play well today,' he said when we finally got back to the hotel.

I did OK, as I remember, but we only drew 3–3 and were thrashed in the replay.

It seemed bizarre that Bobby should keep me out so late before a game. But I suppose his reasoning was that he would keep me out until I was too tired to go partying. And as Bobby was with me, he at least knew that I wasn't drinking.

The following month, after another heavy night's drinking, I was lucky to be alive after my worst car crash.

The promised car from Fulham had never arrived so I had borrowed an Alfa Romeo from the chairman's daughter, which, after a night of drinking, I wrapped around a lamp post outside Harrods at about four in the morning. You get a better class of ambulance around there. The last thing I remember is clipping a kerb, trying to keep the car upright and then flying through the windscreen. Naturally, I wasn't wearing a seat belt and having cut my face to ribbons, I fractured a shoulder blade as my body was catapulted back in the car.

Luckily, there was a guy out walking his dog, who saw it happen and immediately called an ambulance. Even luckier, the medics turned up before the police, who followed on to the hospital but were told by the doctor that I wasn't well enough to receive visitors. And certainly not well enough to be breathalysed.

When I saw my face the following day, it looked like a road map. They'd put in 57 stitches around my eyes and with my shoulder blade also broken, the doctors said it would be three months before I could play again. The side of my face was completely numb for about a year but I was determined to prove them wrong and after putting myself through the mill on the training field. I played five weeks later at Hull, feeling I had already been there and back.

In the midst of all this, I got some bad news from home.

Mum had had a heart attack.

As soon as I was well enough to travel, I flew to Belfast to see her.

If she was shocked at the sight of me, it was a mutual feeling. My mum had always been such a beautiful woman but this time, she looked pale and thin and drawn.

'You want to rest more, Mum,' I said.

'Don't worry about me,' she said. 'I'll be fine.'

I'd seen her looking a little haggard or tired before – who hasn't seen their mum looking like that? But this was something different. There was a sadness and tiredness in her face as well and the change was dramatic. When you haven't seen someone on a daily basis for some time, you notice it more and I was upset by her appearance, though naturally I told her she looked great.

When I got her on her own, I did try to have a quiet word with her about the drink but I didn't really believe it would make any difference. Me talking to her was like Sir Matt talking to me in his office. He knew I was going to sit there nodding, saying, 'Yes, Boss, no Boss' and that as soon as I went out and closed the door, I would do the exact opposite of what I'd agreed. So whether I talked to Mum for two minutes or two hours, it wasn't going to make any difference. I knew that, like me, she wouldn't have listened to anyone's advice.

Believing I would be spending a long time in the States, I

also said to her, 'Why don't you and Dad come and live in Los Angeles in the sunshine?'

But she thought the place was full of wierdos. I wanted to get them away from the Troubles and my dad would have been OK in LA because he could adjust to anywhere. But he's stubborn, like me, and he wouldn't have wanted it to look as if he were being forced out of his own home.

At least there was some good news. Although Angie had vowed not to come back, she felt sorry for me after my accident and phoned to see how I was. We had a good chat and she was impressed that I was throwing myself into training again. We met up for a meal and as things were going well, I said, 'How about giving it another go?'

'You'll only go back to your old ways,' she said.

'No, I won't,' I said. 'Come home and you'll see, it will be different.'

She agreed to move back in but not to the poky little flat that Fulham had provided for us. So we bought a flat of our own nearby, which removed some of the tension from our living arrangements. Things went so well for a while that when I told her I was going back to rejoin the Aztecs in the summer, she said she would come with me. I think she was happier in the States, in any case, though there was another row brewing over my registration because I was supposed to have returned in April for the start of the American season.

But I left that to the authorities to sort out while I got on with playing.

The demons had well and truly returned now, despite making it up with Angie and for the first time in my life, I woke up in the mornings needing a drink to get me going. I had drunk in the mornings in Spain during my first 'retirement' in 1972 but now I was really craving it. I don't know why I was putting away so much. You could say it was because of Mum's heart attack and the fact that I've never been able to handle pressure too well. But to be honest, I've never really needed a reason to drink.

And the real problem was, I enjoyed it. It didn't seem like a big deal.

Before long, I had got a little daily routine worked out, which mainly revolved around drink and, at the time, it sounded perfect. I would get up mid morning, with the sun shining, which was guaranteed at that time of year, and would wander off for a cooked breakfast and my daily Jim Murray fix. Jim Murray was a brilliant sports columnist on the *Los Angeles Times*, who wrote in an absolutely unique style and I couldn't wait to read his piece every morning. I would drop my 25 cents into the vending machine outside the restaurant, pull out the paper, take out the sports section and throw the rest in the bin. Then I'd sit and have hash browns and eggs and endless cups of coffee and read Jim.

By 10.30 a.m., I was gasping for a beer, but most places

didn't open till twelve in LA. I knew a place called Fat Face Fenners, however, which catered for those with a mid-morning thirst, so I'd roll up there for a few liveners. Then I'd go to the beach for a burger and chips – not French fries but American chips – with tortillas and salsa on the side. After that, I'd head down to the Mermaid, a bar on the beach, where I could sit and watch the girls go skateboarding by in their bikinis, and have a kip and get a tan for a couple of hours.

After the business experience I'd gained at Slacks and Oscars, I also felt I was up to running a place there and one day I decided to put the idea to Bobby McAlinden.

'How do you fancy going halves on a bar?'

'I can't afford that,' he replied,

'Come on, you're earning good money here and there's a bar down the road which is going for a song.'

It was a place called Hard Times and after Bobby had slept on it for a couple of days and decided he was in, we bought it and, with great imagination, renamed it Bestie's. And what is the point of owning a bar if you can't be your own best customer, which is what I was? We'd go off there towards the end of the afternoon for a game of pool and some more drinks and it seemed like paradise.

I actually proposed to Angie that summer of 1977, not that I was living like a man preparing to settle down. The girls were coming out of the woodwork and who were Bobby and I to say no? We'd got used to the life of Riley with Ed Peters and, thanks to him, could get to all the best places. So sometimes we'd treat ourselves by hiring a limo and going to Dan Tana's, an exclusive Italian restaurant.

Dan was the chairman of Brentford football club at the time and his restaurant was so hot that there would be big name actors trying to bribe their way in with hundred dollar bills and Bobby and I would just swan past them all. And we'd be treated like royalty, the maître d' enquiring, 'Your normal table, Mr Best?'

We would always order the same things as well – caesar salad followed by spaghetti bolognese, washed down with a couple of glasses of wine. Well, I'd have a couple of bottles of wine and Bobby would have a couple of glasses, which was enough to make him drunk.

The Aztecs had also moved their training headquarters to the Hollywood race track for that season. Now, I liked a bet but Bobby was an absolute racing nut so he basically never went home from training. As soon as we'd finished and showered, he would head up to the racetrack's private boxes entrance. Bobby quickly made friends with the steward there, who would tip him off about which people weren't using their box on any particular day. So there was Bobby, up in this luxurious box, surveying the scene with his binoculars as if he were Lord Astor. And this was a man who had been playing for Glentoran only a few years earlier.

I was having such fun that I didn't really fancy going back

to Fulham and a long winter of English football. I missed the opening games, anyway, while we went through the tiresome ritual of FIFA approving my registration again. And after ten games, I decided I'd had enough and went back to LA. It was the off season there, of course, but there was no off season as far as drinking and women were concerned.

I don't really know how Angela put up with it because I was going missing for days on end. When I did go home, we'd have furious rows, not surprisingly, and one time, when I returned from the missing list, walking in casually as if I'd just been out for the groceries, she was apoplectic. I walked into the kitchen where she was cutting some bread.

'So you remember where you live then?' she said sarcastically. 'What's the matter, run out of money?'

'I'm sorry,' I said, making my usual apologies. 'It won't happen again. But I'm starving. How about making me something to eat?'

I looked a right state and she must have felt sorry for me because she went to the fridge as if to get some food out. She still had the knife in her hand and after opening the fridge door, she swivelled round to face me and pointed it at me.

'George, this has got to stop.' She was waving this knife at me and instinctively I turned my back and the next thing I felt was this stinging sensation in my backside.

'What on earth have you done?' I shouted.

She was immediately apologetic and took me to hospital

for treatment. I don't think she meant to stab me in the arse but she was at the end of her tether and when I'd turned my back on her, she just flipped.

By this time the relationship, as you might have guessed, was falling apart and I was sleeping around all over the place. But when I saw a picture of Angie with Dean Martin's son Ricci, whom she had allegedly been dating, it was that old thing of me wanting what I seemingly couldn't have. In a moment of complete madness in January 1978, I proposed to her and in an even bigger moment of madness, she said yes. I thought marriage would give me the focus I needed.

We decided to fly to Vegas to tie the knot but were both having second thoughts and only just made the flight. We were both suffering from the night before and only Bobby, who came along as my best man, was in any fit state. If we'd been just a little bit more sober, we might have called the whole thing off. Looking back, it was a complete shambles. Angie had sold the exclusive picture rights to the *Sun*, which was romantic, so the rest of the press were chasing us around town, and we had forgotten to get the licence, which meant a detour downtown to get one.

And the wedding pictures were a joke. Angela had just had her hair done and looked like Harpo Marx, while I was wearing some multi-coloured jacket that Coco the Clown would have turned down. The ceremony, such as it was, took place at the Candlelight Chapel. The formalities only took a few minutes and then the preacher asked me to put on the ring.

'We haven't got one' I said, and we all stood there looking sheepish for a few seconds until Bobby pulled a ring off his finger.

'Here, you can borrow this for now,' he said.

That allowed us to complete the ceremony and afterwards we went to Caesars Palace, where I headed straight for the tables and lost every dollar I had on me. We flew back to LA the same night and I went out for a drink on my own which, at the time, just seemed the normal thing to do. It was not as if marriage had been the culmination of a long and steady courtship. We were already living together, already experiencing the problems of an old married couple and the actual wedding didn't change anything. I was still an alcoholic in full swing and when we got back from Vegas, I carried on where I had left off. I think my wedding night drink lasted two days.

I phoned my parents to tell them I'd got married, but I think they had already read about it in the newspapers or heard it on the news. By that time, they were used to me doing things on the spur of the moment and they didn't comment on the suddenness of the wedding. They never criticised anything I did in my private life and it was more a case of 'Well, as long as you're happy.' And I said that I was.

At the Aztecs, events were shaping up – going pear-shaped that is – just like they had at United and Fulham. John Chaffetz had sold out to a local businessman, who asked me which players the club should bring in and then ignored every one of those I suggested. His feeling was that the way to bring the fans to the games was to tap into the Latin character of the city by signing Mexican players. That would have been OK if they had signed some good ones but the players the club brought in were hopeless.

I followed the now-familiar pattern of drinking to forget the football and managing it so well that I even forgot to turn up for training. Then the club would suspend me, I would promise that it wouldn't happen again and a few days later, we would start the cycle all over again.

In the end, I told them that I didn't want to play for them any more and they packed me off to Fort Lauderdale Strikers in June 1978. I flew in to Florida just a few hours before their biggest match of the season against the New York Cosmos.

'Are you ready to play, George?' said the Strikers' English coach, Ron Newman.

'Against the Cosmos?' I replied. 'You bet.'

The Strikers had never beaten the Cosmos but this was just the stage for me, a full house against the most glamorous team in the League. And this was another new beginning. Just as at Fulham, I scored with my first touch of the ball and, running on adrenalin, I got another one later on in a 5–3 win.

It was a brilliant start, which was a turning point for the Strikers' season. We were on a roll after that and, against all odds, qualified for the play-offs and won through to the Conference championship.

We played Tampa Bay Rowdies, Rodney Marsh's team, in a two-legged Final and with the tie all square, we played a third game which was also heading for a draw and a shoot-out as we went into the last period of extra time. We had our five players nominated for the shoot-out, which included me, Ray Hudson, who used to play at Newcastle, and David Irving, who was an ex-Everton striker.

A few minutes before the end of extra time, Newman pulled all three of us off so that we could discuss how we would take the kicks, which were not from the penalty spot but from the 35 yard line, with players allowed 15 seconds to run the ball forward and shoot or to dribble round the goalkeeper. While the game continued on the pitch we sat with Newman in the dugout while he outlined what he thought we should do. I had to interrupt him.

'Why are you telling us? We can't take any.'

'Of course you can,' he said. 'You're my first three takers.'

So I reminded him that a player had to be on the pitch at the end of the match to be involved in the shoot-outs.

'Are you sure?' he said.

'Of course I am. Haven't you read the rules?'

So he had to find three more players to take kicks and,

hardly surprisingly, we lost. I was fuming that the coach apparently hadn't understand fully the American rules of soccer!

With the season over, Detroit Express asked me if I wanted to join them as a guest player on a European tour in September, which seemed like a good idea at the time. The rules appeared to be a lot more lax in the States than they are in Europe, which led to many of the problems with my registration. Fulham went ballistic when they learned I had played for Detroit and complained to the FA. They, in turn, went to the world governing body and on 11 October, FIFA suspended me from playing in any country under their jurisdiction, which covered just about everywhere.

By the following day, I couldn't have cared less if they'd banned me for life. Lying in bed with Angela, having just returned to Los Angeles from Europe, I was woken by the worst phone call of my life and the hardest my dad had ever had to make.

My mum was dead.

CHAPTER TWELVE
PICKING UP THE PIECES

I was aware that Mum's drinking problem had become serious because I'd received several calls from Carol in the months before her death, asking if I could go home to visit, but she has since told me that she knew there wasn't much I could do. There isn't anything anyone can do for an alcoholic. Carol, I think, just wanted someone to give her some support because unless you've experienced it, you can't have any idea what it's like to live with someone with a drink problem.

Over the years I'd got out of the habit of going home because I'd been too busy leading my own life. And when Carol started asking me to go back, I was having enough trouble keeping my own life together. Remember, I'd always run away from trouble and I wasn't inclined to run towards it.

It was tough on her, my dad, and the rest of the children. And it was hard for me to understand because my memories were of my loving, non-drinking mum from my childhood. It's good that Carol can remember her like that, too, so that there was someone else who could tell people what a great mum she had been and prove that I had not imagined all that.

'Mum has really got a problem,' Carol would phone and say, 'but she'd love to see you. It would be great if you could find the time to come over.'

Two years earlier I had managed that trip to see Mum following her heart attack. Now, here I was, flying to Belfast for her funeral with Angela, who hadn't even met Mum or Dad or any of my family. So it was difficult for her as well, although on the journey from Los Angeles, I was more in a daze than anything else. It was only when we got to the house and I saw the state of my dad and sisters that I really broke down. It was the first time I had been at any family funeral or wedding since my grandad's death when I was 11, when I'd sat under a lamp post and cried. There were lots of relatives whom I hadn't seen for years, making me feel almost as much a stranger as Angela.

I certainly did not want to see my mother lying in her coffin, having seen her looking so poorly on my previous visit. I wanted to remember her like my mum, my beautiful, loving mum, not like what she had become. It was hard enough going to the funeral, which, as was still the custom in those days, only the men attended.

Angela, with her Hollywood ways and get-up-and-go attitude, must have seemed like someone from another planet to my sisters and my Irish aunties. But when we came back from the graveyard, she had them all doing these Jane Fonda type exercises in the front room. Bizarre as the scene was, it helped to take their minds off it all for an hour or so. I learned that Angela had continually asked my Aunt Lily to try out the exercises and Aunt Lily, beside herself with embarrassment, had finally said, 'Can you not pick on someone else?'

The girls were in tears of laughter by the time Angela had finished and, as my grandmother said, 'Who would have thought we'd ever laugh again and on this day of all days?'

My dad, as I'd expected, tried to be strong for everyone else but you knew he was breaking up inside. He found alcoholism harder to understand than anyone because he is one of those rare people who, if he goes out to have two drinks, will have two and come home. Even if he goes out with a friend who starts off with the same intentions, and the friend gets the taste for more, my dad will stick to his two. If my dad says it's two, it's two, and if he starts his second bacardi and lemonade at 10 o'clock and he's ordered a car to collect him at 11, he will make his drink last.

I've never seen my dad drunk and he seemed fine the night after the funeral when he came back after a couple of drinks with one of his pals. I was sitting in the lounge waiting for him and had kept the fire going, but I could see he wasn't in the mood to talk. He just curled up in front of the fire like a wounded animal and I knew there was nothing I could say to him. We just sat there in silence for what seemed like hours, until eventually, he let out this long sigh and slowly got up.

As he went off to bed, he stumbled against a couple of chairs and I realised that for probably the one and only time in his life, my dad was drunk. And then I broke down in tears, as much for him as for me.

Dad and I did get to talk, of course. Like me, he felt guilty and responsible for Mum's death, believing he should have done more to stop her drinking and that maybe he was wrong to have taken her out to have a drink in the first place. She was the best customer of the off-licence on the corner.

'You don't know how many times I thought of going around there and putting a match to the place,' he told me.

'Dad, it wouldn't have made any difference,' I said – and I should know. 'She would just have got the booze somewhere else.'

Mum had actually given up for a year after her heart attack.

'We really thought it was all behind us and we had our old mum back,' Carol told me. 'She even used to recount all the awful things she'd done when she was drunk and all the terrible things she'd said to us and laugh about it. But whether she was kidding herself or not, she started drinking again.'

My dad also took her to a hospital for alcoholics but she didn't get past the initial interview. She wouldn't admit that she had a drinking problem so the doctor turned her away.

'I'm sorry, Mrs Best,' he said, 'there is nothing I can do for you.'

At the end, it seemed that my mother just gave up.

Carol said that on the Tuesday before her death, she'd said to Mum, 'You've got to look after yourself.'

'No, I've had enough,' Mum had replied.

She died on the Thursday, aged 54, and was buried on Saturday morning.

We all seemed to share some guilt after Mum's death. My sister Barbara had come home from South Africa with her husband a few months earlier and Mum so enjoyed her company, that she begged her to stay in Belfast. But Barbara and her husband Jim had to go back and she couldn't get over for the funeral. I felt guilty because of all the bad publicity that I had been getting, which I knew upset Mum more than anyone else in the family.

And I felt even more guilty that I hadn't been there for her, which was something I couldn't really change but which made me feel guilty all the same. I felt that her death was all my fault, that if I hadn't gone to England, hadn't done the things I'd done and if I'd only gone home more often, it wouldn't have happened. It's a terrible thing, guilt, and it would be a long while before I could see things as they really were and accept that there was nothing I could have done.

People always want easy answers. But there are no easy answers as to why someone becomes an alcoholic. Do people really think that I like being one, or that I woke up one morning, saying, 'I've had a dreadful week. I think I'll become an alcoholic'?

It is accepted as a disease now, and it's great that it's seen like that because there is such a stigma involved. People think that if you're an alcoholic, you're a drunken bum. But there are no class barriers, that's for sure. Yes, you can be a down and out, living rough on the street and drinking meths but equally, you could be a wealthy company director presiding over a successful business. Or a Belfast mother. Or a world-class footballer.

My mum had a hard life bringing up six children. And she had the added pressure of my fame, which would have been difficult for anyone to cope with, and the worry about what would happen to me, particularly after I quit football. But if she hadn't had that alcoholic gene, or whatever it is that makes us susceptible to it, she would have coped like everyone else coped. If you have got that gene, it can happen at any time and the doctors say that the biggest problem for alcoholics is that, in the early stages, when they have a chance to stop drinking, they have no desire to. Then when they want to, it's already too late.

My dad, true to form, went straight back to work on the Monday after the funeral and insisted that Ian and the twins went to school. He wanted life to go on as normal as possible, though he was to get many cruel reminders of Mum's drinking over the next few months. Every time he got up the courage to clear out some of her things, he would find more of the hiding places where she'd stashed her wine – in her wardrobe, her shoe cupboard – all the places he wouldn't have looked into when she was alive.

I felt guilt over my mum's death but like any alcoholic, (which I was, though unaware of it) I didn't relate it to my own drinking. That may sound incredible but I hadn't admitted to myself that I had any sort of drink problem at that stage. Of course, I knew that I drank too much but I didn't feel I was very different to many other people who drank heavily. And I was still young and relatively fit, so I couldn't equate my situation with Mum's, who'd had a difficult life. Despite the blackouts and cravings, I couldn't see what the drink was doing to me physically. Besides I always – arrogantly – thought I could stop at any time.

If I had related her situation to mine, I would have tried to sort out my drinking then, perhaps made a serious effort to cut it down. But I drank even more heavily after her death, partly because of that guilt, I suppose. I can't say, in any case, that I wouldn't have drunk just as much if she had lived. It was another of those situations in which people want easy answers but to which there aren't any. I knew my binges were anti-social and affected my relationships. But I didn't see them as *harming* me. I didn't see myself as an alcoholic. Not then.

I didn't have an easy fix for my football either. I went back to Los Angeles with Angela and left the lifting of the worldwide ban in the hands of my lawyers, which meant it took lots of time and money, the latter, fortunately, coming from Fort Lauderdale's pockets. When our case against Fulham finally got to court in March, the judge ruled against us, but a few days later FIFA lifted the ban and I was a footballer again, if not a very fit one. And before long, not a very happy one.

At Fort Lauderdale I didn't have much respect for the coach, Ron Newman, and I lost the plot completely after a game against the Cosmos in New York. No one ever beat the Cosmos there but we had signed Cubillas of Peru, who destroyed Scotland in the 1978 World Cup Finals and Germany's Gerd Muller, one of the best finishers in the world. With those two on top form, as well as Hudson and Irving, we took a 2–0 lead with twenty minutes to go and were absolutely cruising, knocking it around and enjoying ourselves. Then, with fifteen minutes to go, Newman took off Hudson and Irving and put on a couple of teenagers, one an American and the other a trialist from Australia. Inevitably, the team lost all its shape and the Cosmos beat us with three goals in the last fifteen minutes.

In the dressing room afterwards, Newman was going round saying 'well done' to all the players.

'What do you mean, well done?' I said. 'We've just lost 3–2 because you took two of our best players off and put on a couple of kids.'

'Well, it's no disgrace to lose here,' he said.

I tore off my shirt and threw it at him. 'I'm starting to get really pissed off,' I said, 'do you know that?'

I said the same in the local newspaper, which probably wasn't a great career move. But after Newman suspended me for failing to turn up for training, the paper ran a poll asking whether the Strikers should get rid of me or Newman. They voted for Newman to go but he still had the owners' backing so in July, I walked out.

I wasn't the only one to make a dramatic exit. Angela had stuck by me after Mum's death, while trying to steer me away from alcohol. But when she realised that it wasn't just a phase I was going through and that I wasn't going to stop drinking, she packed her things and left me a note, saying, 'You're wasting your life, George. You're not going to waste mine as well.'

She flew back to LA and that's where I headed, as well, but this time to live on my own. I hit the drink harder than ever before and there was no one to give me any hassle because no one knew who I was. That was one of the things I loved in the States, I could go into a bar with all these screaming Americans watching grid iron and they wouldn't have a clue who I was.

And if I got talking to anyone and they asked what I did for a living, I would make something up. I loved that anonymity because it also meant that there was no one to shop me to the newspapers.

I'd thought it was all over between Angela and me, but we still spoke now and again and even saw each other. For all our fights and break-ups, there was still a lot of chemistry between us. When we got together one day we were getting on especially well and ended up in bed, which made us think we could work things out.

'Look, George,' she said to me that day. 'If you get help and sort yourself out, we can give it another go.'

'OK,' I said, 'I'll do it. I'll go back to England and get a job and show you I can change.'

Well, two out of three isn't bad. I did go back to England and I did get a job – playing for Hibernian, which was a hell of a way to commute from Chelsea. But I didn't change. If anything, I got worse.

'You don't have to live up here in Scotland,' the Edinburgh chairman Tom Hart – a lovely man – told me. 'Fly up on Thursday, train with the lads on Friday and fly back after the game on Saturday.'

It sounded good enough to me, although that arrangement meant that I didn't really get to know the players, on or off the pitch. Not that it would have made much difference to the performances – if the club had been serious about improving results, they wouldn't have signed me under those conditions. Like all those other clubs after Manchester United, they were looking at me to make them some cash. They were delighted when over 20,000 turned up for my home debut against Partick Thistle in November 1979.

Although Tom Hart had spoken about training with the team on Fridays, with the money I was bringing in, he was happy if I just turned up for the game. Sadly, I couldn't even guarantee that all the time, sometimes turning round and flying back to London after getting to Edinburgh and sometimes not bothering to catch the flight up there at all.

To be honest, I couldn't take it seriously and the alcoholism had kicked in to the point where, if I were in a bar and enjoying myself, I wouldn't leave for anyone or anything.

In February the following year, we were due to play a Scottish FA Cup tie against Ayr United, fatally on a Sunday, which meant that I spent the previous night in my hotel bar. I had only intended to have a few – honest – when the French rugby team walked in. They had just played Scotland at Murrayfield and when the great Jean Pierre Rives spotted me, he beckoned me over.

Now everyone knows how rugby players can put it away and they wouldn't dream of letting me go to bed after a few drinks. Not that I had any inclination to once I got the taste. Jean Pierre is a fantastic guy and I lost all track of time as the session went through the night. I think I was still at the bar when Hibs officials came to pick me up. If they had come any later, that might have been a literal expression.

I was clearly the worse for wear but they were really polite about it, saying, 'Do you think you are OK to play today, George?'

'Perhaps it would be best if I gave this one a miss,' I said – or words to that effect.

Tom Hart sacked me after that but took me back a week later. He was just like Sir Matt, always giving me another chance, which again made me think it was fine to carry on the same way. I wasn't doing much training, either, and I put on more weight at Hibernian than I'd ever done before. I just couldn't be bothered – though if I thought Hibs were bad, they were world beaters compared to my next club.

I signed for San Jose Earthquakes in April 1980, and I was pleased to be going back to California and the sunshine. And, even more importantly, to Angela, who had agreed to move back in with me. I don't know why she agreed to give me another chance. I suppose somewhere in the back of her mind she believed that one day it would all change, I would change, and we'd live happily ever after. I really don't know what kept us together because, although there was a lot of love at first, it was never going to last.

Even if we'd had a hope of sorting out our life together, it was not going to be in San Jose, which turned out to be the worst place ever for me, in just about every aspect of my life. The NASL was also changing, trying to turn it into a more native American League. When I first went, clubs only had to play three Americans but gradually it increased to five and then eight, and most teams didn't have eight Americans good enough to play to the standard the crowds had become used to. So it became more like parks football and the whole thing began to disintegrate from what had been a half-decent league to a virtually amateur one.

And as well as my being out of condition, my right knee was giving me more pain than it had for years. The hard pitches in America didn't help and I would often have to have the knee drained three times on a match day. They would put a needle in before the match and drain all the fluid out and repeat the process at half time and again at the end. I was still managing to turn it on now and again and scored eight goals that season, which wasn't bad in a team that finished bottom of the League.

There was no rest after the season, however, because I'd also signed to play for San Jose in the North American Indoor Soccer League, six-a-side football at which my team mates were a lot more adept and we got through to the playoffs against San Diego. After so much football, I was coming off in agony sometimes, although in six-a-side you're on and off all the time. I had also damaged my toes but I wanted to play against San Diego and for the first and only time, I agreed to have a cortisone injection to allow me to get through it.

It was a bit like when I first had cartilage problems back in 1966 and agreed to play for United until they were out of Europe. It seemed like a pointless sacrifice, however, when we went 6–0 down. But then we started pressing and pulled back to 6–5 down, with me scoring four of the goals. Then, right near the end, one of our Yugoslav players knocked a ball across to me but instead of rolling it, he hit it at a hundred miles an hour.

By now, the cortisone was starting to wear off and I was thinking, 'If this ball hits my foot, I'll never finish the game.' So I quickly shifted my weight and shot with my left foot and it hit the post and came out. That pissed me off more than the pain.

I could have done with a long rest after that but I was due back in Edinburgh to play for Hibernian. I didn't feel that I had much time left to play football and I needed to make as much money as I could in the remaining years. It was easy money, too, since I was not expected to be the George Best of old, though I still got a lot of pleasure when I played well. A football pitch had always been the place where my other problems did not exist, so I was probably also afraid to give up that crutch.

I got back in time for Hibs' fifth league game, against Dundee away in September, which we won 2–1. But in the next month, I only played five more games, and funnily enough, given that I was there to bring in the crowds, only two were at home. My final match was against Falkirk, which we won 2–0 but which only brought in a crowd of under seven thousand.

Hibernian had been relegated to Division One after I'd left for America the previous season, not that my contribution had done much to help them when I was there. And without glamour fixtures against Celtic and Rangers, attendances had dropped off and it seemed that I was no longer a crowd puller. Tom Hart had been quite happy to put up with my frequent absences while I was sucking money through the turnstiles but now that wasn't happening, I was of no further use to him. I had planned to live in Scotland and make a real go of it with the team but before I'd even had time to look for a place, we both agreed to call it a day. In any case, my situation had changed dramatically and it seemed best for everybody if I returned to California. Angela was pregnant.

When Angela told me she was expecting a baby just before I left for Scotland, I was as happy as any other prospective dad and Angela, for her part, thought that it would finally help me to settle down. I know it sounds a horrible thing to say, but in many ways the pregnancy just complicated things and made the situation a little more difficult. I hated San Jose and although we had a nice house, which we filled with beautiful furniture, it was situated in the middle of nowhere. And while I tried to help around the house and get things ready for the new arrival, I soon got bored and would head off on another bender.

I was hitting the bottle harder than ever at this stage and while Angie had had first-hand knowledge of addiction through working with Cher, whose husband Gregg Allman had his problems with drugs and alcohol, I don't think she really understood the grip it can have on you. I think she felt you could just pull yourself together.

But it's not like that. By this time I was *craving* drink – I just couldn't get enough of it. And nothing was going to stop me drinking, not even when Angie started hiding the car keys and all our money. If I couldn't find either I would just go walking, and I mean walking, maybe seven or eight miles until I found a bar. Sometimes, it would take me a couple of hours to get to a bar and if I didn't have any money in my pockets, I would just sit there until one of the other regulars recognised me and bought me one. I turned into a beach bum, actually sleeping on the beach some nights.

The experts always say that alcoholics have to reach rock bottom before they are able to recognise their problems and seek help to take control of their lives. I had gone through some pretty low moments, taking money from Angela's handbag and stealing from the large bottle in the kitchen, where we used to put our loose change. It was a bit like the days as a kid when I stole from my mum's sixpences jar, though this was far more desperate.

My lowest point, however, came one day when I was sitting at home gasping for a drink and could find only a few dollars in the change jar. Angie must have got wise to that one and begun keeping her own quarters and nickels. That money wouldn't last me long in a bar and, as Angie had the car, I faced a long walk to get to one. Even so, I scooped up the change and set off on the road.

I decided to go to a bar I knew at the beach and where I had become a regular. It was one of those typical Californian beach bars, more like a wooden shack, with a deck outside and pretty basically furnished inside. There were a few pine-style tables and chairs for those who wanted food and a long bar where I liked to sit on a stool. That way, it was easier to get talking to people who might buy me a drink on days when I didn't have much money on me. A day like that one, in fact, though things didn't look promising. There were only a couple of other people in, a guy at the far end of the bar and a girl a couple of bar stools away from me. I didn't know either of them.

She was just a normal, plain-looking girl, a bit overweight, about 30 years old and looking as if she might have worked in a bar herself. I think she, the barman and I exchanged a few words about the weather, and how the local football team were doing. The normal bar-room stuff in the States. But it was only chit chat.

After an hour in there, I only had a few cents left, not enough to buy another beer. I sat there nursing what was left in my glass, wondering whether I could ask the barman for credit, tell him I'd left my wallet at home or something. He did know me and recognised me as a regular. I was just thinking about it when the girl slid off her stool and walked off to the toilet. Instinctively, I turned around as I heard her bar stool moving and noticed that she had left her handbag on it. I looked up and saw that the barman was talking to the guy at the other end of the bar and, in an instant, stuck my hand into her bag. I fished around and pulled out a bill, which I stuck straight into my pocket. My heart was thumping at what I'd done and I couldn't face seeing the girl when she came back. So I drained the last of my beer, shouted goodbye to the barman and walked out.

When I got outside, I pulled out the bill and discovered I had got away with all of ten dollars. That made me feel even worse, thinking that it was probably the last ten dollars the girl had on her to get through the day, while I was making thousands a week. But I wasn't going to give it back. I needed it for more drink and I walked to another bar a couple of blocks away to get it.

If I felt guilty about that when I was drunk, I felt even worse when I sobered up a couple of days later. So I went back to the bar and, sure enough, she was sitting there on the same stool.

I went up to her and handed her a ten dollar bill, saying, 'I think this is yours.'

'What are you talking about?' she said.

'The other day,' I said, 'when you were in here and you went off to the toilet, I took this from your purse.'

'What the hell ...' she began, but before she could finish, I interrupted her.

'Look,' I said, 'I know it was a terrible thing to do but my wife's pregnant and I didn't have money to get a cab home. I was too embarrassed to ask you so I just took it – I only meant to borrow it.'

Amazingly, she forgave me, but I refused her offer of a drink. I just wanted to get away. The worst thing, however, was that even after stooping so low, I was still embarrassed to admit to this girl that I had needed the money to buy drink. I had to come up with a pathetic excuse.

If Angela had been there to hear me, she wouldn't have known whether to laugh or cry.

After that I began to accept, at least in Angela's company, that I needed help to sort out my drinking. Angela had often suggested going into rehabilitation but it didn't appeal to me, so when someone suggested Antabuse tablets, which make you violently ill if you drink, I thought that was a much easier solution. Willpower wouldn't come into it – they would simply take the option of drinking away from me.

I began taking them and was feeling good when Milan Mandaric, the generous Yugoslav owner of the Earthquakes, took Angie and me on a weekend trip to Lake Tahoe. We were having a nice, relaxing time but on the second night, as Angie was getting dressed for dinner, I said, 'I'm just popping out for some air. I'll see you at the restaurant.'

I walked straight from the room into the casino bar of the hotel and ordered a large vodka. I felt so good that I didn't really believe it could do me any harm. But after a sip or two, I felt a little nauseous and before I got halfway through it, my heart was beating at a hundred miles an hour and I felt a burning sensation in my cheeks. I rushed off to the gents and saw that my skin was breaking out in big red blotches.

I went back to our room and as soon as Angela saw me, she said, 'Have you had a drink?'

'No,' I said, 'I think I must have had some sort of allergic reaction to the pills.'

I'd been out such a short time that she believed me and somehow, I managed to get through dinner, although I didn't eat much.

I couldn't believe that I couldn't stop drinking even when I knew that alcohol would make me ill. At the time I think I partly excused my actions to myself by making out that I was simply testing the pills out.

But whether I was ready to accept it or not, I was desperately in need of help.

One night I did something completely out of character and, in a way, hit rock bottom.

Now and again, I would go back to Los Angeles and check into a little motel down the beach. Bobby and I had sold the bar by this time but I used to go to a little place called Hennessy's, where a few of the locals knew me. Not that I chatted much to them. I just liked sitting there on my own, having a few beers and watching the world go by. And I had always loved the anonymity I could get in America.

But on this particular night, I got annoyed because the barman didn't know who I was. He'd served me a couple of times and said to me, 'You here on vacation?'

'No I used to live here,' I said, and he just said 'Oh, yeah?' or something, so I thought to myself, I'm going to tell him who I am.

'Do you remember Bestie's bar?' I said when he came over again.

'Yeah,' he said, 'I remember.'

It was the drink talking. I couldn't help myself. I had to say it.

'Well,' I said. 'I'm Bestie.'

The look on his face said it all.

I had come a long way from being the Fifth Beatle.

CHAPTER THIRTEEN
'MY NAME IS GEORGE...'

If anything could change me, I remember thinking, it would be fatherhood.

I've always loved kids and I would keep promising Angela, 'It will all be different when the baby comes along. I'll change, you'll see.' She'd heard it all before, of course, and I'm not sure I even believed it myself. But the pregnancy went OK, and after a couple of false alarms, when she thought she was going into labour, I was in a bar one day in February 1981 when Angie called.

'George, get here quickly,' she said. 'It's coming.'

'Are you sure?' I said. 'I'm just in the middle of a game of darts.'

'Of course I'm sure! Get here as soon as you can.'

I dashed home and drove her to the hospital and our son Calum was born at seven o'clock the following morning, 6 February. We named him Calum Milan Best, the middle name in honour of Milan Mandaric, who was fantastically supportive.

As I watched Calum being born and then cut the umbilical cord, I really hoped this would help to change our lives. And with him being a boy as well, I couldn't have been prouder. I suppose most dads want a son and for a few days after he and Angela came out of hospital, I stayed at home and helped out as best as I could.

Sadly, it didn't last long. Having Calum proved one thing – alcohol had become the most important thing in my life. More important than my wife and even more important than my new-born son. I felt guilty that I couldn't stop drinking even for him and probably drank even more because of my guilt, which is just about the worst vicious circle you could get.

For days on end I was having blackouts and when I came home and stopped drinking, I was getting the shakes and the hot and cold sweats. Angela was having enough trouble trying to cope with Calum, without having to worry about me too. So we went to see Milan and told him that we were having problems and it was agreed that I would seek help at the Vesper Hospital's rehabilitation unit. The club's insurance company were to cover 80 per cent of the treatment costs and I checked in on 2 March 1981.

I might as well have been in prison. They locked you up for the first two weeks and after that you were only allowed out for an hour a day and with two screws – sorry, hospital staff – with you. So a quick drink was definitely out of the question, but I was still craving one. I had agreed to go in because it seemed like the proper thing to do but for it to work, you really have to want to give up. I didn't, so my heart wasn't in the treatment and I probably wasn't a suitable case for it, either.

I spent hours and hours in group therapy, in which everyone has to own up to their worst faults and listen to all the other patients criticising you. I also had to write down six examples of how my drinking had got me into trouble with the police. Only six? Well, that was a let off. That form of therapy has proved helpful to a lot of people and I don't have anything against it. I am just not the sort of person who likes to talk about my inner feelings and found it near impossible to do so in front of a bunch of strangers.

I faked my way through it for just over two weeks and they let me out early. The treatment was supposed to last 30 days but I fooled them into believing I was 'cured', although one of the counsellors, an Irish-American whose background might have helped him to understand me better than the others, said to me one day, 'You might be fooling everyone else but you ain't fooling me, George.'

That was all he said and he was absolutely right.

The doctors laid it on the line for me before I left. They said that in the following 12 months, one of three things would happen – either I'd stay off alcohol, I'd be dead, or I'd be back in the hospital. That sounded OK to me. I thought, 'I'll stay off the booze for 12 months and then I can go back on it and everything will be fine. I'll be able to keep it under control.'

And that's what I did. Even Angela seemed fooled by her new, loving husband, who stayed home and changed nappies and did jobs around the house, like any normal husband and father. I even went shopping and spent two weeks painting a Disney mural on the wall of Calum's bedroom, though I wasn't quite so good with some of the other fatherly duties.

Angela always did Calum's first feed in the morning, which was some ungodly hour like four or five o'clock. But I kept offering to do it, saying, 'Just leave all the stuff out and I'll give him his first feed. You have a lie in.'

She wouldn't let me of course but she got so tired after a few weeks, that she said, 'OK. You get up and feed him.'

We used to put his little baby chair on top of the kitchen table, which was next to the oven. Angela gave me a verbal list of do's and don'ts.

'But the most important thing,' she instructed me, 'is to strap him in his chair and keep your arm across him while you're feeding him because he's lively and he'll bounce about.'

'Don't worry, don't worry,' I was saying, 'I'm not a complete idiot you know.' Just a halfwit, I suppose, because I forgot all about the arm bit and as I turned round to fill the spoon with more food, I heard this thump, followed by loud screams. He had fallen off the table and landed on his head, which brought Angie running from the bedroom, shouting, 'I knew I shouldn't have let you feed him.'

To be honest, after allowing me to take charge, I don't think she'd been able to sleep anyway. And that was the end of my feeding duties.

My dad and the rest of the family were delighted by the news of Calum's birth and perhaps even more thrilled to hear that I'd gone for treatment. Like me, they were still grieving for Mum, who had died after refusing to get professional help. Now that I'd actually been to the Vesper, they were hoping I'd settle down to proper family life and heed my warning.

Dad was also getting a lot of pleasure from Ian, who was turning out to be a good footballer. With four girls coming after me, it had been a long time since Dad had been able to kick a ball about with one of his children and like the baby of most families, Ian was a pretty easy-going kid. Dad kept me posted about his soccer and it was great to know that there was something to capture his interest again.

Of course, I'd seen Ian play myself and he had all the attributes of a professional footballer – speed, strength and, like me, an eye for goal. He was just 15 then and his team had reached a big local cup final, which all the family were excited about. But unfortunately, the London press got wind of it and decided this was a great story – the new Best, Georgie's little brother.

When Ian turned up and saw all the photographers, he told the coach he wasn't playing but he was talked into it and played a blinder, scoring two goals. But he really didn't like the attention, he couldn't hack the possibility of the press chasing him for the rest of his life, as they had with me. And every step of the way, he knew the press *would* compare him to me. So after the game, he announced that he would never kick a ball again and even though lots of people tried to persuade him to change his mind afterwards, he was adamant. For Dad it was a heartbreaker and it just added to the guilt that I already felt about Mum. It was as if my behaviour had stopped Ian from getting the professional career he deserved. And by making a decision like that and sticking to it, he showed that he was a strong-minded person.

The news of this didn't drive me immediately to drink, but I was dying for one most of the time. I tried to keep myself as occupied as possible to keep my mind off it and I was also scared off it by a terrifying incident. Just before I'd booked into the Vesper, I'd received a call from a San Jose detective, who said he needed to discuss something important with me.

'I know you've got problems right now,' he said, 'so I'll come to see you when you get out of the hospital.'

I had no idea what he wanted but, sure enough, he came

to see me after I got out and it was the most disturbing visit I've ever had.

'Do you know the lady who lives opposite?' he started off asking. 'The one with the teenage daughter?'

I said that I did and he followed up by asking if I knew them well.

'Not really,' I said. 'I've seen them out by the communal pool sometimes and have nodded across at them but I don't think I've ever spoken to them.'

He then told me that just before I'd entered the Vesper, a man had broken into their house dressed in an anorak-type coat and with a scarf and a hood over his head.

'What's that got to do with me?' I said.

'Well, the girl says it was you.'

Now, I'm no Rumpole but I said, 'If this intruder was wearing a scarf and a hood, what made her think it was me?'

He said that she recognised my voice.

'And how can that be if I've never spoken to her?'

'Look,' he said almost apologetically, 'you understand that I have to investigate this because she insists it was you?'

But could I honestly say it wasn't me? Maybe I was pissed, maybe it *was* me because I'd blacked out so many times before I went into hospital that it *could* have been me. It frightened me to death and I needed to know what was being suggested. So before he could raise it, I said, 'This person who broke in ... did he do anything to the girl?'

And I was massively relieved when, after a short pause, he said that no, the intruder had just walked out after a few minutes.

I asked how the man had got in.

'Well,' he replied, 'that's what we don't know and there are no clues. Whoever it was left by the front door and set the alarm off, but we've no idea how he got in. So if it was you, you are either a very experienced burglar or very lucky. But we'll be making further enquiries and may have to talk to you again.'

The woman and her daughter were a strange pair and soon afterwards the mother knocked on our door and asked if she could borrow some milk. She had apparently accused me of breaking into her home and now, having never spoken to me before, she was coming round to borrow milk. Very odd. It's not as if I was a contender for the best neighbour award at the time. Apart from coming home at all hours, we had this mad dog which had killed one of the other resident's dogs. So to come and ask me for milk didn't add up at all.

Then, a few days later, I was taking the dog for a walk in a nearby park when a police car drew up besides me. I had seen it from a distance and waved at the officers inside because they were regulars whom I knew. One of these coppers got out of the car and said, 'How are you, George?'

'Fine,' I said, 'no problems.'

Then he asked if the dog was OK after the fatal fight.

'Not really,' I replied.

So he reached out to stroke it and the dog almost had his hand off, which wasn't the best of introductions.

Then the cop put on a serious face and said, 'We've just been to see your neighbour, Mrs So-and-so. You know what it's about, don't you?'

'Yes, about someone breaking into her house.'

'No, she says that you exposed yourself to her and her daughter.'

'You what?' I said. 'Where and when was this supposed to have happened?'

'They saw you upstairs in one of the bedrooms of your house, completely naked.'

'Well, if I was in my own house, I was entitled to be naked. And what were they doing looking into my house. You'd better talk to their solicitors because I think there's something seriously wrong with them.'

'I know, I know,' he said, exasperated, and got back into the car and drove off.

A few weeks later, I had another visit from the detective, who said that they had no evidence to charge me on either the cat burglary charges or for being the phantom flasher of San Jose – so they were dropping the case.

But it had made me think. It was all very worrying. The fact that I'd even doubted my own movements scared me. That I couldn't be sure where I was, who I was with and what I'd been doing. What kind of a life is that? But at least, for the moment, I was clean.

The Earthquakes' side were still failing miserably to live up to their name but once again, after coming off the drink, I was training as hard as I had done for a long time and I was ready for the new season. I knew that no matter how well I played, it wouldn't make any difference to our chances but I wanted to get at least one thing right in my life. I wanted to prove that I could still play, to myself as much as anyone else.

I got 13 goals that summer season of 1981, and one of them was the best I've ever scored. It came against my old club, Fort Lauderdale Strikers, when I got the ball 25 yards from goal and sidestepped a defender. There were three more waiting to pick me off but I dummied left, then right, then left again and shook them all off and as the keeper came out, I knocked it past him. The goal didn't mean anything in terms of the Earthquakes fortunes or the League table. But it meant everything to me in terms of personal pride.

At the end of the season, we went on tour to Europe and I played against my old side, Hibernian in a friendly, which we lost 3–1. It was a pretty dismal performance by us and long before the end I was just going through the motions, but to my surprise, Billy Bingham included me in his Northern Ireland squad to play Scotland in a crucial qualifying match for the following year's World Cup in Spain.

At 35, and having not played for my country for five years, it seemed that I might finally get to play in the World Cup Finals because Bingham's side had an outstanding chance of going through. I also bumped into Bill McMurdo at Hibs, who I'd seen around a lot when I played for the club. He had become an agent for players like Mo Johnston and Frank McAvennie and he agreed to act for me in Britain.

A week later, after I'd played in San Jose's 1–1 draw against Linfield, Bingham dropped me from the squad and said that he thought I lacked the fitness for international football. But it was not the end of my World Cup dream. After Northern Ireland clinched their place in the Finals by drawing 0–0 with Scotland and then, in November, beating Israel at Windsor Park, Middlesborough manager Bobby Murdoch made a bid for me.

'Look, George,' he said to me during my talks with him, 'if you play the rest of the season here, get your fitness levels up and show Billy Bingham that you can still do it, you're bound to go to the World Cup. And we need someone like you to give us a lift.'

This was the first genuine offer to revive my career in Britain since I had left United and a tempting one at that. The Stockport and Hibernian signings were just money-making ventures, both for me and the clubs. But Middlesborough were concerned about relegation from Division One and genuinely wanted me to help revive their team, not just as some sort of sideshow to bring in a few quid. That in itself made the offer tempting and if I had agreed and played for the last four months of the season, there is no doubt in my mind that I would have gone to the World Cup Finals in Spain.

But I didn't join. The timing wasn't right, what with the problems at home and the new baby. I couldn't imagine that Angela would fancy moving to Middlesborough and I didn't fancy playing in another poor team, nor stepping back into the media circus that my return to England would have become. So I said thanks but no thanks, although I was sorry for Bobby, who was shattered when I told him.

At the back of my mind, and the back of Billy Bingham's as well, no doubt, was also the media scrum that would have developed in Spain if I had been part of the squad. A lot of the players I spoke to, like Sammy McIlroy and Big Pat, reckoned it would be great if I went. But although they had done brilliantly to qualify, no one gave them any hope of being anything more than also-rans in the Finals.

OK, to some of the players, just going there was a great achievement but not to me. I never wanted to go to any tournament just to make up the numbers and realistically, that was the case here. I knew that if I worked hard, got fit and played out of my skin in every match, it wouldn't make the slightest difference to the team's results.

I remember the Northern Ireland side making the quarter finals of the World Cup Finals in 1958, when Wales also made it through to the last eight. But Ireland had a freak number of top-class players in that era, people like Danny Blanchflower, Peter McParland, goalkeeper Harry Gregg and, of course, Billy Bingham himself.

I have always believed that the two Irish football associations should have got together and formed one national team. Each side has always had outstanding individuals so if you could have put players like me and Big Pat in with, say, Frank Stapleton and Paul McGrath from the Republic of Ireland side, we might have had half a chance. But politics and money have never allowed it to happen.

The Irish rugby side is united and they've had fantastic successes over the years. But in soccer I think the hangers on and the officials in the two Associations are too frightened of losing their freebies and their status. When they did try a united Irish side, against Brazil in 1974, it was such a fantastic success that they didn't dare repeat it in case people started insisting that they keep it permanently. I think that would have been a great idea.

Under today's rules, I would also have qualified to play for Scotland through grandfather Best, and ironically, they also made the Finals in 1978. But as the rules were then, I didn't have any choice so it was not as if I had any decisions to make or to regret making. I think I should have gone back to England and played a full season but I can't say I regret not doing so because the circumstances just weren't right. And I was finding it too difficult to stay in shape for any length of time.

The one decision I *did* make was to start drinking again when I returned to San Jose. And perhaps deep down, I had been frightened that I might not have been able to stay dry during the World Cup and would end up making a fool of myself.

I'd been off drink for nine months or so but I never for a second stopped missing it. One day I just decided to have a couple. There was no particular reason, there never is one specific thing that starts me off. The amateur psychologists like to think you can point to an incident that triggers off a relapse but an alcoholic like myself doesn't need a reason. As I have learned, it's something inside, something genetic and all you are ever trying to do is control it. I thought that I was now able to contain the cravings, that I could just drink normally, like everyone else, go out and have a few and come back none the worse for wear. I also thought I was getting away with it, as far as Angela was concerned, because I was playing the doting dad and taking Calum out in his pushchair. But after I brought him back, I would make some pretence to go out and sneak off for a few quick drinks.

After so long off it, it didn't take much to get drunk at first. Twelve months earlier, I could have knocked back twenty pints or a bottle of vodka but the first time back on it, I was gone after a couple of pints. But once it gets back into your system, God, it's lovely, and before long I was craving more and more and going off on three-day binges again. I was back in black-out territory.

The doctors at the Vesper had painted an accurate picture of what would happen when I left in 1981 – that the next twelve months would see me either dead, dry or back knocking on their door. I certainly wasn't dry but I was at least alive and ready to put myself through another dose of rehabilitation. This time, they weren't prepared to take me unless I completed the whole thirty days, which I managed and even ended up with an Alcoholics Anonymous medallion. The trouble was that I still didn't feel at ease with group therapy. I did what I had to do, standing up and saying, 'My name is George and I am an alcoholic,' but I couldn't tell my secrets to other people and in any case, how could I ever be anonymous?

Even in the Vesper, people knew who I was and would ask for my autograph. The doctors told me that I would have to attend AA sessions regularly for the rest of my life but I couldn't see myself turning up for meetings and having that happen all the time. It wasn't even that I was not ashamed about some of the things that I'd done. It's just that I've always been a shy person and I'm not comfortable talking about myself. Even writing this book was difficult for me at times. Group therapy works for a lot of people and AA do a great job. I particularly like their Serenity Prayer: 'God grant me the serenity to accept the things I cannot change, courage to change the things I can, and wisdom to know the difference.' But sadly, AA is not for me.

If I had been able to continue in therapy, it would no doubt have helped. But on my own, that medallion was never going to be worth more than a loser's medal and I was soon drinking again. This time, Angela couldn't take it any more and we agreed that I would go back to England and live with her parents, which sounded a bit like the Vesper but with better food and less therapy. It was really an ultimatum from Angela and the idea was that if I behaved myself at her parents, she would return with Calum and we could be one big happy family again, but even that was a delusion – we had never really been that.

I had been having an affair in San Jose with a girl I'd met on one of my long nights out and, true to form, as soon as I got through customs at Heathrow, I phoned a friend of Angie's who'd been a regular at her pool parties, but who was also now back in the UK. She agreed to have lunch with me, although I had a lot more on my mind and we ended up having an affair. So much for the new leaf. I was hoping that a change of environment might help, which it had done when I first went to America until the demons kicked in. But as bad as San Jose was, I wasn't prepared for the culture shock of Southend.

I had given Angela's mother and stepdad some money to help them buy a house there, on the understanding that if they ever sold it, I would get a share of the profits. But it didn't look anything like a des res when I first saw it. The place had been owned by some old man who hadn't done anything to it for years. When they bought it the place stank and there was wall-paper hanging off the walls.

Angela's stepdad, Joe, had started to clean the inside of the house up so I got started on the outside. It was the worst kind of work I'd had since I was an apprentice boot cleaner at Old Trafford. If I wasn't out with a wire brush, I was scraping the garden wall or painting the gate. Then I started painting the walls of the house, but after I'd done the front and the side – the parts that you could see from the road – I figured it was time to down brushes.

I felt that Angie's mum used to nag a bit. Joe was really easy-going and when we'd finished for the day, we'd go down the local Conservative club for a game of snooker and a few drinks. I was supposed to be dry but Joe couldn't have cared less. He would have his half a pint of bitter, that's all he ever had, a half. And a cigar. He was a bit like my dad, who believed in doing everything in moderation. Unlike me, of course, and if I felt like sinking a few, he would let me get on with it. Joe had been a bookie and he still liked a bet, but again, not in the sort of amounts that would affect the family finances.

I'd been back in England less than a month when I was asked to play in an exhibition match in Belfast, which gave me the chance to see Dad and the rest of the family. On the way back, I bumped into an old friend, the actor, George Sewell, at Belfast Airport. George was famous for playing hard man roles in gangster films and TV series like *The Sweeney*. But I have to say I was much more interested in his companion.

She was a stunning blonde (yes, another one!) whom he introduced to me as Mary Stavin, a former Miss World. Just my type in fact, despite the unhappy ending to my brief affair with Marjorie Wallace. She was trying to get started as an actress, so I found out from George when they were performing in Birmingham next and I turned up the following week.

I hadn't suddenly discovered a new love for the theatre. But I *had* suddenly discovered a new love in my life.

CHAPTER FOURTEEN
OLD HABITS
DIE HARD

Mary didn't tell me at first that she was living with the footballer Don Shanks, who was renowned as a bit of a hard man on the field. But then I don't suppose it would have made much difference to me. It certainly hadn't in the past and I was hardly a free agent myself, even if I never stopped acting like one.

We managed to keep things quiet at first, or at least as quiet as a famous footballer and Miss World could have hoped. But the paparazzi were starting to get busy and it was inevitable that it would get out sooner rather than later. We were snapped having dinner together in June 1982 and of course, someone quickly passed the good news on to Angela. This time there was to be no reconciliation, and this time, neither of us wanted it.

Angela didn't phone up and slag me off or immediately demand a divorce. She was past caring and had her hands full with Calum. And in fact, when we did next speak, she made a joke of it.

'That's typical of you, George,' she said. 'I knew there would be another woman eventually, there was bound to be someone. And being you, of course, it couldn't just be any woman. It had to be Miss World.'

We both accepted the marriage was dead and we agreed that she should sell the place in San Jose and all that expensive furniture and split the proceeds.

Like so many of my relationships, the one with Mary developed quickly. We got on really well and we laughed a lot. In fact, on our first date, all we did was talk and laugh. I went to see her in her dressing room before she performed in a play in Birmingham.

'If you fancy a coffee afterwards,' I said, ' I'll be in my hotel room.'

'Aren't you staying to watch the play?' she said.

'No, it's not really my thing, but I'd love to see you for a coffee and you can tell me all about it then.'

She was supposed to catch the eleven o'clock train but after she turned up in my room and we began chatting, she decided to catch the midnight one. But we were getting on so well, just talking about our lives, that she stayed all night. We ordered sandwiches and wine from room service and just sat on the bed chatting, though I did make a clumsy attempt to kiss her at one point and fell off the bed as I made my lunge.

A few days later, she phoned to say she was leaving Shanks and I helped her to move into the house of a couple she knew in Windsor called Geoffrey and Madeleine Curtis. About a week later, I moved in myself. We couldn't live there permanently, of course, so a few months after that, we resettled into a flat in the Barbican, in London, which was one of the worst moves I've made because I ended up hating the place.

Soon after arriving back in England, I'd received one of those brown envelopes from the Inland Revenue, which everyone loves so much. I thought, as I'd been working abroad, that I might have been due a rebate. But instead it was a demand for £17,996 taxes, which they said I owed them from my earnings at Fulham.

I just didn't have that sort of money and when I spoke to the Inland Revenue, I explained that I had separated from my wife and had a lot of capital locked up in our property in America. I offered to pay them £10,000, with the rest to follow in six months. But they wouldn't accept it. I stalled them a bit longer because I also hoped to make a tidy sum from the sale of my flat in Putney, which I had bought during my Fulham days.

I had appointed agents to sell it and everything in it and was expecting a nice surplus from a flat in such a fashionable location but the agents told me that everything had been swallowed up in expenses.

'What expenses?' I said. 'How many expenses can you incur in selling a house?'

But they just fobbed me off, saying, 'You know, telephone calls, paper work, removal lorries.'

I suppose I should have followed it up but I wasn't in the right state to do so. There wouldn't have been a massive profit because we hadn't put that much down, but I was expecting at least £10,000.

If I'd invested more of the profits I'd made from the early days of Slacks and Oscars, I would have been a rich man. But I had gambled most of those away or used them to fund holidays and by 1982 both clubs were run down and my shares worth next to nothing. They had both had a good run, since anyone in the business will tell you that five years is the maximum life for a club. There are always exceptions, like Tramp and Stringfellows, which go on forever. But the unwritten law is that in five years, fashion changes and people move on and if you're sensible, you move before that happens. Also, one of the great attractions of my clubs had always been that I was in them most of the time. But I'd paid only fleeting visits over the previous six years.

I didn't have time to dwell on my tax problems because I was too busy trying to make a living. I was asked to do some football analysis work for TV South in Southampton and on the strength of that, I was hired by ITV as a World Cup commentator in Spain in the summer of 1982. So I did get to the World Cup after all, wearing earphones rather than the green shirt of Northern Ireland.

I didn't feel any regret about not being in the side because I had known when I turned down Middlesborough six months earlier that I was putting myself out of contention. The lads did fantastically well to finish top of their opening group, beating Spain 1–0 in the final game after they had been reduced to ten men.

But as I had predicted, they were sure to get a stuffing somewhere along the line and it duly arrived in the second stage when they were hammered 4–1 by a brilliant French side, which included Michel Platini, Jean Tigana and Alain Giresse. And I am not fooling myself that the scoreline would have been any different if I had been on the pitch.

The competition gave me a brief respite from the Inland Revenue but negotiations resumed when I got back. I say negotiations, but they refused to compromise and insisted that they would apply for a bankruptcy order if I didn't pay them in full. I kept asking for more time but in November 1982, they were as good, or as bad, as their word and I was declared bankrupt owing £22,000 to creditors.

It seemed incredible after all the money I had earned in my career and was still earning. But although it wasn't a nice thing to be bankrupt, I had suffered worse humiliations in my time and it wasn't something that interfered with my daily life.

The TV work gave me an incentive to try to give up the drink – or at least, to control it – and people were always sending me things through the post that were supposed to offer cures. If it wasn't Alcoholics Anonymous, it was some other self-help group, some of them from complete fruit cakes who reckoned they could get me off the drink for good. Most of the leaflets that came through the door promising foolproof cures ended up in the bin but there was one that attracted me from a group called the Conservation of Manpower. Don't ask me why they were called that, or why I was attracted to their pamphlet, but they were based somewhere on the Thames and one day I thought I would give them a try.

I phoned the guy who ran it and arranged an appointment.

So I went along and this guy had a little chat with me, asking how I felt on a scale of one to ten. Just as well, because at the time, I felt around minus six. After our chat, he gave me some mixture to drink, I never found out what it was, and then he sat me in a chair with a headset on and said, 'I'm leaving you for a while now.'

As he left the room, he turned out the light and the next thing I remember was waking up about half an hour later. I hadn't heard anything through the headphones but maybe there was some subliminal message played through them because I felt a real buzz, a really nice feeling which persisted for a few days afterwards. And amazingly, I just didn't feel like a drink.

After that, I started going to the place about once a week, and it was always the same procedure. As the treatment went on, I was feeling closer to ten out of ten and I began to believe in the treatment because every time he switched the light off and left me, I fell asleep immediately. It was one of the few things that I've ever known to suppress my cravings but inevitably, after a few months, I got a phone call from a press man, which began, 'We understand you've been going to the Conservation of Manpower ...'

So I stopped going. I knew that if I went again, the place would be crawling with press men and photographers and I wasn't going to give them that satisfaction. It was a shame because it worked and didn't involve me telling my inner feelings to a lot of other patients, like AA.

I still had no idea what I was going to do with my life. I didn't know whether the TV stuff would last, nor the celebrity appearances which Bill McMurdo arranged. He set up quite a few lucrative deals, which only required me to turn up and sign autographs at shop openings or football promotions. I also played in quite a few exhibition matches. So I had a big decision to make when, out of the blue, I received a phone call from Big Ron Atkinson.

Big Ron, who is one of the most flamboyant men in the game, had been manager of United since 1981 and had brought a lot of flair to the job.

'Look,' he said, after some polite chat, asking me how I was and what I was up to, 'instead of fannying around with TV work and telling people how you used to play, why don't you come back and show them instead?'

I was staggered.

'Are you serious?' I replied. 'You're asking me to play for Manchester United again?'

'Well, if you're a fraction as good as you used to be, you'll do for me,' he said. 'Why don't you give it a go and see how it works out. I don't expect you to be running at your age so just do your own thing, knock the ball about y'know, stroll around the park. We've got plenty of others to do the running.'

It was tempting, particularly because the offer came from Big Ron, whose teams had always played football the right way, the way I liked to play, with formations based on attacking skills rather than defensive ones. I also knew that he was someone I could talk to, someone with a big sense of humour who didn't treat players like schoolkids, like some managers did. Had he taken over United instead of Tommy Docherty in 1972, I might never have left. I might even have produced some of my best football since I was only 27 when I left in 1974.

But that was then. I was now coming up to my 37th birthday and hadn't played at the highest level in League football since leaving United. I did give it some serious thought but I was afraid that I might go back and make a fool of myself or, at the very least, ruin the memories fans had of me. I'm sure they would have been sympathetic but I didn't want someone pitying me. I had to face facts – at my age, I could never play the way I'd done in my prime and if producing a few pieces of magic every game would have satisfied Big Ron, that wouldn't have been enough for me. He even said that it didn't matter if I didn't play a full ninety minutes but it did matter to me.

So again I said thanks, but no thanks.

Instead, in March 1983, I joined Bournemouth, who were struggling in the old Third Division, the bottom League. That might sound ridiculous but I was happier with the arrangements at Bournemouth, whose managing director, Brian Tiler, just wanted me to bring a few people through the turnstiles. Atkinson had wanted me as a serious performer, albeit for only a part of the games, which would have meant a lot of hard work getting into shape and a lot of expectation.

At Bournemouth, it was the same deal as I'd had at Dunstable, Stockport and Hibernian. I didn't have to train much, I just had to show up, do a few tricks, earn the club some money and everyone was happy. Everyone understood each other. Most of those clubs got their money back from my first game, so that it almost didn't matter if no one showed up for the second one.

Bournemouth certainly had no complaints because they

pulled in over 9,000 fans for my debut against Newport on 26 March, which was double their usual gate. I played four more games for Bournemouth, the last one against Wigan in their final home game of the season.

Towards the end of 1983, my wife Angie came back from America to live with her parents. It would have been impossible for her to have gone back to her old job with Cher when she had Calum to look after, so she decided to stay with her folks for a while in the house I had helped to buy.

After a year apart, we got on pretty well, though it was a different relationship when we saw each other. There was no longer any chemistry between us, no chance of us slipping back together, as we'd done so many times before. But at least we weren't fighting any more, and she was quite happy for me to see Calum as often as I wanted. He was only a toddler, of course, and she didn't trust me to take him out for the day at that age. So she would bring him to the flat and sometimes leave him with Mary and me while she went off to meet some friends.

But I felt Mary never showed the slightest interest in Calum, would never hold him or even take his hand. I thought she might at least have taken an interest in the child of her live-in lover. But our relationship was starting to fall apart at this time. Mary was desperate to make it as a film actress and desperate to be famous. She was so single-minded about this that she was perhaps worried she might become attached to Calum and that it could impinge on her ambitions.

She had persuaded me to make a keep fit record as they were starting to become big business in the fitness-conscious Eighties. She also kept talking about going to Los Angeles to find her fame and fortune, which I'd already tried. But I wasn't interested in any of it.

One day in May 1983, she finally walked out, saying, 'George, I've made up my mind. If I'm going to make it as an actress, I've got to go to LA.'

'Do what you have to do,' I said, 'but I can tell you that you're going to have a tough time. You might be a former Miss World but there are hundreds of beautiful women walking the streets of LA and there are even more good actresses.'

She left, anyway, and I flew off on a tour in the Far East with Bill McMurdo, playing for a couple of teams in Hong Kong and then for the Brisbane Lions in Australia. A guy called Ed Marconi owned them and we had some pretty good attendances in the three games I had agreed to play for them. So he asked me to play one final match, a special game he was trying to organise against their biggest rivals – I can't remember what they were called. It wasn't part of my deal, so he said, 'Tell you what, George. It's bound to be a big gate, so I'll split the attendance money with you.'

The Lions game turned out to be my last club appearance. One odd thing about Bill was that he had a beard and long hair, not dissimilar to my own, so the kids in the Far East would sometimes mistake him for me and ask for his auto-graph. Now you would expect any normal person to have told them that they'd got the wrong man but Bill would take their books and sign my name.

Meanwhile, I had managed to save enough to put down a deposit on a flat in Oakley Street, Chelsea in June 1984. I had never liked the Barbican, which seemed all concrete and no personality. That June, I also met my new girlfriend, Angie Lynn – who wasn't Miss World but could have passed for one, instead making her living as a glamour model. We had met in Blondes club in the West End, which was appropriate since she was another of my beautiful blondes. And as with my other long-term girlfriends, we hit it off pretty quickly and although she had been dating Chris Quinten, the *Coronation Street* actor, she moved out after agreeing to come to Norway with me.

That was to be the start of the most tempestuous relation-ship of my life.

Talk about two tempers and two clashes of wills.

I don't know how it started but we were always standing each other up or running out on one another. She had a flat in the Cromwell Road, not far from me, so it was a question of your place or mine during our early courtship, which was more like warfare at times.

I stayed at her place one night that summer and when she

got up before me in the morning, she shouted into the bedroom, 'Just taking the dog for a walk.'

Naturally, I thought nothing of it but when I got up around midday, she still wasn't back.

'Sod it,' I thought, 'I'm going out for a drink,' but when I tried the door, it was locked and I didn't have a key, and all the windows were barred as well. I was getting angry but I thought she was bound to be back before too long, though when she still wasn't back that night, I thought of phoning the police. Then again, after my experiences with them, I thought better of it.

There was no drink in the flat because, like me, Angie was someone who went out to drink. We weren't the sort to do it quietly at home. So my tongue was hanging out by night time and I didn't know what to do to get out. I didn't have my phone book with me, I didn't know where Waggy was at the time and even if I rang him, how was he going to get into the flat? Also, I kept expecting Angie to walk in at any moment but it was the following night before she turned up.

And, would you believe it, she walked in as if nothing had happened, still pulling the dog on its lead.

'Where the hell have you been?' I said. 'I'm dying of thirst here!'

'Oh, I got invited to a party.'

'What do you mean, you got invited to a party? You only went out to walk the dog.'

'I know,' she said, 'but I bumped into someone I know who invited me to a party and I was meaning to come back and let you know but I just seemed to lose track of time.'

'And what did you do with the bloody dog?'

'Oh, I took him with me.'

It was absolutely amazing, the way she could just stand there explaining things so casually, as if she'd simply come home five minutes late.

On other occasions, our exchanges got physical and often in public places like pubs and nightclubs. One of us would say something that set the other one off and we'd end uptaking swings at each other. Paintings would get knocked off walls, windows would get broken and the police were called to several establishments to warn us about our behaviour. How it never got into the press is beyond me but it was one of those classic, can't live with and can't live without situations.

She used to go to a seedy little club just off Regent Street and when she'd do her disappearing act I would normally find her in there.

'Why do you come to a dump like this?' I'd say.

'To get away from you,' she'd reply.

And that would start us off. I'd tell her to leave and she would tell me to piss off and then we'd lay into one another.

We were both absolutely besotted by one another and when things were good between us, it was fantastic. But when we fell out, it was fireworks.

Drink was nearly always involved so in a desperate attempt to get off it for a while, I went to Copenhagen to have Antabuse pellets sewn into my stomach. The Antabuse pills I'd taken in America had helped for a while but if I'd wanted a drink, all I had to do was to stop taking them. So I decided to have them sewn in so that I couldn't be tempted and I had to go to Denmark because the operation wasn't legal in England at the time. I had the pellets put in twice but as soon as the treatments had finished, I was back in the pub.

I was knocking it back heavily and after another big fallout with Angie in November 1984, I headed off to Blushes in the Kings Road. I could easily have walked there but for some reason, decided to take the car, promising myself that I wouldn't drive it home.

After I'd had a skinful at Blushes, I went across the road to a late disco and had a few more, leaving at about half past one, when I decided to go to Tramp. I walked out into the Kings Road, intending to get a taxi but it was pouring down and, as any Londoner knows, you can't get a cab for love nor money when it's raining.

I stood in the street for ten minutes or so and then thought, to hell with it, it's only a five-minute drive to Tramp. But I was in no fit state to drive five yards and I was pulled up by the police almost directly outside Buckingham Palace. They needn't have bothered with the breathalyser because it must have been obvious that I had no hope of passing it, but they went through the formality anyway and carted me off to Canon Row police station, where I was charged and bailed to appear at Bow Street magistrates court the following day.

They didn't let me out until six o'clock the following morning, Saturday, 3 November, and this time I did take a cab home and went straight to bed. I didn't wake up until early afternoon, when I decided, having been denied my final drinks at Tramp the following night, to go back to Blushes for an eye-opener.

When I walked in, it was like one of those scenes from a Clint Eastwood movie, where everyone stops drinking and talking and looks at you.

Of course, I knew a lot of people in there and one of them said, 'What are you doing here, George?'

'What do you think?' I said. 'Having a drink like everyone else.'

'But there's a warrant out for your arrest,' he said. 'The cops are after you.'

'What are you on about?' I said. 'Are you winding me up?'

'No,' the guy said. 'It's been on the news. You were supposed to be in court at nine o'clock this morning.'

I couldn't believe it. I'd only been let out of the police station at six. So how did they expect me to get back to court by nine? Remember, I wasn't exactly stone cold sober when I left the nick and I assumed that my court date was on Monday. I didn't know courts sat at weekends.

While I thought about what to do, I decided I might as well have a drink.

And then I had another. And another. And another. I did take time out to phone Bill McMurdo to tell him what had happened and for him to organise the legal side of things, although he had already heard about it on the news. It seemed that I was the only one in London who didn't know that there was a warrant out for my arrest. He told me he'd try to sort it out, and arrange for me to just turn up in court on Monday. So I carried on drinking and when I got tired of Blushes, I did a circuit of a few clubs, all without any attempts by police to arrest me.

I finally got back to Oakley Street around seven o'clock Sunday morning, to find the place surrounded by reporters. They told me that the police had been there looking for me and were waiting for them or me to come back.

I went inside, which was probably not the brightest move, since the press no doubt informed the police and within minutes, the place was surrounded. There must have been twenty officers in all, which made me wonder whether anyone was policing the rest of Chelsea that day. The inspector in charge rang the bell and told me over the intercom to come out but I hung up and tried to form a plan of action. I didn't think they would smash the door down so I decided just to stay there until Monday morning.

After an hour or so, the commotion outside seemed to

have died down and I couldn't even see any police. I assumed they were only hiding but reckoned if I were quick, I could get to the flat across the road to stay with a former girlfriend called Diana Janney. I phoned her and asked if I could spend the day with her.

'What for?' she said. 'What's going on? What were all the police doing outside your flat?'

'Just leave your front door open,' I said, 'and I'll be over in five minutes to explain everything. It's nothing serious, believe me.'

She wasn't convinced it was the greatest idea but eventually agreed. So I quietly opened my front door, took a big breath and sprinted – well, as near to a sprint as I could manage, across the road, which was only 20–30 yards.

As I did so, I heard one of the cops shout, 'Get him, boys' and half a dozen of them came flying behind me. It was like something out of the Keystone Cops, even to the point where they all careered into the front door of Diana's flat just as I slammed it in their faces.

If Diana had been perturbed to see the police outside my flat, she was even less amused that they were now pounding on her door. And by this time, the Special Patrol Group had turned up, who looked like the sort of lads who could make a nasty mess of your furniture. She must have wondered whether I'd killed someone and was at least relieved when I told her the truth. But it was still a hopeless situation for both of us.

'Look, George,' she said, 'I think you'd better give yourself up. You're only making things worse for yourself.'

There was no way out, in any case. So for the first time since this whole thing had started, I did the right thing and went out to surrender. Before I did so, hoping we could deal with this in as dignified a manner as possible, I called out through the door, 'OK, I'm coming out!'

I thanked Diana and opened the door and eight policemen came dashing at me, almost spilling over into the house.

'OK, guys, I'm giving myself up,' I said, trying to take the heat out of the situation.

But they were obviously up for a fight after being messed about all day and they pushed me roughly against a wall before handcuffing me. Then they started bundling me towards the paddy wagon, with one of the cops giving me verbal abuse all the way.

'You little Irish wanker,' he was saying. 'You Irish scum.' Which seemed way over the top when I was under arrest on a drink driving charge. I also thought that the show of force was excessive for a man who was giving himself up voluntarily anyway.

I was getting more and more pissed off as they shoved me roughly into the van when this mouthy copper put his face right up to mine.

'You little shit,' he said, 'you think you're a big star but you're just another piece of Irish dirt.'

After making one good decision to give myself up, I quickly reverted to making my most stupid one yet. I head-butted one of the policemen.

After I'd been officially charged with drink driving, failing to appear for a court hearing and assaulting a police officer, I was taken to Canon Row where I was held overnight.

The following morning, at Bow Street magistrates courts, my solicitor applied for a one-month adjournment, which was granted by the stipendiary magistrate, Ronald Partel, and I was released on £500 bail. So after all that fuss about my not appearing in court on the Saturday, the case was being put off for a month anyway.

My solicitor warned me that I could go to jail, since courts didn't take too kindly to assaults on the police.

He came round to the point of view that it was unlikely I'd be jailed, so instead of electing for trial by jury, we agreed to accept a magistrates' hearing, at which I would plead guilty and throw myself on the mercy of the court. Angie and I were having one of our better spells and she was in the Bow Street public gallery when I appeared before stipendiary magistrate William Robins on 3 December. Apart from confirming my name and pleading guilty to all the charges, I didn't say anything in court, still believing that I would probably get a hefty fine, or a suspended prison sentence or, if they did jail me, 30 days at worst.

But Mr Robins was a far cry from Sir Matt, or Tom Hart of

Hibernian or my dad, who had all shown leniency for my past misdemeanours. It was almost as if, at last in my life, someone felt they needed to get tough with me. He banned me from driving for five years, but that was the least of my problems. He sentenced me to three months in prison. And then he put the boot in by saying, 'I regard assault on the police as an extremely grave matter. Those who commit it do so at their peril. I see no reason to distinguish your case from others because you happen to have a well-known name.'

They took me straight down to the cells but fortunately, not directly to jail, because my solicitor managed to get a High Court hearing a few hours later, where Mr Justice Skinner granted us leave to appeal and I was released on a surety of £500.

But I was only delaying the inevitable.

I'd been confident before the magistrates' hearing but I didn't have much hope of the sentence being quashed in the High Court. The hearing was set for Southwark Crown Court on 17 December, just two weeks away. That was the longest fortnight of my life. I was absolutely dreading stepping back in the dock.

The night before, Angie and I went to a Chinese restaurant. I don't know how I got my food down because my insides were churning but I was trying to make a joke of it, saying things like, 'Will you wait for me, darling?'

© POPPERFOTO

Running from The Law. Denis and me showing off
our foot speed and physiques in pre-season training.

*Man of the cloth.
Outside one of
my boutiques.*

*Field of dreams.
I am starting to feel
isolated on and off
the field, 1969.*

With fiancé Eva Hareldsted. She later sued me for breach of contract.

And to think I used to support Wolves! Receiving the normal treatment from a defender.

*Stripped for action with new boss
Wilf McGuinness at the start of
the 1969–70 season.*

*Showing my heading skills
with the LA Aztecs and
(left) on Hermosa Beach.*

*Opposite:
Wearing the green
of Northern Ireland.
I would have liked to
have worn it on more
than my 37 occasions.*

Here's one for grandfather 'Scottie' Best. Playing for Hibernian, 1979.

Taking a corner for Fulham while I was still pulling in the crowds, 1977.

Posing in my final league strip for Bournemouth, 1983.

Another one of my collection of Miss Worlds! Mary Stavin slightly overdressed for my Bournemouth debut against Newport in March 1983.

With Calum and niece Ann on a trip back to Belfast.

Posing with the Beverley Sisters at a function to help promote the National Lottery.

Saying a few words for the Boss during his testimonial at Old Trafford.

Renewing old rivalries. United versus City six-a-side before Sir Matt's testimonial match.

With Alex and Phil on holiday in Portugal.

Sharing a book and a seat with the missus during a long day in the sun.

Wedding Day, 24 July 1995.

You may now kiss the bride! Alex and I begin married life.

*The much loved and much missed Shay Brennan
with wife Liz at the wedding reception.*

Presenting the final shirt I ever wore to Hiroki Miyagi, friend and business partner in World Football Shop Best in Toyko. I wore it in an exhibition match before Manchester United's World Club Championship game in 1999.

Ian Wright and me making a commercial for the football pools in Sweden.

Like fine wine, star players mature with age. The 1968 European Cup winning team at a reunion dinner in Dublin. Plus guest stars Harrey Gregg (fourth from right) and Denis Law who missed the final through injury. I'm the one without the bow tie.

At the Manchester United Disabled Supporters' dinner with Sir Alex Ferguson, Chas Banks (left) and Phil Downs.

Arriving at the TV Awards presentations with my lovely wife.

their last-minute Christmas shopping, knowing I was going to spend mine in jail.

No one who hasn't been inside can have any real idea what prison is like and, believe me, nothing could prepare you for Pentonville, which I'm told hardened cons believe is one of the worst in the system. The stench of the place hit me as soon as I stepped down from the van, the smell of excrement, rotting food and body odour. Just the smell made me dread the thought of spending three months in there, though the governor said to me, 'Hopefully, you shouldn't be in here too long. Just keep yourself to yourself, don't get involved with anybody and you'll be shipped out to an open prison in next to no time.'

I knew enough about Pentonville to know that it housed some pretty tough criminals, so I was relieved when they told me that I'd have a cell to myself. It was humiliating enough having to go to the toilet in a bowl, without doing it in front of a complete stranger. And when everyone emptied their slops into the toilet in the morning, the smell was enough to make you throw up. It certainly didn't put you in the mood for breakfast, which was virtually inedible, in any case. Yet you counted the hours until meal times because they were the only occasions you were guaranteed to get out of your cell, if only long enough to collect your food on a tin tray and bring it back. You knew that breakfast was 7.00, lunchtime was 12.00 and dinner was 4.30, which was a bit earlier than I was used to taking it.

The rest of the time, I would just lie on my bunk, wondering what Dad and the family would be thinking and feeling frustrated that I couldn't even speak to them to let them know I was all right. And you can't have a visit until your seventh day inside, which in my case fell on Christmas Day, when no visitors were allowed. We even had to eat our turkey and Christmas pudding in our cells, which is a very sobering experience, I can assure you. And as usual, we were locked in for the night at 7.30 pm, and for the only time while I was inside, I did shed a few tears.

The day after Boxing Day, however, I was transferred to Ford Open prison in Arundel, Sussex, which after Pentonville, was like a holiday camp. You get so bored locked in your cell all day that it was almost a treat to ride in the prison van and when we arrived at Ford, I felt almost happy. I got the same speech at reception, 'Don't get involved with anybody, keep yourself to yourself.' Being an open prison, you could also get anything brought in if you had the money and the warders knew all about it.

'They'll try to talk you into drugs and drink,' the governor told me, 'but if you keep yourself clean, you'll get out of here with full remission.'

He didn't have to warn me off drugs, because I've never fancied trying them and I had decided that I didn't want to drink, either. It was drink, after all, that had got me into this mess in the first place and with a drink inside me, it might cause me to do something that would keep me in prison longer than was necessary – and there was no way that I was going to serve the full three months. I got the shakes for a few days but I'd defy anyone not to have those in Pentonville. But I was fine once I moved to Ford.

I decided to keep my nose clean and take something positive from the experience by getting really fit, and going to the gym every day. In Pentonville, you were lucky if you got to walk around the prison yard for four or five minutes a day but at Ford there was plenty of time for exercise and recreation. There were no cells – and no slopping out either. It meant that I lost my privacy because I had to share a dormitory with eleven other prisoners but it was a price worth paying. And being an open prison, my dorm mates were not high-category prisoners.

I got quite friendly with the two lads who worked in the gym, who were both really fit. And we also played a bit of wall tennis. I wouldn't say we were pals but I got to know them quite well. I also got on with the head screw, a lovely man who had a handicapped son and who asked me to sign some pictures for him, which I was happy to do.

The lads who ran the gym had their own little primus stove, so we would cook egg and chips a few times a day if we fancied it, and you could also order a takeaway if you wanted to, and the delivery boy would throw it over the fence to you. It was mad stuff, really, considering you were supposed to be in prison. But you weren't locked up and they told me that I could walk out at any time but that if they caught me, I would be sent back to Pentonville. I wasn't going to allow that to happen and I'd had enough of the cops and robbers game.

They had a football team at Ford who were let out to play away games, which could have been an incentive for me to play or coach them. Nevertheless I had no intention of getting involved in any capacity because I knew that the press would get wind of it and I wasn't going to give them the satisfaction of taking my picture in prison garb. But the rumour obviously went around Fleet Street that I was going to play and they turned up mob-handed for Ford's next away game. They didn't get any pictures of me and they caused such a commotion that one of the players decided it was too good an opportunity to miss and did a runner.

The only scare I had in Ford was when some group from Belfast wrote to say that they were going to spring me. As if I couldn't have sprung myself simply by walking through the gate one night. The governor called me into his office and showed me the letter he'd received from them.

'Do you think this is serious, George?' he asked, 'because if it is, I might have to recommend that you be sent back to a closed prison.'

'I don't know who these people are,' I said, 'but I can tell you, I'm not going anywhere.'

'OK,' he said, 'we'll leave things as they are for now and see what happens. You'll be out of here soon enough, anyway.'

I suspected the letter was a hoax but I wasn't frightened about them coming to get me out, just of going back to Pentonville.

Things were so relaxed at Ford that the normal limits on mail didn't apply to me, either. They were bringing sackloads of letters to me from fans and well-wishers. I wrote to Dad for the first time in a long time as well, telling him that I was OK and behaving myself and for him not to worry. I apologised for putting him and the family through more bad publicity and I told him that I knew what I did was stupid. But in any situation, you can only react the way your instincts tell you and I'm not one to drive myself crazy by wishing I could turn the clock back. I just thought I'd try to make the best use of my time inside by staying dry and working out.

Dad was great about it. He blamed a lot of my problems on the press, believing they always portrayed me in a bad light and that affected other people's views of me. I don't think my wife, Angela, was surprised and, luckily, Calum was too young to understand.

I wrote to Angie Lynn a lot, too, and I'm glad I never got the letters to her mixed up with the ones I wrote to my dad because I don't think he could have taken it. Angie and I had fought like cat and dog on the outside but now that I was banged up, we both wanted each other desperately, which is probably a reflection of both our personalities. We used to write the most obscene letters to each other detailing what we planned to do to one another in bed when we got out. It was postal sex. And we repeated the same things to each other across the table when she came to visit me, which only served to frustrate me further since I was hardly in a position to put any of it into practice.

I'd been given a release date of 8 February 1985, assuming that I kept out of trouble and qualified for full remission, so Bill did a deal with a newspaper for my exclusive story of life inside, and they booked flights to Mauritius for Angie and me on 9 February.

Angie was there to pick me up at the prison gates and as we headed home, we both had only one thing on our minds. We started tearing at each other's clothes as soon as we got through the door of Oakley Street but, as randy as I felt in my head, it wasn't happening physically.

'I don't believe this,' said Angie, and started teasing me, which made it worse. But eventually we laughed about it and she said, 'Don't worry about it. It will be all right. We've got plenty of time for that.'

Believe it or not, it can even happen to George Best!

That was a first for me and it was strange that it should happen with Angie because our relationship had always been so physical – and thank God it *was* again once we arrived in Mauritius and booked into the Le Touessrok Hotel. It was a fantastic hotel on the East Coast of the island and the paper had booked us into the honeymoon suite and left flowers and champagne in the room. It was a beautiful room, with twin baths facing each other, though in those circumstances, one was normally enough for us. I had taken such places for granted all my life as a footballer but after prison, I really appreciated it.

I wasn't tempted by the champagne because I was enjoying being fit and wanted to keep up my training during our two weeks on holiday. The weather was fantastic on our first morning there and the photographers took all their pictures and I did the interview, after which they left us alone to enjoy a two week holiday in the sun.

But the following day, it was pissing down as I went on my daily run and it carried on raining for the next six days. And when you're on a sunshine island, there's not much to do when it's raining all the time and the pair of us got depressed and started snapping at one another. So much for the 'honeymoon' couple.

Before the week was up, as I was walking past the bar on the way to my room after my run, I just thought, 'Fuck it, I fancy a drink.' I turned round and went into the bar and knocked back three large vodkas, which tasted fantastic. Naturally, after so long off it, it affected me more than usual, though I thought I was OK when I walked into our suite. But Angie could tell immediately.

You've had a drink, haven't you,' she said.

'Sure I have,' I said, 'we're supposed to be on holiday.'

'You promised me you were staying off it,' she said, 'but you couldn't even manage a week.'

'Well,' I said, 'there's nothing else to do around here', which wasn't the greatest compliment.

'That's it, George,' she said, 'it's over.'

The rest of the holiday, if you could call it that, was a disaster. Angie was upset that I'd gone back on the booze so quickly but I thought she was being unreasonable after the time I'd spent inside so I carried on drinking. Not that I had much choice. I had reached a point where once I started, I couldn't stop. I still thought I could control it but I was at a stage where I was either off it all the time or on it all the time. There was no longer any halfway house.

When we got back to London, and Angie kept to her word by moving out of Oakley Street, I soon started to miss her and decided on a third course of Antabuse injections to help me stay dry. As usual, they told me to take it easy for a while afterwards and not to get my stomach area wet. But I did both, by starting training too soon after the operation and also by getting wet. Once the stitches broke, the tablets started to come out and I couldn't stop them. I ended up having to go to a plastic surgeon to repair the damage.

Angie and I got back together after a couple of months and I hoped everything would work out. But we were both soon back to our destructive ways. Without the help of the

Antabuse, I couldn't keep off alcohol and after a row one day in the summer of 1985, I caught a cab to Heathrow and jumped on a plane to Marbella without telling her.

I turned up at the Skol Hotel, where they told me they were full. But being a regular customer, they managed to find me a room for two weeks. Then I settled back into my normal routine, shandies when I got up in the morning to get me ready to face the day, beers round the pool, early drinks with the old men in the tapas bar next door and into Puerto Banus in the evening. Funnily enough, I wasn't interested in chatting up any other women. I used to come back at night and sit on my balcony alone with a bottle of wine and be quite happy.

The crazy thing was that after a few days, I started to miss Angie and I would phone her three or four times a day, normally when I'd had a few.

'I'm really sorry I ran off,' I would say, 'but I'll be home soon.'

'Well, why don't you see if you can get a flight tomorrow?' she would say, and I'd be promising I would and we'd start all that dirty talk again. But we went on like that for almost two weeks – it was absolutely nuts.

Finally, I phoned and said, 'I'm coming home in three days on such-and-such a flight' and she said, 'I'll be waiting for you.' But when I got home to Oakley Street, all I found was a note saying that she had gone to Ibiza. She'd planned to leave on the exact date I got home and we continually did that. I would disappear and when I came home, she'd be gone and when she came home, I'd disappear again. We were like a couple of big, daft kids.

In the times when we were in the same country together, it was as passionate as ever and we even talked about getting married. We started to plan it seriously when, in September 1986, she told me she was pregnant. I thought that this time marriage and a child would make all the difference, though the timing was ironic because my divorce had just come through. Angela and I hadn't seen any need to rush into the divorce courts and neither of us wanted a big, public slanging match. So we waited until we had been apart three years before filing for the papers on the grounds of separation and they were finalised in the spring of 1986.

I was about to jump straight back into another unsuitable marriage but Angie lost the baby in December. Both of us were disappointed at the time but I think we both probably felt relief as well. We took it as a sign that things were not meant to be. Consequently we quickly cooled on the marriage idea. Looking back, it was for the best all round because it would almost certainly have ended in a terrible repeat of what had happened with Angela. Probably worse, because my relationship with Angie was so much more volatile and because my drinking was just as big a problem as when I'd been in the States.

A few times, when Angie had left me and I was pining for her, I'd go hammering on the door of her flat and she'd call the police to move me on. The last time that happened was in February 1987 when, drunk and disorderly as they say, I was so angry that she wouldn't let me into her apartment that I put my fist through her window. Then I walked home, leaving a trail of blood for police to follow, if they were so inclined. She did call the police, but they didn't charge me. It was definitely the end of the affair.

If we hadn't broken up, we would have ended up killing one another.

A few months later, I saw a beautiful, dark-haired girl in Blondes nightclub. I didn't know it at the time but her name was Mary Shatila and she was part Egyptian. Her half-sister Fiona was with her and what I also couldn't have known at the time was that Mary had nodded at me and asked, 'Who's that?'

'That's George Best,' Fiona said. 'He's a womaniser and a drunk. Don't even think about going out with him.'

I've had better notices but a couple of days later, I got the chance to make a personal introduction when I bumped into Mary at Blushes. I only spoke to her briefly but managed to get her phone number and we started going out.

We quickly became an item and within weeks she moved into Oakley Street. After my marriage and the relationship with Angie Lynn, this was like the quiet after a storm. Mary was really soft-spoken and easy-going, though she was a strong person inside. She also had a business background and offered to try to help sort out my tax affairs, or at least discover how I had managed to go bankrupt after earning so much money. So she asked Bill for the accounts books from the day he had begun handling my affairs and started digging into the payments, going into them in fine detail.

Mary also realised that I couldn't go on making money from exhibition matches for much longer, and she wasn't the only one who had come to that conclusion. My knee was not up to playing on a regular basis and my TV work was sporadic. So she suggested that I should try to get on the public-speaking circuit. When she first raised the idea, I thought she was nuts.

'There's no way I'm getting up and speaking in front of a bunch of strangers,' I said.

'Why not?' she retorted. 'You've got lots of stories to tell and the public love you.'

I wasn't keen on the idea at all but when my pal Kenny Lynch agreed that it was a good idea and he would be happy to go on stage shows with me if it would help, I thought it might be worth a go.

'Why don't we try to get you and I together with Bobby Moore?' he suggested, and as I liked Bobby, too, I decided to give it a try.

We started a round of engagements, though being shy, I found it awkward at first and didn't like it at all, which is why it was brilliant to have a showbiz professional like Kenny along. It's horses for courses, I suppose. I don't know whether Kenny would have fancied running out at Real Madrid's ground to play football in front of 120,000 people, something that didn't bother me in the least. But whereas he was completely relaxed when he stood up to speak in front of a few hundred people, I was absolutely terrified.

Before long, Mary, who was now acting as my agent, was getting bookings for me to speak on the lunches and dinners circuit, which were becoming big business. I still couldn't say that I enjoyed it but I began getting better at it and I realised that people were pretty easily satisfied. They weren't expecting some great speech from me, just a few stories about United and, of course, my affairs with the two Miss Worlds, and then the chance to ask me some questions.

So I developed a little routine where I would speak for a few minutes, crack a couple of jokes and then throw it open to questions. And very quickly, I found myself in huge demand. I could end up doing six or seven dinners a week, sometimes doing lunch and dinner engagements on the same day. I could do a lunch in Edinburgh and a dinner in Cardiff and the following night I might be in Huddersfield. It was a mad but lucrative circuit.

Also Jim Boyce, Billy Kennedy, Malcolm Brodie, John Smedley, Derek Wade, George Keenan and Dad helped to arrange a testimonial match for me at Windsor Park on 8 August 1988, which we thought would help to raise a large sum of money to solve my tax problems. I went into training for two months beforehand because I didn't want to go on to the pitch looking like I was four stones overweight. It was pure pride. I knew the people of Belfast would turn out in big numbers for me and most of them didn't have much money to throw around. So I wanted to go out and give them a show, remind them of the good old days.

And I wanted to do it for me, too. I didn't want to run out with people like Paul Breitner, Liam Brady and Ossie Ardiles and be puffing like an old man after five minutes. I got myself down to just above my old playing weight of 10 stone 10 pounds and I've got a photo taken during the game which gives me great pleasure because I look just like I did in my heyday. It poured down with rain for three days before the game but Windsor Park was still packed with 25,000 people, including my dad. My team won 7–6 and I scored with a chip over the keeper which gave me as much pleasure as some of my best League goals. So did the cheque from the receipts, which amounted to some £110,000.

After that, it was back to singing for my supper – and my lunch – again, though we got off the treadmill early in 1989, when Mary booked Denis Law and me on a tour to Australia, where we were to appear with a Scottish comedian called Joe Doherty, who lived over there.

We were packing places out but when we turned up at a little place called Newcastle, not far from Sydney, which used to be a mining town, it was more ghost town. We booked into this little hotel in the middle of nowhere, which is where the show was to be held, and we seemed to be the only guests. Well, except for a reporter from one of the Australian newspapers, who had come to do a piece on me.

'This is going to be a disaster,' I said to Denis after we'd checked in. 'We're in the middle of nowhere and I can't see how we're going to get anyone in.'

I said the same to the organiser, but he just shrugged it off.

'No, we'll be all right,' he said, 'I've sold a few tickets and out here, people tend to just turn up on the night.'

So Denis and I went off for our normal afternoon kip.

Once we'd woken up and got dressed for the show, we went down to the bar at the back of the hotel for a drink and there were only a couple of other people in there.

'I think it will be a pretty short show tonight,' I said to Denis.

The organiser came in to see us and we said, 'How's it going out there?'

'Oh, not too bad,' he said.

So we went out, expecting about a dozen people and the place was packed to the rafters, all mad Scots and Irish ex-pats, some of whom, we were told, had driven six or seven hours to get there. It was a fantastic show and afterwards we retired to the bar, where I agreed to speak to this reporter, though I quickly got the impression that he wasn't intending to write a favourable piece.

He made the mistake of trying to keep pace with me in the drinking stakes, which wasn't a good idea. I'd been off it for two months while I trained for my testimonial but I had missed drinking every day and now I was making up for lost time. We all learned the consequences of the journalist's attempts to match me the following morning. The woman who owned the hotel came out blazing as we were checking out and demanded, 'Who the hell was in room 6?', which was the reporter's room.

Apparently, he'd spent all night throwing up – over the bed, on the carpet, everywhere. And his newspaper article was pretty sick-making, too, on the lines of how a once massive superstar like me was having to scrape a living doing small town shows. In fact, I was making a fortune, picking up four or five thousand pounds for an hour's work. But naturally, I didn't tell him that.

On my return from Australia I began to get closer to Mary's daughter, Layla, who was about three or four-years-old when we started going out together. I quickly became 'Uncle George' to her and I became closer and closer to her, probably because my relationship with her mother was going so well. I've always got on well with kids in any case. And I probably got close to her because my own son was 6,000 miles away in California and was still too young to travel on his own. Layla's father was Mary's estranged husband, a Lebanese businessman who used to fly to Paris to see his daughter. Soon after we got back from Australia, in 1989, he phoned and said he wanted to see Layla so Mary took her to Paris and the next thing I knew, she was phoning me, saying that he had disappeared with her.

'There's probably some innocent explanation,' I said, but after a day or two, Mary flew home alone.

She was freaking out, like any mother would be in that situation, and presumed that her husband had taken Layla back to Beirut. So after a month or two without even a word, I decided to do something about the situation. I had been telling a friend of mine about it and he suggested that I get in touch with a former SAS man he knew, who still kept his hand in, so to speak. I phoned this guy and arranged to meet him in Scribes in Kensington, the club owned by Terry Venables, the Spurs manager at the time.

I was sitting at a table when this enormous guy walked in, about 6 ft 3 ins with broad shoulders and a real military bearing. He reminded me a bit of Grandad Withers – he had that same air of authority, and he was immaculately dressed as well.

He sat down and ordered a drink.

'So I understand you have a problem, Mr Best?' he said.

'Yes, my girlfriend's little girl has been abducted,' I replied. 'My girlfriend was married to a Lebanese guy and we believe he has taken her back there.'

He nodded. 'And what is the name of the gentleman who has taken the little lady?'

I told him and he replied, 'And I take it you would like to get your girlfriend's daughter back.'

'Well, that's the idea,' I said. 'What do you think the chances are?'

He went quiet for a moment and then said, 'We don't have a problem with the snatch, Mr Best. That would be the easy part. The hard part would come after you got her home. You know the father may try to come and snatch her back again and I don't think I have to tell you what the outcome might be or what you might have to do to stop it.

'So I would suggest you sit on your hands for a while and hope that you can eventually get in touch and sort this out through negotiation before thinking of embarking on such a drastic course of events.'

He didn't have to spell it out. So although Mary and I were becoming increasingly distraught, we decided to sit tight and see if she could get her daughter back through more official channels. I think it was sheer desperation that drove me to contact this SAS guy. I wanted to do anything I could to help. Later, after we split up, I was pleased to learn that Mary had managed to get in touch with her husband through family contacts and was seeing her daughter again.

With Calum so far away and with Mary separated from her daughter, children had suddenly become very important in my life. I guess being around kids brought me back in touch with my own childlike qualities, which I think have stayed with me throughout my life. I know there are people who still believe that I've never really grown up! Perhaps being forced to live in the spotlight from such a young age has made me more mature in some ways and less in others.

While we were still in Australia, Denis and I had done some work at schools for physically and mentally handicapped kids, which I always enjoyed and at one school, they presented me with a scrapbook in which each of the children had done a painting of me. I thought that was great.

As at other schools, the kids all wanted to play football with me, so we went out in the playground and were having a kick around when I looked through the classroom window and noticed that one little girl – she must have been about eight or nine – was still sitting there reading on her own.

I stopped and called one of the teachers over and pointed at the girl.

'What's wrong with her?' I asked. 'Why isn't she playing with the rest of the kids?'

'Oh, we've given up on her,' she said. 'We just can't get her to communicate with the others. She won't even mix with them. We've tried all sorts but nothing has worked. She's in her own little world.'

'Can I go to talk to her?' I said and the teacher just laughed.

'You'd be wasting your time,' she said. 'She certainly won't speak to you.'

'Well, can I just go in and say hello?' I said.

'If you want to,' the teacher said. 'But don't say I didn't warn you.'

I walked quietly into the classroom and shut the door behind me and as soon as the girl saw me, she pulled the book up in front of her face, the way kids do. So I walked round behind her desk to see what she was reading. It was one of those picture and word books and she was on the alphabet page, which was illustrated with animals and fruit. You know the sort of thing – A for apple, with a big picture of an apple beside the letter, B for banana, C for cat and so on.

I just looked for a while and then I reached out and pointed at the apple and said, 'Banana!'

Absolutely no reaction.

Then I walked round the front of her again and leaned over the book to point at the apple and shouted 'Banana!' again.

Still nothing.

So every few seconds, I would do it again and after about the sixth time, she looked up at me and shouted 'Apple!' back.

'No. Banana!' I said.

'Apple!' she said.

I knew I was on to something so I pointed at the banana next time and said, 'Apple!'

'Banana!' she replied.

Then I pointed to the cat and said, 'Dog!' and she was joining in the game now and seeing the joke.

After a few minutes, we were both rocking with laughter
and there were tears streaming down the girl's face. But
despite the tears, now that her face was lit up, she looked just
like a little angel.

CHAPTER SIXTEEN
UPS AND DOWNS

I was earning bundles of money by the end of 1989 but unfortunately, not much of it was reaching my bank manager because I was spending it as fast as it came in. If I earned £5,000, I would spend £5,000 and worry about the bills when they arrived.

Not that you get bills from casinos, where a lot of my cash was going. But with money in my pocket again, I rediscovered my love of gambling and, like my drinking, once I started, I couldn't stop.

Mary tried to keep hold of the money from my speaking engagements so that I wouldn't gamble it away but it was *my* money, I'd earned it, and if I wanted to play, I would. And even on nights when I had success at the tables, I went home with less cash than I'd started because I got in the habit of keeping the chips and taking them back to gamble the following day.

The gambling gave me a buzz, just like it had when Colin Burne and I had that winning streak in Manchester. And I didn't worry about things like bills and bank statements. I never have and I couldn't tell you what is in my bank account at the moment. I'd come through some bad times and felt I needed a bit of fun and with money coming in thick and fast, there didn't seem any reason why it shouldn't continue to do so. I felt that there would be plenty more where that came from.

The saddest time of that year came when I went to see Angie and Calum one day and she said, 'George, I've got something to tell you. I'm going back to work in the States.' Naturally, Calum would be going back with her, which would mean I'd see a lot less of him.

As he'd grown, I'd enjoyed my visits more and more, taking him to the seafront at Southend and kicking a ball around with him. But Angie was much better equipped than me to bring him up and her work prospects in the States were better than in England. So reluctantly, I agreed that it was probably for the best.

I spent a couple of days drowning my sorrows after Calum left. And I was also drinking heavily when I was invited on to the *Wogan Show* in 1990 for an appearance that I wished I had turned down. I was told to be at the studio at a certain time, which I didn't pay much attention to but which turned out to be three hours before the show went on air, leaving me all that time to kill in the Green Room, which is how TV refers to the hospitality suite.

And of course, the hospitality mainly came in liquid form, which I took full advantage of.

People have suggested that some of the *Wogan* people might have almost been hoping I'd get drunk because the show's audience figures were down and they needed something sensational to win back viewers. I don't think that's true but I do know that it wasn't a good idea to lock any thirsty person in a room with lots of booze for three hours and especially not someone with my reputation.

Naturally, I wasn't intending to get drunk and when I finally got on, I thought I was OK. But it was obvious to everyone else that I was half gone and the interview only lasted a few minutes.

Wogan asked me about all the women I'd been out with and I said, 'Terry, I like screwing, all right?' And when he tried to change the subject by asking what I liked to do with my time, I replied, 'Screw.'

The worst thing was that I thought I'd got away with it, that though I might have been a bit tipsy I had come across as reasonably coherent. But when I saw the recording the following day, it was obvious that I had been completely out of it. It wouldn't have been so bad for some idiot who can't string two words together at the best of times. But when you know that, in normal circumstances, you're quite intelligent, it's awful to see yourself coming across as some mumbling drunk.

After the storm broke in the newspapers about my performance, the *Wogan* people vowed never to have me on the show again but they got so much publicity out of it that they changed their minds. Mary was upset at the way I'd come over but she blamed the TV company as much as me. She thought it was madness to put temptation in my way like that.

Despite the *Wogan* experience, LBC radio in London invited me to become a commentator, providing professional opinion alongside their football expert, Tony Lockwood, which kept me out of mischief on Saturday afternoons.

It also brought me into contact with a lot of my old football pals and on one memorable afternoon at Sunderland's Roker Park ground when they played West Ham, I found myself sitting next to my old pal and former Fulham team mate Bobby Moore. A couple of fans spotted us and nudged their mates and eventually, everyone in the stand turned round to wave at us, which was nice.

'Fancy a cup of tea, Bestie?' Bobby said to me, at half time.

'Please, Bob,' I said.

So he went off to get the teas but being Bobby, he didn't just get a couple of cups of tea, he came back with meat pies and chips as well. I was thinking to myself, 'This is the man who won the World Cup for England and he's fetching me a meat pie.'

But that was Bob, always generous, always thinking about other people and with absolutely no side to him – he treated everyone the same. Before Bobby died of cancer in 1993, Alan Ball says that he received a phone call from him and, as he was later to discover, so did all his other 1966 England team mates. Bobby just chatted, without mentioning that he only had days to live. That would have been utterly typical of him, wanting to say his final goodbyes to his colleagues without wishing to alarm them.

I had been hoping that the money from my testimonial would not only allow me to clear my bankruptcy but leave a tidy surplus over to rebuild my life. To protect the money, I had put it in a trust fund for Calum but Stoy Hayward, the insolvency practitioners appointed by the bankruptcy court, were trying to get their hands on it, saying that I now owed almost £100,000 in back taxes and interest. As I'd gone bankrupt in 1982 for just £22,000, that figure didn't make any sense to me and I must give Mary credit for the way she set about delving into my financial affairs and looking for answers.

In September, 1991 I was recommended a solicitor called Bryan Fugler. Mary and I went to see him, taking along all the paperwork we had.

'We'd like you to tell us what the problem is and how we can sort this out,' I said.

Bryan was absolutely brilliant, going through it all seemingly in an instant and then summing up the situation in terms that any layman could understand.

He took over the case and it took him just six months to sort out a situation which had been going on for nine years. On 5 May 1992, I wrote a cheque for £32,500 and my bankruptcy was discharged.

McMurdo had done a lot for me but I felt it was time for a change. As luck would have it, around this time I bumped into a guy called Phil Hughes who ran a knitwear shop and a souvenir shop in the West End. He's a Manchester United fan from Wales, whom I met in Blondes one night. We got friendly really quickly and later on, we drifted into a situation where he began acting as my agent.

The stage shows with Denis were still going strong and once I learned to cope with my nerves, I loved doing them because if you went on at eight o'clock, you knew you would be off at nine thirty, whereas with the dinners, you'd get there for cocktails at six and could still be there in the early hours of the morning. Of course, you didn't have to stay until that time but once I had got the taste of the drink, I was happy to do so.

In 1993 I did the most successful tour of the lot with Rodney Marsh, BBC radio commentator Peter Brackley and a lad from Southampton called Mike Osmond. It was the same format, a few stories and a few jokes, followed by a question and answer session. And the most exciting booking of all was the London Palladium.

When I was first told we were to play the Palladium, I thought it was a wind up but it turned out to be true and proved a fantastic night. I just felt privileged to walk out on that stage where so many big names had appeared before me. So that was the highlight for me, though soon afterwards, Peter developed stage fright and didn't want to do any more dates.

In 1993, Rodney and I signed up for Sky TV's Saturday football show. This starts with us and a couple of other ex-footballers like Frank McLintock, Clive Allen or Alan Mullery previewing the big games. Then, when the matches kick off, each of us watches a selected game on TV, which cannot be shown to viewers because of the copyright laws. So the viewers are just watching us watch football on television, giving them verbal updates on what's happening. I thought it sounded crazy when they first told me the format, but it's become an enormous success.

With the bankruptcy discharged and the money coming in, my life was back on a relatively even keel and the pain of my final days at Manchester United were well behind me. But all the old memories flooded back when the news reached me in January 1994 that Sir Matt was dead. He was 86 years old and hadn't been well for years but it was still a shock when he finally went. He was one of those people you never imagine dying. And his funeral, on January 27, was painful for me not just because I was saying goodbye to Sir Matt but because of the memories it stirred of my old life.

I hadn't seen some of the 1968 team for years so it was strange meeting up with Bobby Charlton, Nobby and Shay again, particularly under those circumstances. We'd been part of a very special United side but there wasn't much reminiscing when we were reunited at Old Trafford on the morning of the burial. It was a typical funeral, all small talk, and everyone feeling a little awkward.

The club laid on a bus to take the 1968 players to a Requiem Mass at Our Lady and St John's Roman Catholic church in Chorlton cum Hardy and it was amazing to see the turnout in the streets. It was the sort of day you associate with a funeral, and a typical Manchester one, absolutely pouring down, yet there were thousands of people outside Old Trafford and lining the streets. They had banners and flags and black and white photographs of the Busby Babes, which they held up to the windows of our bus. You'd have had to have been over thirty to remember Sir Matt's feats as a manager yet there were hundreds of young kids out there with their parents, who obviously knew the legend and simply wanted to pay their respects to a great man.

There were over ninety past and present United players,

and Sir Alex Ferguson flew the entire first team squad from Portsmouth where, as a fitting tribute to Sir Matt, they had won a Coca-Cola Cup tie the previous night. A couple of thousand people couldn't even get into the church and had to listen to the service on specially erected loudspeakers. I remember the Bishop of Salford describing Sir Matt as a world celebrity 'clothed in modesty and charm' which I thought was beautiful.

After the service, the cortege made its way back to Old Trafford and stopped at the Munich Clock, outside the East Stand, on Sir Matt Busby Way, which is permanently dated 6 February 1958, the day of the crash. After coffee and sandwiches at the ground, most of the lads made their excuses and left. But Bobby Charlton, Noel Cantwell, Maurice Setters and I had been invited to the burial at Manchester's Southern Cemetery, so we got back on the bus for the most emotional ride of all, at least for me.

The route took us through Chorlton, where Sir Matt had lived and where I'd spent almost my entire United career. We passed so close to Mrs Fullaway's house that I could have reached out and touched the front door and we also went past the bus stop where I used to hide from Sir Matt. I thought of all the times I had seen him driving down that road and it made it so much more emotional for me.

I started thinking of all the fun times I had had during my time there and that first day at Mrs Fullaways, when Eric McMordie and I had found Manchester so strange and decided to run away. Memories of the time I had slipped that note to Steve Fullaway's girlfriend, asking her to go out with me, and the time we arrived home covered in blood after fighting over a little bit of fish all came flooding back. Plus the times, later on, when I used to dodge police patrol cars on the way home from nights out. My whole life flashed before me, even if it seemed like a lifetime ago that I had lived in that house and first dreamed of being a star footballer.

I had to dry my eyes before I got off the bus but the tears started again when they lowered Sir Matt into the ground alongside his wife, Jean. I thought of him lying in his coffin, dressed in his club blazer and tie, as immaculate in death as he'd been in his life. I'll never forget Matt's son Sandy leaning over as they lowered the coffin and whispering in my ear, 'You know he loved you.'

It was the hardest day I'd had to go through since my mother's death.

Mary had done a terrific job in getting me on to the speaking circuit and in helping to sort out the bankruptcy, but romantically, I was starting to feel indifferent towards her. Maybe it was because she was so easy-going, so forgiving when I got drunk or when she found girls' telephone numbers in my pocket.

Like all relationships, it had begun to change and not for the better. Despite living with Mary, I had cheated on her with a few different women. But in July 1994 I met a young, blonde girl in Tramp called Alex Pursey. I invited her out and discovered that she was a flight attendant with Virgin Airlines, although she wasn't like you imagine the stereotypical air hostess. She was a bright girl, very bubbly and, after some of the women I'd been out with, very normal.

I took her out to dinner a couple of times and inevitably we were photographed coming out of a restaurant. When Mary saw the pictures in the papers, she went mad. She had always forgiven me before or tried to ignore stories like that, hoping that it was just a fling or a one-night stand. I'm not sure how, but perhaps she sensed that Alex might be more than that because she agreed to a newspaper interview in which she painted a pretty black picture of me, detailing all the drunken escapades and the women I'd bedded. I was furious when I read it.

'How can you say all these things about me when you say that you love me?' I said.

'I do love you,' she said, 'but there is nothing in the article that isn't true.'

Alex obviously realised that as well, because she stopped returning my calls and was, in any case, working on Virgin's North American route, which meant she was away from home a lot. She had also told me that she was just getting over a long-term relationship with John Scales, then a Wimbledon player, and I thought that maybe she wasn't ready to get involved with someone else.

I let things drop and it wasn't until January 1995, five months later, that I spotted her in the Dover Street Wine Bar, a favourite haunt of mine. She was having dinner with a party of girls, who seemed to be having a lot of fun so I walked over and said, 'Hello, Alex. What's the celebration?'

'It's my birthday party,' she said, which gave me a perfect opening.

'Well, in that case, we'd better have some champagne.' I ordered a few bottles for her and her friends and after sharing a glass with her, left her to enjoy her party. But before I went, I said, 'I'll call you tomorrow' and when I did, she answered my call for once and we began going out again.

This time – maybe because she had had a chance to get over John and I'd been coming to the conclusion that Mary and I had reached the end of the road – it seemed much more like a proper relationship rather than a casual affair.

And despite our age difference – she was celebrating her 23rd birthday that night, while I was only four months from my 49th – we seemed to get on really well and would chat on the phone for ages. It got into the papers again, though Alex had been terrified about what her parents would think about her going out with George Best and told them that it was all lies. She said she was seeing someone famous but couldn't tell them who it was.

Mary knew, naturally, and waved the paper at me one morning.

'How can you do this to me after all I've done for you?' she said. 'I've made you the centre of my life these last eight years and done everything I can to sort out your problems. And now you humiliate me again.'

'I know you've done a lot for me,' I said, 'but that's the way it's supposed to be in a relationship. It's give and take.'

But when women do things for me, everyone always talks about them as my backbone. Angela was portrayed that way and now it was happening with Mary, as though I'm some hopeless little dog who, if I hadn't been trained to do things, wouldn't be able to fend for himself.

Most of the women I've had long-term relationships with have ended up slagging me off in the press. Angie Lynn is one of the exceptions and I'm pretty sure Alex wouldn't do that either. But so much crap has been written about me that I can't be bothered any more. I just use the press as much as they use me. But I do get upset when my former girlfriends are portrayed as angels, while I'm always the helpless bad guy.

That sort of attitude always pisses me off because if it had been the other way round, and Angela or Mary needed help, I would like to think that I would have looked after them. That was my final row with Mary, who moved out a week or so after my collision with Alex at Dover Street.

I left Mary to sort out her stuff from the flat. But a month or so later, when I was going through my things, I discovered that she'd taken my keepsakes from that visit to the handicapped school in Australia, the scrapbook containing the children's paintings of me and a photograph of me and the little kid with the alphabet book. I had been planning to get that photo framed, so I phoned her.

'Why have you done this?' I said. 'That picture means a lot to me and it can't mean anything to you. Why did you take it?'

She said that she must have got it mixed up with her things, having left in a hurry, and would send it back, along with the scrapbook. But I never got either and that left me with a bitter taste. Mary had been good for me and we'd had a solid relationship for almost eight years. But I didn't feel any guilt about splitting up. Our relationship had lasted longer than my marriage and I had done my best to get her daughter back.

So at the end, I just felt angry with her, although of course I was delighted about her reconciliation with her daughter. Mary and I did talk about marriage a couple of times but we never got round to it and it would have been a mistake.

My relationship with Alex developed as swiftly as all the others had done and even survived meeting her parents, Cheryl and Adrian, who is the director of an industrial belting company. Alex was a well brought up girl, who was educated at public school and she was unbelievably nervous when I finally went with her to meet her mum and dad, whom she didn't think would approve of me. They might not have done but when we met, we got on brilliantly. As they were both virtually the same age as me, it was perhaps not surprising that we were on the same wavelength.

I found them really easy-going, not at all stuffy, as I had suspected they might have been, and once I had cleared that hurdle, the romance between Alex and me really blossomed. I wouldn't say it was all plain sailing, even then, because I did go off on the odd long boozing session but she didn't make any big deal of it and in the summer of 1995, I asked her to marry me.

Naturally, this was a great story for the newspapers – ageing footballer marries Virgin trolley-dolly half his age – and poor old Alex got a taste of what I'd been through in the press for years. The papers loved me when I was scoring great goals and dating Miss Worlds. But when it suited them, they were only too happy to paint me in a different light as someone who wasted his talent. Even when I began making a lot of money outside the game, I was portrayed as a drunken loser. I suppose it's the old story about building someone up just to knock them down, and the British press do that better than anybody.

Alex was depicted as some gold-digging bimbo, which was not only unfair but ludicrous since she'd been brought up in a wealthy family home in Cheam, Surrey. I might have been back on my feet, financially, but I was no great catch. It was purely a love job between us and not just in the physical sense. We got on well and found that we laughed at the same things and it really did feel right for me. The age gap was obviously a big issue for the newspapers but I was probably more worried about that than Alex. She just sees people for who they are, rather than counting how many grey hairs they have, even if mine were starting to grow rapidly.

When Alex and I began dating and she got her first taste of the press, I said to her, 'This is the way it's always going to be.'

'I'm used to it after six years with John Scales,' she replied.

'Alex,' I said, 'I don't mean to be rude but I don't think it's quite the same.'

She didn't think it was funny at the time but she does now.

We got married on 24 July 1995 at Chelsea registry office and after the wedding, I took Alex to Belfast to meet my family, which was also emotional for them and me because the last time I had taken a wife home, it was in the most awful of circumstances. But Alex is so easy-going and natural that I'd defy anyone not to get on with her. Dad and my brothers and sisters probably didn't know what to expect after Angela, but they took to Alex straight away.

Ashleigh, my sister Grace's child, who was about five and a half at the time, was born with hydrocephalus, or water on the brain, and had to go to a special school. But considering that doctors had said she would never talk or walk, she was doing brilliantly. A taxi took her to school each morning and once a week, she was dropped off at my dad's house on the way home.

We happened to be at Dad's one day when the taxi turned up and I looked out of the window and waved at Ashleigh as she was getting out. She had been told that I was bringing my new wife and when she saw me waving, her face lit up and she came running in. She walked with a bit of a limp and her arm was very stiff but she ran up and gave me this enormous hug.

'I love you, Uncle George,' she said, 'I love you.' Then she looked up at me and said, 'Where's Alex?'

She's behind you,' I said. 'You ran right past her.' She turned round and saw Alex and gave her a big smile before running up and hugging her and saying, 'I love you, too, Alex. I love you.'

And Alex just couldn't hold back the tears.

Ashleigh was the greatest little kid you ever met, always happy, always smiling, never complaining. It always seems to be that way with kids who are born with problems like that. It broke my heart to see her in that condition and it was one of the things that made me wonder about whether there was a God or some supreme being because it seemed so unfair.

Why should Ashleigh be the way she is when you have all these nutters in the world living perfectly healthy lives? Why a little girl who's never brought anything but happiness to anyone? There is no logic in that for me. I guess it made me reconsider some of the blessings I have had in my own life, and how randomly such gifts are given to people. I have often felt burdened by the way my life turned out and wished that I could have done things differently. But Ashleigh's courage made me reconsider this and I was humbled by her warmth and optimism.

A year later, Grace phoned to tell me that Ashleigh had died after a seizure. Her funeral was set for 22 May 1996, my 50th birthday and a day on which I was already committed to appearing on BBC television.

BBC 2 devoted their whole evening schedule to me, six programmes in all, and I was due to appear live in one. It was almost impossible to get out of that and, as it turned out, Grace and the rest of the family were quite relieved when I told them I couldn't go to the funeral because they knew what sort of circus to expect if I turned up. They wanted it to be little Ashleigh's day and after the life she'd had, she deserved to be put to rest with dignity. If I'd been able to go, I wouldn't have allowed the media to stop me but it would have been hard on the family, who were not used to it.

It didn't leave me in much of a party mood, though. I went home for a nightcap and a little cry.

As we settled into married life, Alex began looking after the accounts and collecting money from after-dinner speeches, while Phil made the bookings, taking over from Mary. Knowing my weaknesses, Alex began to keep an even tighter grip on the purse strings than Mary, getting my money into the bank before I could blow it in the casino. We'd had a few skirmishes over my drinking and gambling and in September 1996, after a particularly bad row, I stormed out of the flat and started on a three-day bender. I had a couple of speaking engagements in the diary but once I started drinking, I didn't give them a thought. In that situation, if you've got a drink problem, nothing else counts in your life. You surrender all normal rationales and reasoning.

Consequently, I didn't turn up for the Sky show, either, locked into a session which had taken priority over everything.

People always ask, 'How could you stay out drinking when you had a living to earn?' but that is introducing logic to the argument. Alcoholics don't operate on logic or reason, they work on impulse and once a drinking session has started, it has to run its course, regardless of any other demands on your time which any normal person would react to.

When I finally got back home, there was no sign of Alex or any of her things. I phoned her parents' house, where I guessed, correctly, that she had gone. But when her mum said that Alex wasn't there, I left a message for her to phone me and a few days later, she got hold of me at the Phene Arms. I told her how much I missed her and begged her to come back.

'Well, if I do,' she said, 'will you stop behaving like this?' and of course, I said yes. Alcoholics will always take the line of expediency, telling loved ones what they want to hear. And at that precise moment, I probably believed my lies myself.

The marriage rollercoaster continued, and after she moved back in, one day in April 1997, after a particularly bad row, I did a money hunt around the house and rustled up £300, with which I set off to the Palm Beach casino. I was in a self-destructive mood, seeming almost to want to lose all the money to punish Alex, and began playing two roulette tables at once, spreading the chips all over the place.

Hardly surprisingly, it wasn't long before I was down to my last chip but I got a winning spin with that and then my luck started to change, just as it had in Soames in Manchester all those years earlier. I'd only been playing with £25 chips (only!) but as I started to win, the croupier was giving me bigger and bigger denominations. I ended up with single chips worth £1,000 but as I had now won £11,000, I decided to call it a night. At least as far as the gambling was concerned.

I stuffed all the chips into my pockets and wandered off to the Dover Street Wine Bar for a few nightcaps, arriving home around three or four in the morning.

I thought the coast would have been clear by then but Alex was waiting up for me.

'Where the hell have you been?' she said as soon as I walked in, 'as if I don't know. You've been gambling, I presume?'

'Yes, if it's any business of yours,' I said. 'I've been to the casino gambling with *my* money, the money I earn from all those dinners.'

'How much have you lost?' she said.

I smirked at her and said, 'As it happens, I've done quite well' and began fumbling around in my pockets, pulling out all these different coloured chips.

Chips, mind, not cash or a cheque.

Her mouth dropped open as they piled up on the lounge table and she started to count them.

'Bloody hell, George,' she said, when she'd finished, 'there's over £11,000 here. Why didn't you cash them in?'

Then, knowing my habit of reinvesting gambling winnings – which was the way I saw it – and having been trying to get together enough cash to redecorate the flat, she said, 'Don't go and blow this all back, George. We can really do with this money.'

She was obviously determined that I wasn't going to blow it all because the following day, when we'd made up and I was about to slip out and take on the casino again, she was ready and waiting and insisted on accompanying me back to the Palm Beach. And after I'd lost a grand back to the casino, she persuaded me to cash up and go home.

Towards the end of 1997 and early 1998, I was growing increasingly depressed.

A court case over the ownership of the Oakley Street flat was due to be heard in May 1998 and the thought of losing it was getting me down. It wasn't just that it was my home. It was that it had come to represent everything I was worth. If I lost it, what had I achieved in life? What did I have? Perversely, I was drinking more to try to forget about it, which was causing more rows than usual with Alex, and that in turn would result in me hitting the booze even harder.

It was the classic vicious circle. On one occasion, we were coming home from Alex's parents in Cheam when we began having a row in the car and she just skidded to a halt on a country road, opened the door and pushed me out.

'How am I supposed to get back to Chelsea from here?' I said. 'We're in the middle of nowhere and I've only got a tenner on me.'

'Good' was all she said – and with that she sped off.

It was about midnight by this time and a cold night and as I started walking, not knowing which direction I was headed in, there was hardly a light to be seen. After about twenty minutes, I saw some lights in a building ahead of me and when I reached them, I saw that it was a pub.

I tried the door, which was locked, and when I looked through the window and saw that there were people inside drinking, someone just shouted out 'Private party, mate.'

So I shuffled off again when I heard the pub door unlocking.

'We didn't realise it was you, George,' a guy said. 'Come in and have a drink, mate.'

So I went in and someone bought me a glass of wine and then another.

'Any chance of getting a cab?' I said.

No problem,' they said and after another glass of wine, a cab pulled up outside.

I got in and told him where I was going and I let him get a good few miles down the road before, fingering my tenner, I asked, 'How much does the fare to Chelsea work out?'

I didn't want to tell him I might not have enough to pay him until we were much closer to London.

'Well, normally it works out around £20,' he said. 'Is that all right?'

'Well, not really,' I said, 'because I've only got a tenner on me.'

He went quiet for a second and then said, 'No, I said it's *normally* twenty quid but for you, it's free.'

So thanks to the kindness of strangers I'd had a good night that ended well. Not only did I manage to get home on my own, but I'd also enjoyed a few glasses of wine – and still had my tenner.

Not all my rows with Alex ended as happily. Another time, after a couple of days of drinking at various haunts, I staggered into my local, the Phene Arms, a small corner pub tucked away just behind Cheyne Walk. It's a cosy little place with flock wallpaper and a circular bar and is full of locals from all walks of life, from actors to firemen.

As I slumped into my normal corner seat, I saw another of

the regulars, who was a locksmith.

'You're just the man I'm looking for,' I said. 'I've got a job for you.'

'What's that, George?' he said.

I handed him my house keys and said, 'I want you to go round to my flat and change the locks because Alex and I have split up.'

He looked a bit embarrassed because he knew Alex and knew that we were always breaking up and getting back together again. But he went round to my place and was just starting on the locks when Alex walked in.

'What the hell do you think you're up to?' she said.

'George told me he wanted the locks changing', he said, but as you can imagine, she sent him off with a flea in his ear.

We made up as usual. But though, when we did so, we both said that we loved one another and she insisted that she was totally happy, I wasn't convinced that she was. She was so much younger than me, after all, and I suppose I might also have been frightened that she might one day go off with a younger man.

Also, when we were getting on well and spending all our time together, I sometimes felt stifled. I've always told every woman I've lived with, 'Look, there are times when I just want to go off on my own for a few days', which I suppose is how everyone feels in a relationship. I had said the same thing to Alex early on and she said she understood but if I ever suggested going off to Amsterdam for a weekend on my own, she went nuts.

I used to love going to Amsterdam, not because I wanted to pay for a woman or smoke dope. I just loved sitting in the old square having a couple of beers and watching the world go by. I have always been that way. Maybe 'loner' is too strong a word but I've always enjoyed being on my own and I can be on my own in a crowded room. I can just sit there quietly and am perfectly happy.

In fact, one of my ex-girlfriends once said to me, 'We had some wonderful silences together.'

Alex and I can sit and talk about most things but I couldn't tell her what was really worrying me – that she might leave me. I suppose I thought it would make me sound weak. The prospect of another failed marriage was just too much to contemplate. Life just didn't seem worth living at times.

The New Year of 1998 did not seem to bring any respite to what I saw as my problems. If anything, I felt my life situation was more hopeless than ever because I didn't think Alex and I would last as a couple and I was worried that I could lose my flat. I might have been great at coping with pressure on the field but I've clearly never been able to handle it in normal life and I've never liked confrontation. In the past, I had simply run away from those situations and tried to sort them out when I got home, but this time I decided to take the ultimate way out. I couldn't talk to Alex about my greatest fears about our relationship. But as I drank more and more, the answer came to me.

I would run away and top myself.

Once I'd made the decision, it seemed not just like the perfect solution for all concerned but the obvious one and as I started planning it in my mind, I was almost looking forward to it. I would lie awake for hours at night plotting the exact details, which shows you what a state I was in. There I was, lying next to this beautiful young woman, who was my wife, and I was plotting to kill myself.

I'd had enough of people telling me what to do, to stay off the drink, to look after myself properly, to do this and that, so I decided that I would have one last month of doing all the things I loved and then just put an end to my life. I've always liked the sun so I decided I would fly to somewhere hot, with a lovely beach and eventually settled on the Bahamas.

I was planning to take a nice lump sum out of the bank and book into a luxury hotel, preferably on the beach, and spend four weeks eating my favourite food and doing all the wrong things. Women didn't come into my plan, I just planned to sit around the pool or on the beach, eating whatever took my fancy and knocking back all my favourite drinks – beer, wine, vodka, champagne, brandy.

In my mind, I suppose I saw it a bit like my trip to Spain back in 1972, when I'd first announced my retirement, just getting up when I felt like it, having a drink when I felt like it, eating whenever I wanted to. And just having no one to bother me, no one to tell me that I shouldn't be doing this, shouldn't be doing that.

And at the end of the four weeks, I would say to myself, 'Well, I've had a nice month' and then go to my room with a bottle of champagne and some strong pills and put an end to it all. I even thought about which pills would be best for the job and how many I would need, though I reckoned that a bottle of Nurofen or some similarly strong painkillers would do the job. But then I thought to myself, maybe I won't be able to get the pills because people might realise what I'm planning.

So I decided on plan B, which was to go to my room at the end of the last day of my perfect month and sit in the bath, Roman style, and slit my wrists. That was an option that would be a lot more bloody and a lot harder to do but I reasoned that after a couple of bottles of champagne, washed down by a bottle of Louis XIII brandy, I wouldn't feel a thing.

I had spent weeks thinking about suicide up to that point and I believed I had it planned to perfection. But I kept imagining what my body would look like to the person who found me and what affect it would have on them. And I started thinking, 'How can I put someone through that?'

Before I could find a satisfactory answer, events took a dramatic turn.

CHAPTER SEVENTEEN
FIGHTING
BACK

At the start of 1998 I had reached the lowest point I think I have ever been. The thought of losing my home made me feel like such a failure, that I had almost nothing to show for all that I had done in my life. I felt pathetic and even considered just giving up and ending it all. It's difficult to describe my feelings but my mind was all of a jumble. I had been going on benders to escape from all the hassles in my life.

But when the case finally came to court in May 1998, it didn't turn out half as badly as I had feared. My fortunes had changed so dramatically within a matter of hours that the relief was incredible. I can honestly say that I felt a huge weight had been lifted. I put all my depressed thoughts to one side and began looking to the future with renewed optimism.

Alex and I moved to another flat almost immediately in Cheyne Walk, a few hundred yards from the Oakley Street premises. The only difference from my point of view was that, to get to the Phene, I had to remember to turn right when I stepped out of my front door, instead of left.

It wasn't just the flat business that had made me so depressed. It was everything – especially my relationship with Alex, which had been under a lot of strain, partly because of my insecurity as I was still not sure that a young girl like her would want to stay with me for long. I felt under the weather a lot of days too and my right leg, which is never great at the best of times, often caused me pain.

But after the court case it was like a big black cloud had lifted and my mood seemed to change with it. I am a great believer in the expression that things often look better in the morning and if I had any more nights thinking about the possibility of ending it all, I would wake the next day, chiding myself and saying, 'What was all that about?'

Eventually, I stopped thinking about suicide altogether. I felt more confident about the future, particularly after finding a new home, and life in general was looking up again. Alex and I were more settled, the work was pouring in, including a sell-out show in Ireland entitled 'An Evening with George Best'. And offers were coming in from the oddest sources.

Soon after the court case, during one of my frequent visits to Henlow Grange health farm, I was interrupted by a call from

Phil who said, 'How do you fancy opening a new betting shop for Victor Chandler?'

Chandler owns one of the biggest bookmaking empires so I knew it would be a classy occasion.

'That's fine, Phil,' I said. 'Where is it?'

'Hong Kong,' he replied.

So Alex and I jetted off first class and found ourselves booked into the Peninsular Hotel, which is one of the best in the world. Our suite was fantastic, with a jacuzzi overlooking the water and two mini-bars, which is what I call luxury. Yet the place also reminded me of my mad house in Bramhall in Manchester since there were buttons to open and close the curtains electronically.

I discovered that I would not be opening a betting shop in the traditional sense, after all, since they are illegal in Hong Kong. I was there to launch a betting *service*, which entailed punters phoning a Chandler number in Gibraltar to place a bet, thus presumably spending a fiver on the call before even beginning to gamble away any money.

It sounded crazy to me but we had a fantastic lunch in the Shangri-La restaurant, where we were served live prawns, which were rendered comatose by being doused in champagne.

After this, I was told that the audience were ready for my speech. I looked up and saw 250 sets of oriental eyes and I panicked.

'I can't speak to this lot,' I said. 'I have enough trouble with my Belfast accent in England!'

Fortunately, they had an interpreter so I just spoke for a few minutes about my football career, wished the venture well and sat down again.

It wasn't your everyday speaking engagement but jobs like that were becoming commonplace, flying to the other side of the world for a few minutes' work. I even got invited to Sydney, Australia, for a 'Celeb behind the bar' night, which was a neat bit of typecasting and required me to stand behind a bar talking to punters for an hour. All nice work if you could get it.

At 52 years of age, with a new wife and a regular income, I ought to have been living a quiet and settled life. But even now, I was managing to get into the sort of scrapes that you normally associate with teenagers. I am sorry to say that one of them, in September 1998, was witnessed by Calum, then 17.

Calum was on his usual annual summer visit to stay with me when we popped into the Phene one Sunday lunchtime. He only has the occasional pint and was drinking Coke that day when a van screeched to a halt outside and a dozen blokes jumped out and burst in, immediately setting about me with their fists. I shouted to Calum to get out of the way and began fighting them back, with a few of the locals piling in. Then, just as quickly as they'd rushed in, my attackers all rushed out again and sped off in the van. Fortunately, Calum was unhurt, though when I pulled my shirt up, I discovered a kaleidoscope of bruises.

'What was that all about?' Calum said, when we'd got our breath back.

'I guess they don't like losing at pool,' I replied.

I explained that, a few nights earlier, a pal and I had been playing pool for money against some of my attackers and it had turned a bit nasty when we kept on winning. Following the attack on me I never even bothered getting the police involved.

It was just another normal day in my chaotic life.

Calum had got into the habit of coming over to stay with me for three or four weeks every summer, which I really looked forward to. He'd grown into a real, strapping lad and a good footballer, probably good enough to make it as a professional from what I've seen of him. But in California, the schoolkids only play soccer, as they call it, for a few months in the summer and the coaching, as I discovered in my time there, is hopeless.

He did tell me once that he wanted to come over and play for Manchester United, but to reach that level he would have needed to have started playing here when he was eight or nine, which was just when his mother had taken him back to America.

I did once ask Sir Alex Ferguson to look at him but Calum

never played in England and it didn't happen. Nowadays, he is more interested in modelling.

It may sound hypocritical after the way I've led my life, but I also make sure that Calum doesn't drink too much when he's with me. If we go out for a meal, I'm quite happy for him to have a glass of wine but when he goes out with his friends, I tell him to limit himself to a couple of beers. I'm pleased to say that, like me as a teenager, he is more interested in girls than drink. And a good-looking, tanned, athletic, 6ft 3in Californian lad doesn't lack for female company when he's in England.

It's strange, however, to find myself playing the concerned dad for the first time in my life. One night, after he'd gone out to a nightclub, I was lying awake in bed, wondering where he'd got to, and constantly checking the time. It was three o'clock in the morning when I heard his key in the door and turned over to go to sleep. But then I heard him chatting on the phone to some girl. He was talking all lovey dovey and it went on for half an hour.

Eventually, I climbed out of bed and walked out of the bedroom.

'Calum,' I shouted, 'we're trying to get to sleep. So get off that phone.'

He made his excuses to the girl and hung up and as he went to bed, he shouted, 'Dad, do you know something? You're becoming a right boring old fart!'

That was a first.

We've also spoken about his upbringing and whether he felt that he missed out because he lived with only one parent. But he understands that his mum and I didn't get on and that I had lots of problems to deal with. He's also got plenty of friends in California from broken marriages. Considering all the potential headaches, including having a dad who is always making headlines, my relationship with Calum has worked out better than I could have imagined.

That year, 1999, I took Calum to a game at Old Trafford. At the time Manchester United were in the middle of what was to become the most momentous season in their history. And in the fifth round of the FA Cup, as coincidence would have it, United were drawn against Fulham. A coincidence because I had been seeing quite a lot of Fulham since they had been taken over by Mohammed Al-Fayed. He is also the owner of *Punch* magazine, in which I had been writing a column since August 1997.

The first time I went to a game at Craven Cottage as his guest was hilarious. We had a fantastic meal and plenty of drinks beforehand but it was a chilly evening so when we went up to the directors' box to watch the game, I was thinking that Mohammed, who was only wearing a suit, would get pretty cold. But no sooner had he taken his seat in the box than this assistant came sprinting up the stairs with half a dozen over-coats over his arm. It was as if Mohammed was back in his

Harrods store as he tried on a few of the coats, the helper saying, 'I think the brown one would suit sir best tonight.'

For the FA Cup tie at Old Trafford, Mohammed invited me to fly in his private plane with him. There was only one problem with this – the match was on Valentine's Day and because he travels with so many minders, there was no room in the plane for Alex.

She wasn't best pleased when I first told her, but I suggested that she fly separately and meet me at Manchester Airport, so that we could go to the game together and stay at my favourite hotel, the Midland. Being a young romantic herself, Alex also cooked a special meal the night before, and even managed to get some heart-shaped candles for the table.

Before I left the following morning, she gave me a Valentine's card and looked a little miffed, not to mention surprised, when I didn't hand her one in return. She said, 'Haven't you got anything for me?'

'Of course,' I said, 'but wait till we meet up in Manchester.' I had already arranged for a dozen red roses, champagne, chocolates and perfumes to be delivered to our suite at the Midland Hotel, planning to take Alex there before the game.

Sadly, the flights were late and by the time we met at Manchester Airport, there was no time to go to the hotel. We had to go straight to the game. In the taxi there, she said, now a little irritated, 'So where's my card, darling?'

'To be honest with you,' I said, not wanting to spoil the surprise, 'I've been that busy that I just didn't get round to it.'

'I don't believe you!' she said. 'After me cooking that meal and everything?'

She carried on sulking throughout the afternoon but after the match we'd planned an early meal in Chinatown, which meant that we'd still get back to the hotel in time for her to enjoy the flowers and champagne. But everywhere in Chinatown was packed and after forty minutes waiting for a table, we went back to the Midland. As we were starving by now and the French restaurant in the hotel had a table, we sat down to eat without going to our room first. I wasn't going to give the surprise away at that stage but every now and again, Alex would say, 'I can't believe you didn't get me anything.'

Anyway, we finally finished a wonderful meal and retired to our suite. There was no sign of the deliveries in the bedroom when we went in, so I said to Alex, 'Could you pop into the living room and get me a Perrier, please darling?'

I was expecting to hear her squeal a few seconds later as she saw the flowers and the rest before running back in, throwing her arms around me and saying, 'Darling, you *did* remember' and the day would end on a romantic note. But nothing.

Instead, she walked back in with the Perrier and said, offhandedly, 'Someone's delivered some champagne and roses to the room.'

I said, 'Yes, me. Who do you think had them delivered?'

'Well, anyone but you,' she said. 'You were too busy even to get me a card.'

'That was just to wind you up,' I said, 'so that I could make it a big surprise.' But she wouldn't have it. I had done such a good job convincing her that I hadn't had time to buy her anything that I couldn't change her mind!

United beat Fulham 1–0 on their way to winning the FA Cup, strolling to a 2–0 victory over Newcastle at Wembley. They also reclaimed the Premiership title they had lost to Arsenal the previous season, pipping them by a point to make it a League and Cup domestic double. But the greatest excitement revolved around their success in Europe, where they had reached the Final of the European Champions League for the first time since our team won it in 1968.

There was no way I was going to miss that Final, against Bayern Munich in Barcelona's Nou Camp Stadium. What a great setting for a Final of that stature. The Nou Camp is one of the most atmospheric stadiums in the world and there was a record crowd of 90,000 on the evening of 26 May 1999. I got goosebumps just sitting in the stands with Phil and imagined running out on a night like that. The other great nights in my career flashed through my mind as the teams came out to thunderous applause. But Manchester United looked tired after their long season and went behind in the sixth minute to a goal scored by Basler. I expected United to buck their ideas up after that but the Germans continued to dominate the game and hit the woodwork twice towards the end.

There seemed no way back for United so with a minute or so to go, I nudged Phil and said, 'Come on, let's get out and beat the rush.' We had a car outside waiting to take us back to our villa-hotel, which was only a few hundred yards up the road. The driver was listening to the radio commentary and just as we leaped into our seats, Teddy Sheringham hit the equaliser for United. And even before we had reached the hotel, Ole Gunnar Solskjaer had scored United's winner.

It was unbelievable stuff and we jumped out of the car and ran in to the hotel to watch the re-runs of the goals. It was a choker to miss such a dramatic finish but Phil and I took a magnum of champagne to our villa and watched the entire game on the box again. And we must have seen the goals about a thousand times.

Some people suggested that I would be upset if United won the Champions League because it would mean that my team mates and I from 1968 would no longer have the distinction of being the only ones from Old Trafford to do so. But that's nonsense. We're all United nuts and want the side to win everything. And it doesn't matter if the club wins the European Cup a million times. We were the first United team to win it and no matter what anyone says, they can't take that away from us.

I think there is also still a lot of nostalgia surrounding our side because of the style in which we played, though I have to say that Sir Alex Ferguson's team is the best in the club's history. That honour has to go to them because of all the trophies they have won and because of outstanding players such as David Beckham, Paul Scholes and Jaap Stam.

But it will be fascinating to see what happens when Sir Alex retires as manager. It will be a similar situation to 1969 when Sir Matt quit as manager and you have to wonder whether the club will handle such a big retirement any better this time.

It will also be interesting to see if it leads to a mass exodus of star players.

After all the upsets of the previous few years, I was probably too content towards the end of 1999 and I began drinking more than ever. I was also putting on weight, partly because I wasn't eating properly. It led to an embarrassing night at the prestigious Northern Football Writers' dinner in Manchester in October.

I've had my problems with the press but the football writers have always been good to me and I was happy to accept an invitation as their guest speaker. To make sure I was on top form, I didn't even have a drink on the train going up. In fact, I slept for most of the way. But I had a few at the reception beforehand and then started on the wine when I sat down for dinner.

I suppose I had been knocking it back so much over the previous weeks that it was just a question of topping up. And the waiter, though I'm not blaming him, made sure my glass was full all the time.

I still thought I was OK when I got up to speak, which was a good three hours after we'd first sat down. But it was obvious to everyone else that I was gone, especially when my first words were, 'Where's my fucking drink?' Anyone who knows me will tell you that I'm not much of a swearer and it's something I would never do in public when I'm sober. I feel mortified just thinking about what I must have said.

I only managed a few more minutes when one of the organisers tugged on my sleeve, and said, 'Great job, George, you can sit down now.' I walked straight out and off to my room, leaving an embarrassed Alex to sort things out. It wasn't until I sobered up the following day that I realised what a fool I'd made of myself. And naturally, it was all over the papers. Phil, who I'd finally taken on as my official agent, was inundated with calls the following day.

A month later, for my father's 80th birthday, my sisters Carol and Barbara arranged a surprise party at a plush restaurant in Holywood, just outside Belfast. My dad guessed that they would organise something for him but knowing all the bashes that I had missed over the years, he didn't expect me to show up. To throw him off the scent completely, I phoned him a few days before his birthday to ask him how he was going to celebrate it.

'Oh, I think the girls have arranged a lunch or something,' he said.

So I made sure I arrived there early – which was a first – and was at the bar getting a drink for Ian when my dad came in. I ducked behind the bar and let my sisters find him a chair. Then I shouted across, 'Excuse me, Mr Best, would you like a drink before your meal?' He looked across, startled, not believing that he had really heard my voice, and when he caught my eye, his face was a picture.

It was the start of a fantastic day. But when I was about to leave, Carol pulled me aside and said, 'Are you looking after yourself, George?'

'Of course I am,' I said.

But according to her, I was well out of it, although as usual I would probably have been the last to see that.

I had started to feel increasingly poorly by the end of '99 and had begun getting pains in my stomach, which I put down to my poor diet. Rather than going to the doctors I helped myself to a brandy cure. I thought any illness was just the result of my heavy work schedule, all the dinners and the TV work. But when I wasn't working, I was spending more and more time in the Phene.

I know this may sound ridiculous but it didn't cross my mind that the drink was doing me any physical damage – well, not of a life-threatening kind. Anyway, in my head, even when it was as clear as day to everyone else, I did not believe that I had a major drink problem – and one that could kill me. You could say that once again I was unable to see what was staring me in the face.

I was, however, determined to be on my best behaviour for a tribute dinner in my honour in January 2000, organised by the Football Writers Association. They had been planning the event for almost a year and after my less than impressive effort in Manchester, they were extremely nervous about the evening. But this time I made sure I kept a close eye on how much wine I was drinking. I wanted it to be a successful night and I didn't want to embarrass my dad, who made his first trip to England for five years to be there.

It turned out to be a great night and I got a standing ovation from the writers, as much out of relief that I had not spoiled things as much as appreciation of my oratory. I was really touched by their kindness.

It made me feel great, emotionally, but physically, I was becoming more and more run down. I didn't realise it but I was on a real downward spiral, healthwise. Alex had started to notice it but if she mentioned anything to me, I just brushed it off. I told her it was nothing and that when the work eased off, we'd have a week in a health farm, which would restore me to normal.

Little did I know that I was not to feel normal again. And

this 'under the weather' feeling, as I described it to anyone who queried my health, ended up as suspected liver failure.

CHAPTER EIGHTEEN
A SUITABLE CASE FOR TREATMENT

The first morning I spent in the Liver Unit at the Cromwell Hospital in February 2000, I was mystified to receive a get-well card signed by about 15 people, which arrived in an envelope without an address or a stamp on it.

I couldn't work out how it had got to me or who had sent it until I recognised a couple of the signatures as being those of Everton players (keep working on the joined-up writing lads). This still didn't make any sense until I picked up a paper and saw that they were playing at Chelsea that weekend and realised that they must have been staying at the Swallow Hotel across the road. It was lovely to think that they had taken the time to do that and, as you can imagine, it was the start of an avalanche of cards and flowers from all over the world.

We got so many flowers and potted plants that my room quickly became full and Alex had to keep taking them home. There were get-well messages from Meg and Noel Gallagher, Jilly Johnson and my old showbiz pals Kenny Lynch, Tarby and Michael Parkinson. Plus, of course, thousands of cards and flowers from ordinary fans.

I've always been amazed at the number of letters I still – and continually – get from people, all these years after finishing my playing career. Sometimes they are addressed: 'George Best, Chelsea, England' and they get to me. Some of these letters are not even from football supporters – they're just from people who seem to want to wish me well. The most surprising bouquet of flowers, though, came from Tottenham footballer John Scales. Another nice gesture from one player to another, you might think, except for his previous relationship with Alex. I didn't know whether he was being kind or taking the mickey but decided to give him the benefit of the doubt!

Naturally, on this occasion I also got plenty of letters and notes from newspapers offering telephone number sums to tell my story and Alex was getting others pushed through our letterbox too. We tried to stem the calls coming into the room by using Alex's maiden name – Pursey – so that only our real friends could get through. As far as the papers went, we knew from past experience that it's better to join them – you can never beat them – so I agreed to talk to a couple of them. I also allowed them to take some pictures as part of the deal, although they were hardly the most flattering ever taken of me and certainly not shots I would want on my bedroom wall!

Slowly, I settled into the routine of hospital life, which was a lot more hectic than I could have imagined it. It was like Waterloo Station most of the time, with people constantly popping in with menus, bottles of water or to change my drip. They seemed to change it so regularly that after a few days I had arms like a junkie's and they were struggling to find a vein in which to insert it. I couldn't get out of bed in those first few days so my only use for a bottle now was for what came naturally. And that was quite frequent since I was now drinking water in the same quantities that I had been drinking alcohol – by the bucketload. I had to keep drinking it to flush out my system and to reduce the jaundice, though I was amused when I heard Bob Monkhouse's crack that I was being lined up for a part in *The Simpsons* when I got out.

My old pal and former team mate and fellow Sky regular Rodney Marsh popped in to see me, which was touching because I knew that, at the time, he was wrapped up in a court case involving a driving offence. Sky TV were brilliant, telling me not to even think about trying to go back on until the following season. In the meantime, Alan Mullery, who lives near to my in-laws in Cheam, where we've bumped into each other once or twice, stood in for me as usual.

My son Calum phoned from California and so did his mother, my ex-wife Angie.

Best of all, of course, was the arrival of my father from Belfast. It must have been difficult for him to see me in that condition, particularly after what he went through with my mum. When I was taken into the Cromwell, I was just a few days short of my 54th birthday, the same age as Mum when she died. But Dad is just my dad – he never changes and is never judgmental. And the lovely thing about him is that we're so close, we can just sit in a room together and not speak for hours but we both appreciate the other's company. Both know there is a mutual respect. So just having him sit at the end of my bed was fantastic. Naturally, we talked, we talked a lot, but we are not the sort of people who feel that we have to fill every break in a conversation with empty words.

Mostly, my daily visitors were Alex and Phil and we would sit around like we used to at home or in the Phene, doing the crossword together and at times competing against each other over the answers. In the afternoons we'd watch the normal quiz shows we watched at home – *Fifteen to One* and *Countdown*, both of which I love – and I had also received a get well card from William G. Stewart, *Fifteen to One*'s presenter.

Being a private hospital, I was a bit miffed that we seemed only to have the five terrestrial channels so I said to Phil, 'Are you sure we can't get Sky on that?' He fiddled about for a bit and then Alex had a go but we couldn't find any other stations.

None of us is what you would call an electronic wizard. Eventually, bored at being unable to watch all the big football games, I said to a nurse, 'Do you think that the hospital would mind if I get my pals from Sky to put a dish up on the wall outside my room?'

'Why, what's wrong with it now?' she replied and to my embarrassment, picked up the remote control and pressed a button which turned it to Sky. This was about a fortnight into my stay.

Most people tend to lose weight in hospital because the food is so bad and they may not have much appetite when they are ill. But I could hardly lose any more weight and having hardly eaten for weeks, I was down to about seven and a half stones. As the pain in my stomach started to ease, I began making up for lost time. It helped that the Cromwell had a pretty good menu, better than some places I've eaten in in my time. And it helped even more that I've got a lot of friends in the restaurant trade who, like most creative people, have a lively imagination.

I was delighted when Michel, the maître d' from Scalini's restaurant in Walton Street, London, walked in one day, carrying a big bag. I knew he hadn't brought the traditional hospital gift of grapes or flowers since there appeared to be something moving in the bag. He'd brought me a couple of lobsters, which he proudly displayed before commandeering the kitchen to cook them for me.

A friend at Casa Carlo, a restaurant in which I have a financial interest, brought me a T-bone steak and Alex would also turn up with home-made fare. I was not allowed anything cooked in salt though, nor anything spicy, which for some reason also included baked beans, to which I've always been partial. Fortunately, there was no ban on chocolate or ice lollies, for which I've never lost my taste but for which I now had an unbelievable craving.

I developed a particular liking for Calypo lollies, though Phil and Alex would scour the shops looking for different makes and flavours that I might like and I would be as excited as a child when they brought them in. I also started eating wine gums, possibly on the off chance that they might actually contain wine.

One day, I went through a pack of them while watching a movie but saved all the black ones for a treat at the end, which I had last done when I was about six. I collected them all under the sheet and was just cramming them into my mouth when, to my embarrassment, a nurse walked in and caught me in the act. If she had been a psychiatrist, she might have noted this incident as proof of my obsessive nature.

Anyone who has been in hospital for any length of time will know that you need these little treats to keep you going. As I started to improve, the highlight of my day became taking my drip, stand and all, on a 100 yard walk to the coffee shop down the corridor from my room.

On good days, I would even take the lift up to the roof garden and watch London going about its business. After a while, however, you can't help but get restless and a bit depressed. I was ticking off the days at first but then it turned into weeks and I wasn't seeming to make any progress with my blood count, which would determine when I got out. Until it became appreciably higher, Professor Williams was not willing to risk letting me go until my platelets had built up.

These are the smallest type of blood cells and a deficiency of them, known as thrombocytopenia, can result in you bleeding to death from the smallest of cuts. That explained my problem when I scratched that spot on my leg before I was admitted.

To cheer ourselves up, Alex and I planned various holidays – to Barbados, to Venice, to Monte Carlo, all sorts. But we could never get around to booking any. Pavarotti used to get me through a good few hours, too, as I wasn't able to read for too long because it gave me a headache. My eyes gave off such a bright yellow light that I could almost have read in complete darkness and I did start reading the story of Harold Shipman, a nice cheerful book in my condition, although it at least comforted me that I was in so much better professional hands.

When I was finally discharged from hospital at the end of April 2000, with only a portion of my liver in proper working order, I was finally free of pain but still felt about a hundred years old.

Alex and I had hoped to go on holiday almost as soon as I got out but for the first few weeks, I had to go back to see Professor Williams almost on a daily basis, so that was out of the question. Also, I was so exhausted that I doubt if I could have made it as far as the airport. Just walking a couple of hundred yards down the road to sit outside the pub and drink a coffee tired me out.

We got a little red setter puppy which I called Red because I'd always wanted another dog and now that I was off the booze, I thought I would have plenty of time to take him for long walks. But exercise would have to wait. I spent most of my days just slumped in front of the TV, and most afternoons I would take a siesta.

The Professor warned me that recovery would be a slow process but I didn't expect it to be at such a snail's pace, though at least I had plenty of time to sit and think about how I wanted to spend the rest of my life. The three of us – me, Alex and Phil – had more or less decided that it would be suicidal for me to go back on the after-dinner-speaking circuit because there would be so many temptations to drink. But that would leave a big hole in my diary and my income.

Sky TV said they would take me back as soon as I was ready, which meant I'd have regular money coming in during the football season. But we needed more than that to live on and I had spent a few months' wages buying new clothes when I came out of the Cromwell. I was still a couple of stones beneath my normal weight and the big old tracksuits I used to wear before going in just hung off me.

We also had to sort out somewhere to live because Alex and I had also come to the conclusion that we ought to move out of London. We were already thinking about it when I read an article by Jimmy Greaves, who is a recovering alcoholic himself, in which he said that his move from London to Essex had helped him to give up. I'd always been one to run away from problems but this time it wouldn't be so much running away as making a clean break.

Naturally, you can get a drink wherever you are. You can even go into a supermarket and get a drink these days. But it's a question of escaping from your old haunts, breaking the old pattern of behaviour and trying to build a new life for yourself. The other benefit of moving out of London was that I wouldn't have newspaper reporters permanently camped outside my home, waiting for me to fall off the wagon.

Just before my 54th birthday the Professor gave me permission to go abroad, so Alex and I spent a romantic weekend in Venice. Then in early June 2000, we went off for our usual summer holiday in Corfu, where we stay at a beautiful villa owned by a friend of ours. We had our bags packed, had called a cab to take us to the airport and were just about to close the front door when the phone rang.

We normally have the answerphone on permanently and only pick up the receiver if we hear a familiar voice. So it was weird that I should even think about picking up the phone when we were in a hurry to get out. But something made me walk back inside and pick it up, to hear the voice of Liz Brennan, wife of my old team mate Shay. He had collapsed and died while playing the second hole of the Cortown golf course in Wexford. He was 63.

If the bookies had opened a book on which of our 1968 European Cup winning side would die first, Shay would have been the rank outsider, with me doubtless the odds-on favourite. The timing of that call was also so odd, as I'd just survived eight weeks in hospital after almost drinking myself to death, while Shay had dropped dead on a golf course. They believed he had had a heart attack.

It didn't exactly put me in the holiday mood, especially as the first thing we had to do when we got there was to order some flowers for the funeral. And after a couple of days, I just lay in bed thinking about all the good times I had had with Shay over the years and I just couldn't stop blubbing. I was crying so much that the noise woke Alex.

We all like to think we're hard men but I'm a big softy, really. I'll cry all the way through sad films and I said to Alex, as she turned on the light and saw the state of me, 'I'm a big soft so-and-so, aren't I?'

'Don't be silly, you go for it,' she said, then she turned off the light again and put her arms round me as I finished my tears for my mate Shay. His death got me thinking about life in general, and particularly my own life – how things had changed so much since our glory days at United. The holiday turned out to be a bit of a disaster, anyway, spoiled when I began getting terrible pains in my right leg, which I discovered, when we got home, had been caused by an infection.

Before going away, we had made an offer on a cottage near Alex's parents' house in Cheam, Surrey. We had thought of moving abroad somewhere hot, to Spain, Portugal or even Florida but because I needed to be in England during the football season, we had also been looking in England and the place seemed idyllic. However, we had taken a couple of property brochures with us on holiday and our eyes nearly dropped out when we saw some of the magnificent places you could get in France, some with their own lakes and a few acres of land. And all for the price of a cottage in Surrey. We made our apologies to the owners of the cottage and decided that we'd move to France.

Before taking any further steps, we went to pay our condolences to Liz, though she soon had us laughing with her stories about the big fella. Shay was a typical Irishman, who loved the simple things in life. As long as he had a pound or two in his pocket, everything was right with the world. He loved a pint, he loved a smoke and he loved a bet. He wasn't a massive gambler but he studied the horses and Liz, being the careful one, made sure that he didn't fritter away the nest egg they had returned to Ireland with by putting it away and doling out fifty quid a day pocket money to him. Shay would take the paper to the pub with him at lunchtime and study the form, while sipping a pint or two and occasionally lighting up one of his little cigars. Then he would go to the bookies to put on his bets.

He also joined the local golf club and Liz was delighted that he was keeping himself in trim, thinking when he left home that he was off to play another 18 holes. But when she went to the club to collect his things after his death and mentioned to the secretary how keen Shay had been on the game, he said, 'Well, he could have fooled us, Mrs Brennan. We hardly ever saw him on the course.'

Apparently, Shay would turn up most days and only play a couple of holes before retiring to the club house, so it was amazing that he should actually die with a club in his hand, rather than a pint glass. The secretary took Liz to Shay's locker and when they opened it, there was a battered shoe box inside.

'My jaw dropped open when we opened it,' Liz told us, 'because it was stuffed to the top with money. And not just Irish punts and English fivers but notes from all round the world, German marks, francs, pesetas, kroner.'

When they added it all up, it came to a considerable sum, and Liz never did discover where it came from.

Professor Williams was pleased with my progress but in the middle of July, I stormed out of our flat after a row with Alex and went straight to my old local, the Phene.

Funnily, enough, I wasn't craving a drink at that point, just ordering a coffee. But as I drank it, one of the regulars tipped me off that the landlord had phoned the press to tell them I was there. So I walked out in a huff and wandered off to the Dover Street Wine Bar, which is owned by a friend of mine, whose name is also George.

He gave me a warm welcome, asked me how my health was and said, 'What are you having?'

'Bottle of champagne,' I said instinctively.

I had not come out with the intention of drinking but maybe, in the back of my mind, I saw it as a way of hurting Alex. Professor Williams had made it clear to me that I could not drink again, saying, 'It's not a question of easing up, George. Just one more drink could kill you.' Alex was told this too and I knew she would be frantic if she discovered I was drinking again after all the time she had spent looking after me and trying to get me off it.

I had abandoned any thoughts of suicide years before, but when I went out that day, I really didn't care what happened to me. And after all I'd put away, how could a single drink kill me?

For the first time, the champagne didn't even taste nice. It tasted like crap, actually, and having been off it so long, I was tiddly after a couple of glasses. So I decided to take the rest of the bottle home to Alex as a peace offering, which seemed like a good idea at the time. But wandering round the streets of

Chelsea for a couple of hours clutching a bottle of champagne wasn't the best move I ever made, especially with half of the country's press just waiting for that picture.

By the time I staggered home, dawn was coming up and I went and sat on a park bench overlooking the river, just to be on my own with my thoughts. Then, after a while, I got up and went home and as soon as I walked in, Alex ran over and snatched the bottle from me.

'How could you be so stupid, George?' she said, waving the bottle in front of my face. 'How many of these have you had?'

'Six' I said, and toddled off to bed.

The press made a meal of it, of course, and totally exaggerated the story, reporting that a park ranger had found me asleep on that park bench, which was a complete lie. And one paper printed a mock-up wanted poster with my face on it which they urged pub landlords to stick on their walls as a reminder not to serve me.

As if that would have made any difference. If I wanted a drink, no one was going to stop me, not my wife, not my family and certainly not the press. They had hounded me for years and I had learned that they would print whatever they wanted anyway, so I certainly wasn't going to be lectured by them. I felt pretty silly afterwards but I'm an impulsive person and I knew that I couldn't be sure I would stay off it. When those demons get into my head, I can't fight them.

Alex and I quickly made up. We are probably like most married couples. We get on brilliantly for most of the time but now and again one of us will take offence over something trivial and it will be blown out of all proportion. It doesn't help that we both have a temper, once we're roused, and we're both stubborn. So instead of one of us acting as peacemaker, we both dig our heels in and a tiny incident turns into World War Three. Then, when we make up, we're like first time lovers again.

When Alex and I fell out again in August, I flew to Belfast to see Dad and the rest of the family. When they asked me where Alex was, I said, 'It's over. We're getting divorced.'

I had this weird idea in my head that I was going go do a permanent disappearing act so I got my sister, Barbara, to take me to see one of those luxury caravan homes on the beach in County Down. I had this idea that I would buy one and hide away from everyone, as if that were possible for me anywhere in the world, let alone in Northern Ireland.

I just wasn't thinking straight but looking at the caravan and seeing that countryside again (which I had hardly visited since I was a boy) made me homesick. So a few days later, when I made it up with Alex, I said to her, 'What do you think about moving to Northern Ireland? There are some gorgeous places near where Carol lives.'

She was a bit surprised at first but said, 'If it will make you happy, I'm willing to give it a try.'

'We don't even have to live there full time,' I said. 'You can get so much more for your money over there, we can keep this place on as well.'

Alex was brought up in the country and liked the idea of having a bit of land, where she could keep horses. But I was still a bit worried about her because she's only a kid and I didn't know whether she was ready to live anywhere remote.

We looked at a couple of places, but neither of them was quite right. However, one day, we were driving around Portavogie and spotted this big old place opposite the sea. It was also perched halfway up a hill which meant that it had wonderful views of the ocean.

There was a For Sale sign up so we thought we'd see if we could have a look round there and then. We probably wouldn't have done it in Chelsea, but we just drove up the drive and banged on the door and the old boy who owned it was only too happy to give us a tour of the house. The décor wasn't to our liking but it was a big, four-bedroomed property and we could see the potential.

We went back to see it again but had already made up our minds to buy it. And we got on really well with the chap, who said that he was an old sailor, though I reckon he must have owned the fleet because he was obviously not short of a few bob and had a beautiful old Rolls in the garage.

We bought the land for the princely sum of two pounds

and a considerable amount more for the house, still undecided about how we were going to divide our time. We weren't sure whether we should live in Chelsea and use the house for long weekends or to live the other way round. But from August, onwards, we were spending more and more time in Ireland doing the place up. We had to start almost from scratch in every room and as it began to turn from a shell into a home, and a beautiful home at that, we couldn't bear the thought of leaving it for the majority of the time.

We finally decided that we would rent out our flat in Chelsea, so in January 2001, we moved into the house in Portavogie full time. Since then, we've turned it into our dream home and have had the garage converted into a snooker parlour, with a full-size table and a corner bar.

Dad and Carol, whose house is literally two minutes from mine, were naturally delighted because it meant we could see each other every day if we wanted and make up for all the lost years. Our dog, Red, adores it, too, because he can walk for miles, and it seemed a perfect compromise for Alex and me because the flight to London is less than an hour from Belfast City airport. I can easily get back for my Sky engagements and if we make a long weekend of it at our Chelsea flat, she also gets time to see her family and friends.

I still worry whether there's enough for Alex to do in Portavogie because it is a tiny place, but she is the sort of person who can mix with anyone and the locals love her. One or two of them told me that they were a bit concerned about what she would be like because wives of stars sometimes develop airs and graces. But Alex has never seen me as George Best, superstar; just as myself.

After that one incident when I fell off the wagon in London, I knuckled down and told myself that I had to stay dry. But unless you're an alcoholic, you can't know how hard that is and every day was tough, every day I was thinking about drink. I've never needed an excuse to go back on it but after all the treatment I'd had, all the help I'd had, this time I probably did need to find a reason, however feeble, to have a drink.

So one Saturday night, sitting in the car taking me to Gatwick Airport after doing my Sky show, I was saying to myself, 'It's been a long day and I really deserve a drink,' and when I got to the airport, I went straight into the first-class lounge and poured myself a large glass of red wine.

I only had the one, which probably wouldn't have done me much harm. But it felt like I was beating the system, somehow, especially after being told by the Professor that a single drink could kill me. And, of course, having got away with it once, I began doing it quite regularly and sometimes drinking more than one. It wasn't even that I needed the buzz from the alcohol or that I wanted to get drunk. In fact, I didn't want to get drunk. I think it's just that rebellious streak in me, that mischievous thing. You think you are being clever, a bit like a naughty schoolboy, doing something that you're not supposed to and getting away with it.

Not that I can get away with it with Alex. She has been with me long enough to know when I've had a drink, even if I'm not falling about or slurring my words.

Given the fact that so much of my liver has been permanently damaged, it's obvious what more sustained drinking could do to it. I know people will accuse me of being selfish for even thinking of drinking again, particularly when I've had so much treatment. Jim Baxter, the former Scottish footballer, who died in 2000, received hate mail after he said, following two liver transplants, that he still had the occasional glass of wine. Normal people, those without a drink problem, obviously thought that was crazy and ungrateful. But I could understand it. Personal problems had caused me to contemplate suicide but if, on top of those, I had really thought that I would not be able to drink again, I would probably have gone through with it. That is proof enough that my mind doesn't function like that of healthy people. So why wouldn't I risk a couple of drinks, especially as I'd managed a few before without any particularly bad effects?

My problems with alcohol have also left me with an inefficient immune system, which means that I'm more susceptible to bugs and illnesses than other people. So when I developed a cough and cold in February 2001, I was having a lot of trouble getting rid of it. I wasn't 100 per cent fit, in any case, so I didn't think much about it, just took the normal medicines that you get over the counter at the chemist's. Then one day, I took Red for a walk down the beach and got caught in a terrible storm and came back absolutely soaked. I had a bath and dried off but I couldn't stop coughing and I was gasping for breath. It was really quite frightening so I didn't argue when Alex said, 'I'm taking you to the doctor's.'

The doctor examined me and booked a hospital appointment to have some X-rays taken. And as soon as they got the results, they took me in. It turned out that I'd contracted pneumonia. Typical me, I couldn't get anything normal. It had to be pneumonia and not just that but bronchial pneumonia, with a build-up of fluid on the lungs which the doctors couldn't get rid of. For the first few days, I needed an oxygen mask to help me breathe.

I had a private room in the hospital but it wasn't anywhere near the standard of the Cromwell, and Belfast folk don't understand the meaning of the word private. People were trying to wander in to my ward every five minutes, either other patients or relatives who were visiting them, wanting me to sign autographs and pictures or whatever. But on the second day, Phil had a word with the hospital and they put a security guard on the door to stop it. And once again, cards and flowers and self-help books and religious pamphlets started arriving from all over the world.

Michael Parkinson and Jimmy Tarbuck called me, as well as Manchester pals like Waggy and Colin Burne. But when Alex Higgins, who has been suffering from cancer, called Phil to say that he wanted to see me, Phil told him that no visitors were allowed.

I used to bump into Alex occasionally in Manchester but we were never exactly pals. I've never been enamoured of people who use those immortal words 'Do you know who I am?' and I've often heard Alex use them. In my experience he can also be a little aggressive when he's drunk, the complete opposite to me. I had no wish to see him. But one day, the door opened and Alex's head popped round it.

He looked absolutely terrible after his throat operation and he had a scarf wrapped around his neck, presumably to hide the scars. He looked a lot worse than me. We said hello to each other and then he pulled up a chair and sat right beside the bed and said, 'Give me your hand.'

'What for?' I said.

'I'm going to read your palm for you,' he said.

Now if there's one person I don't need giving me advice or telling me what's going to happen, it's Alex. But he's also a persistent character and he insisted on giving me the 'reading', holding my palm and telling me that I would be out of hospital in a few days, that I'd live till I was 80 and that there was nothing wrong with me.

Once I came out of hospital after a couple of weeks, I was confined to the house again, sitting around brooding and thinking about drink. And before long I was saying to myself, *What's the point of going on if I can't have a drink?*, and I drove down to my local.

I'm a regular because we've been eating meals there since we first arrived in Portavogie. But they'd only ever seen me drink tea or soft drinks before. So Francis, the landlord, seemed a bit unsure when I ordered wine but he served me anyway. Alex went nuts when she found out and came storming into the pub to take me home. But I wasn't in the mood to be ordered about so she just left me there.

We had a row when I got home and the next day we made up and I apologised and said it wouldn't happen again. But it has happened a few times since and Francis and the other bar staff have learned to cope with it. The way Francis sees it is that he can't stop anyone drinking and if he didn't serve me then I would go somewhere else, where they might be happy to ply me with as much as drink as I want. He tries to keep a lid on my intake and he will drive me home if he doesn't think I'm capable and before now, he's driven Alex around to try to find me when I've gone missing for a couple of days.

Not long after coming out of hospital, Alex and I went to London for a weekend and had another blazing row and I flew back to Ireland on my own. I went to see my dad, having had a few drinks first, though he didn't seem to notice. But Carol was there and realised I had been drinking.

The following day, a Saturday morning, she came round to my house.

'George,' she said, 'am I getting to know you again after all these years, just to lose you?'

I tried to pretend that I didn't know what she was talking about.

'I'm not going anywhere,' I said.

'If you carry on the way you are with the drink,' she said, 'you're not going to be here. You know it took Mummy.'

'Well, Mum was overnight,' I said.

'No, it wasn't overnight,' she said. 'You weren't here, we were, and we lived with it, day in, day out, for years and we saw what it could do to a person, how it could change a person. We don't want to see it happen to you.'

By March 2001 my drinking was getting out of hand again and Alex was in near despair. I would go without a drink for a week or two but then I would be craving it again and I don't mean craving in the way that normal people mean it. For me, the craving is irresistible. I know I can't keep off it and had just been hoping that the medical people would develop something which could stop the craving.

The Professor gave me some pills for that, which helped for a while, and he even upped the dosage when I said the craving was still there. But I still wanted to drink so we began discussing having the Antabuse tablets sewn into my stomach again, if only to help me in the short term. But I'd ended up having plastic surgery the first time I used them so I wasn't 100 per cent sure. And you also risk dying if you drink when they're inside you.

Alex didn't want to try to push me into anything because she knows that can have the opposite effect on me. But I knew she was hoping and praying that I'd go for the Antabuse. The biggest danger about having Antabuse, of course, was that I'd go on a bender without thinking and end up killing myself.

We were due in any case, to see Professor Williams in London in early April for a general check up. We were sat in his office, discussing things generally when he was paged to see someone urgently and left us on our own for a few minutes. You know how awkward those moments can be, sitting in a hospital, even when you are man and wife, but I had already made up my mind.

'When the Professor comes back,' I said to Alex, 'I'm going to ask to have the Antabuse.'

And Alex's little face lit up like all her Christmases had come at once.

'Are you sure, darling?' she said. 'That's brilliant. I'm sure it's for the best.'

The medical term for it is disulfiram implantation, and I had to see Dr Graham Lucas, consultant psychiatrist at the

Priory Hospital, Sturt in Surrey, so that he could assess my suitability for the treatment. He wrote back to Professor Williams, saying:

> *I saw George today alone and then with his very supportive but understandably concerned wife, Alex. He is coherent, rational and capable of objectivity about his alcohol abuse. Mood is appropriate and cognitive function satisfactory, insight is intact and there is no evidence of denial. Nevertheless, he recognises mood swings and Alex perceives them as vulnerable situations. Despite his very genuine wish to remain abstinent, the risk of impulsive behaviour still remains, as they both fully appreciate. However, it is understood that physical risk is potentially fatal if there is further alcohol consumption. Therefore, in the circumstances, the procedure of disulfiram implantation is fully justifiable. They both understand the potentially fatal implications of drinking alcohol following such implantation. Nevertheless, the matter now rests entirely with George and to pressurise will be counterproductive.*

I thought that was a fair and honest summing up of my situation and Alex's and even though I wasn't so enthusiastic about the Priory programme, I agreed to accept all the conditions set down by Dr Lucas.

CHAPTER NINETEEN
KEEPING BUSY

The first implant of Antabuse was in April last year and since then I haven't fancied or needed a drink, though they have also got me on some new pills which help to suppress the craving. It's such a simple operation and though you have a painful stomach for a couple of days afterwards, I can put up with that. Originally I had hoped that after a year of having the implants I would be strong enough to stay off the drink on my own, but I've decided not to take any chances and am still having the operation every three months.

In fact, now it's me who has to remind Professor Williams when it's time for the next batch. The pellets can last as long as six months before they totally dissolve but I've decided it has to be new ones four times a year for me – just to be on the safe side. I'm absolutely determined to stay on the wagon. And that means my dad, sisters and brother, Calum and, most importantly, Alex are happy. It's a bit weird but I really like the operation now. As I feel the anaesthetic taking effect and I go into unconsciousness I can hear the nurses telling me to imagine something pleasant. I always picture a massive hammock stretched between two huge palm trees. Unfortunately, even though I head for it as quick as I can, the anaesthetic acts so fast that I've haven't yet managed to climb into it.

Being off the booze has also done wonders for my health. My blood count is up and the jaundice isn't so bad; even the swelling on my feet has reduced – despite what one supposed journalist recently wrote about me. Ted Macauley was a friend, or so I thought. But he wrote some stories for the tabloid press saying I limp heavily, my legs are misshapen and grotesquely knotted and my feet are swollen three sizes more than they should be. I might not look quite as dashing as I did in the Seventies, but this was utter cobblers. Funnily enough, Macauley hasn't called me of late. I wonder why? A guilty conscience perhaps? Whatever the reason, I just hope it stays that way. I do bear grudges.

Actually everything, apart from my energy levels, is much better. I am still sick some mornings, but now it is, say, once a week. In April last year, it was every day.

But it is taking a hell of a lot longer to get back my strength than I thought. I still need plenty of rest and sleep. The professor did warn me it was going to take some time – it's over a year since I stopped drinking. Now, instead of champagne cocktails, I have to swallow a cocktail of pills. My daily intake includes pills to improve my circulation, stop water retention, help my blood clot normally, keep my stomach settled, as well as the ones to suppress my craving for alcohol.

Being so weak, however, has meant that I've had to spend a lot more time with Professor Williams in London than I think either of us would have liked. It's also meant that just as we got the house in Portavogie how we wanted, I was there less and less. Our whole escape from England was falling apart. The house in Ireland was meant to be the one, our dream, but after a year and thousands and thousands of pounds of work we realised it would never be right for us.

It was an idyllic hideaway by the sea and meant I could be close to my family. But it took me a 14-hour round-trip every Saturday to do my football commentary on Sky and not much less every time I went for check-ups. It was hellish and not the kind of thing a man in my health should have been doing twice a week. On top of that, we were so remote that going to the 'local' supermarket took Alex almost a day – if she forgot something, it would drive her bonkers. And then there was the weather. I had remembered the summers as being so warm, but we had to have a log fire burning all through July and August. I think we got one sunny day. We both thought: 'Great, it's the start of the summer.' Our neighbour soon put us right. 'What do you mean? Today is the summer,' was his reply. It was just so cold and because I had no weight on me the wind was cutting me in half. I couldn't even step out of the door without coming down with something.

So for much of last year, Alex and I were camping at her Mum and Dad's in Surrey. It made sense, but as fantastic as Adrian and Cheryl are, it didn't make us happy. In the end, we decided to move back to England. My family were pretty devastated – or made a good play at it – but they knew that practically it was proving too difficult.

Alex pushed for us to house hunt in Surrey. It's where she grew up and, as I said, where her mum and dad live. She wanted to be near them – but not too near. And I'm sure they were getting a bit sick of the sight of us. We were there for months: late summer, autumn, Christmas, New Year... They were perfect hosts and very patient. I'm not sure I would have been.

They also made Christmas and New Year great fun. Both were family affairs. Alex's sister and her boyfriend and her gran all came round. And I just made it back from Ireland after seeing my lot. To me Christmas should always be celebrated full on. I love the lights, the tree and the pressies. I love the whole thing. On Christmas Eve, we put out a glass of wine and mince pies for Santa and a carrot for Rudolph. Then we all trooped off to bed. When we woke up, we immediately grabbed our presents from under the tree. The best bit was watching the dogs tear open theirs. They were just like little kids: totally overexcited. Red went mad. There was also lots of TV, Trivial Pursuit and stuffing our faces.

When it comes to Trivial Pursuit, Alex and I are the celebs. But the rest of the family always stop us winning by sending the game into chaos. They all scream out the answers and eventually the game just collapses. They've never let us win yet. At midnight we all had a drink – a soft one for me. Then I made a few phonecalls to my dad, sisters and brother and Calum. He was in LA for the holidays with his mum Angie. After that, I shuffled off to bed – a pale imitation of my former self – as I was presenting on Sky the next day. Alex and the rest of them stayed up until the early hours getting up to no good.

In some ways, 2001 wasn't the best of years for Alex and I. Me catching pneumonia and both of us realising we would have to give up the house in northern Ireland were pretty low points. But towards the end of the year things were starting to buck up. In November we did a Christmas TV ad for Marks and Spencer and I started my new career as a journalist. I must admit I am not a great fan of celebrities endorsing products. A lot of it is a big con, but when M&S asked us to do it I said yes on the spot. Marks has been the one and only place that I buy my undies and socks for 40 years now and their trousers have always fitted me like a glove without having to be taken in or up. When I said to the Marks and Spencer big wigs what a big fan I was, I think they thought I was taking the Michael (sorry, couldn't resist that one). In the end, they realised I was serious and when we finished shooting packed me off with a stash of shirts, jackets and trousers as a bonus. Alex didn't fair quite so well: just one top. But it was lovely and I thought that it was about time I got the gifts – usually she gets given everything. However, she did go and spend a day shopping on the King's Road to make up for what she called her 'shortfall'.

I started my weekly column in Night & Day magazine in the *Mail on Sunday* at the beginning of November and I've taken to it like a duck to water. Some people might say I love nothing better than talking about myself and sounding off. I can't totally disagree! I've always been an opinionated sod, so now it's just nice to get paid for it. But really it's great to be able to have the platform and I hope I never disappoint the readers. I never pull my punches, I always say it as I see it. The reaction has been amazing. Mike Summerbee's wife told me recently, 'I love reading your column because you say things we all want to say, but don't dare.' Barbara Windsor says, 'It's the first thing I do on Sunday. I can't wait to read it.'

It's also good to show that, despite what some people have said about my brain being marinated in alcohol from all those years I drank, I can still hold my own on any subject. And, there's the added bonus that at least I know there is one place where the stuff written about me is true. A heck of a lot of the other stuff that appears is utter codswallop – to put it politely.

I think I did give the editors at Night & Day a bit of a shock early on, though. After only three weeks, they thought I was a goner. It would have been the briefest career as a columnist that even the cut-throats on Fleet Street had ever known.

Alex and I had gone to Cyprus for business and then a few days holiday. The first day went well, but when I woke up on the next morning, my temperature had gone sky high and I had a throbbing headache. Within minutes, I started shaking and shivering. It was getting worse and worse, and I could tell that Alex was getting really scared. To be honest, I was scared out of my wits as well.

The hotel had a doctor on call and by a bizarre twist of fate he knew Professor Williams. The two got on the phone, chatted for a while and decided I had to go into intensive care without delay. I was there for four nights, with tubes coming out of me from the strangest places and people fussing around. There were also all sorts of tests and scans, as well as a blood infusion. This was not quite the break I had hoped for, but all in all I felt better being in the hospital. Eventually, the doctor decided that it was just an infection – I pick up anything that's going around.

However, the press made a meal of it. Either I was dead, dying or had HIV. They seemed desperate for me to kick the bucket. Being stuck in hospital with the Press camped outside is quite stressful. It wasn't what I needed when I was so ill. I was pretty pissed off, more for the sake of the doctors and nurses at the hospital. One sleazy reporter even rang up insinuating I was HIV positive. My reply to the scumbag who hassled the poor staff which such stupid questioning: 'I did have HIV two years ago, but not the kind he's thinking of. For me, it was more a Heavy Intake of Vodka. What an idiot.'

Having said all that, it was quite fun reading my obituary. And it also inspired me to write my own goodbye, which I published in my column soon after. Here's a little bit of it:

The most important things in the world to me are my wife, my son, my family and my friends. I know that sounds corny but I mean it from the heart. This last year has been a second chance for me, a second chance at life. It started the day I went into the clinic and told Professor Williams I wanted Antabuse implants permanently.

At that point Alex knew our lives were going to be different. That my behaviour of the past was in the past. I've never told Alex this but she has saved my life. She saw the good in me when most others couldn't. And she's stayed with me when any sane woman wouldn't. Even if I feel terrible every day, I say a big thank you to God. I have been so lucky to find her. I've never regretted a day I've been with her.

My real regret in life is not seeing my son growing up. It's something that really hurts. But now I look at Calum and how he's turned out. He's such an amazing person. Every time we talk on the phone, he finishes it off by saying, 'I love you Dad', which considering I wasn't around is a great compliment.

Alex and I would love to have kids. This time I'd be there 24 hours a day, seven days a week. I've been given this second chance and I'm going to grasp it. I know I won't get a third.

I'm not frightened of death as long as everyone around me is taken care of. I've put almost everything in Alex's name, so from that point of view there will be no problem. We've never spoken about me dying, I don't think we need to. I've tended to recover quickly. But one day I won't.

I'd hate leaving Alex behind. This is the first time I've been truly in love. I felt it straight away with her. It was a hell of a decision to be together. There was my track record, the age difference, my drinking. Everything was against us. But seven years on we're still together. And things have got better and better.

Alex is strong enough to handle most things, but I hope she'll find someone else. Someone good enough to look after her. She's intelligent enough to know the difference between a good one and a bad one. After all, she chose me!

When Alex read that she started crying. We had talked about me dying, but I don't think I'd ever been that open before. And we had talked about babies – a lot. For a while last year Alex was obsessed. Whatever it took, she was prepared to do it – I was exhausted. She even woke me up at three one night to go over names. James, Alexander and Abigail are her favourites.

To be fair, it wasn't just her. I was as keen and it had been the plan ever since we got married that we'd have kids when she hit 30. She is 30 now, so watch this space. Initially Alex was a bit worried about her own health. She'd been a air stewardess for two years and that can really screw up a woman's system. We had her checked out and she's fine. Unfortunately, I'm not so good. I guess you could say, I'm firing blanks. Apparently, the liver affects your sperm count and as there isn't much left of my liver, my count is at rock bottom.

There is hope, however, soon after I came back from Cyprus, Professor Williams and I decided I should have a liver transplant. It was something we'd been contemplating for a while. I wasn't so bad it was desperate, but my immune system was constantly getting knocked back because my liver couldn't cope. Now, we decided it was pointless trying to manage my condition. Any time I went away – Cyprus, Malta, Italy, Ireland – I just gave up the ghost. The other reason we came round to the idea of a transplant was that I'd been off alcohol long enough by then. I'm not sure I would have been accepted on to the scheme much earlier. The problem with some alcoholics is that once they've had the transplant they think it's fine to drink again. I know that was something Alex was worried about. Worried that if I got a new liver, I'd hit the bottle as soon as I could. I know quite a few people who've been given a new liver and have immediately started boozing, so Alex was right to be apprehensive. There was no way any of us could have survived if I'd gone back to my old ways. And really I am a little scared of that possibility as well, so even after the operation, I've decided to continue having the Antabuse pellets put in my stomach. That makes me feel more at ease – and means Alex and Professor Williams can sleep at night.

If I drink after the transplant, the professor says that he'll have to pack his bags and flee the country. I know what he's saying, quite a few people are going to be tut-tutting when I have the operation. Some holier-than-thou types have already had a go at him, as well as me, sounding off about me not be entitled to a transplant because I did the damage to my liver myself, by my choice to drink and my past lifestyle. In their book I do not a deserve a second chance, they think there are others who are more deserving out there. But thankfully, Professor Williams hasn't listened to their claptrap. He knows how serious I am about a permanent recovery. I won't let him down. He has put his faith in me.

John Humphrys has had a pop at me already. His column in the *Times* was so muddled it was hard to tell what he was really try to get at, but basically he was talking claptrap. Alcoholism is a disease. I didn't set out to do this to myself and now, with help, I'm trying to recover. I think I deserve my chance of living a normal life just like anybody else and I'm not draining valuable NHS resources, I'm going private.

Now it's just a matter of fixing the date. Unless anything drastic happens, I'm hoping it will be very soon – I've been on the list seven months. I'll go in, rest a bit afterwards, take a holiday, and then get back to work in the autumn.

I know that's a bit idealistic, a donor liver doesn't just come along when you click your fingers. No one can predict when it will happen. The liver can come from someone who has died or be part of a liver from one of my relatives with the same blood type. But there is no way I would let any of my family go through the operation. It's very dangerous and potentially life-threatening. So now, I'm waiting for the right donor, waiting for someone to die so I can live. Some people get a bit queasy at the thought of someone else's liver being put inside them. I won't. The way I look at it that person has gifted me something, gifted me life.

I have heard talk that soon using pig livers for transplants could be the norm. I have to say, that is something else I would never contemplate. It is just too freaky. Walking around with another human's liver is one thing, but a pig's? Not for me. Instead, at the moment, I'm walking around with a bleeper so the doctors can get me into hospital as soon as possible when the right donor liver comes. We have to be contactable 24 hours a day and Alex, Mrs Organised, has already got my overnight bag packed. She seems very keen to get rid of me!

I've had all the pre-op tests already, general stuff looking at my heart, blood and arteries. The aim of these is to eliminate any side effects. Professor Williams and the rest of the team are very pleased with my results. I've also sat down with the surgeon, my own doctors and people who have already had the operation to run me through the whole procedure from start to finish. If all goes well, I should be sat up in bed in three days and back at home within two to three weeks. After a year, I should be in tip-top condition – though I will always be on medication.

Professor Williams did one op quite recently and the man was up and about within the week which made me feel pretty positive. I've also had a lovely letter from a lady who has also had the transplant. Beforehand, she had always been tired and short of breath, now she's done parachute jumps and has had a baby. I only hope I feel that good when it's all over.

Of course, there is always the possibility the operation might fail. There is an 80 per cent chance of success. I haven't dwelt on the worse case scenario. For me, it has always been about being positive. I'm a great believer in that. My thinking is that if I'm negative I might reduce my chances by 5 per cent to a 75 per cent success rate. If I'm positive, however, I'll increase my chances by 5 per cent to an 85 per cent success rate. I'm just focusing on having that new lease of life – and seeing Red's face when I finally get my arse out of my chair and give him a run for his money round the garden.

Unfortunately, having the op has meant I've had to postpone a charity event in Marbella that Professor Williams and I were going to host to raise money for the Foundation for Liver Research. I've already raised £50,000 through a dinner at Old Trafford and had hoped to raise £200,000 in Marbella, with an evening do and celebrity golf day. I'm still planning to do it, though. But now it will just have to be a little later, when I can force everyone to dig deeper into their pockets.

Waiting for the transplant has also meant I had to give up any ideas of going to the World Cup in Japan and South Korea. That was a big forfeit for me. I really wanted to see England and the Republic of Ireland play. I thought they both had a chance of getting through the group stages and wanted to be there to see it. However, all the hype around the England team was ridiculous. There are some good players, but each time there's a tournament everybody just expects to much from them. We need a little more realism about the skills of the home teams as well as the talent of likes of France and Brazil. As for Ireland, well, without Roy Keane the team are half what they were. But Mike McCarthy did the right thing sending him packing. I probably agree with much of Roy's gripes, but there can only be one boss of a football team and it wasn't him. Roy speaks his mind, which I love, but sometimes he does it too much. He needs to learn to keep his trap shut. He over-steps the mark. The way he had a go at his Manchester United teammates towards the end of last season, saying publicly that they weren't trying, was plain silly. All players at that level give it their all, and what he said was just insulting and some-thing that doesn't foster team spirit. At times, I think we all have to sit back and look at ourselves. Watching United's match against Arsenal at the end of the season, Roy did noth-ing. He was the one player who didn't have a good game. And

I hate to point out that when Man U did win the treble, Roy wasn't in the team. All that said, my bet is that this season United will be pretty rampant. Their pride has been hurt and they'll be hungry for revenge. The players and Fergie have got a point to prove.

We found our new house right at the end of last year and moved in pretty sharpish in January 2002. It was such a relief to have our own four walls again and doing it up has taken Alex's and my mind off the impending transplant. We've both been focusing just on that for too long, which I'm sure has turned us both a little stir crazy. Talking about curtains and carpets has brought us back into the real world – all be it one full of soft furnishings.

Alex fell madly in love with Flint Barn as soon as she set eyes on it. Me? I can live anywhere as long as there's a TV and a bed. Funnily enough it's quite similar to the house in Portavogie. It is a converted barn with lots of land for dogs and Alex's horses – that's her next hobby. We've been there about seven months now, but already it feels as if we've been here for ever. Alex is cooking in the kitchen all the time, I stoke up roaring fires in the living room and watch TV, and Red, our redsetter, shoves us all around demanding first choice of every sofa, chair and bed in the place. As well as settling in, the two of us have been drawing up list after list of things we've got to do or buy before our house warming – all the Sky boys are invited, as well as Michael Parkinson, Dennis Law, Rod Stewart,

Barbara Windsor, Gail Porter, Angus Deayton and Mohammed Al-Fayed. We can't wait.

The house is perfect. Well, to us it is, though it wouldn't take much to please us. I guess you could say we were on the rebound from Ireland when we bought Flint Barn. We saw it and realised straight away it was right. Ireland – but with much better weather! The asking price was a little over our budget, but I knew if I could get Alex to start wearing all the clothes she buys more than once we could afford it. I'm still working on that one.

We signed, sealed and moved in within six weeks. And unpacking took no time at all. We left a lot of stuff behind because the house in Ireland was so much bigger. We gave my family all the electrical stuff, Barbara sold most of the furniture for us, and other things like the snooker table in the games room we left for the new owners, whoever they may be. So all in all, there was a lot less to dust off and decide where to put. Alex and her mum and dad got stuck in and I orchestrated things from my sofa chair – funnily enough I took a turn for the worse that day and had to rest up with lots of hot cups of tea being delivered to me to stop my throat drying up from all the coordinating I was having to do. It was a hard day, I can tell you.

Ever since, I've been a permanent fixture in the main barn, which we've turned into our lounge and dining room. The sun streams through the windows on both sides and heats up the room a treat, though the barn is so big, with slate floors and a high beamed roof, that it can get a little cold in mid-winter. Fortunately, the open fire is enormous and once lit makes the whole room really toasty.

We've filled the barn with lots of wooden furniture, mostly made from reclaimed railway sleepers. They've been on quite a journey. First Australia, then relaid in South Africa, then transformed into furniture in Ireland and now they're in England. By the chimney, I've got a bit of a nautical thing going on – a bit of a shrine to our last house. Soon I've got a big ship's wheel arriving from Ireland. I haven't told the missus yet.

Alex and I could never be called minimalists. We're more Olde Worlde, into fireplaces and rocking chairs. Well, I'm into rocking chairs – part of my homage to the great Val Doonican. Alex is more into thrones. She bought a couple of wooden ones motifed with lions a while back. I call them the Posh and Becks Thrones – but I think ours are a bit more tasteful. Well, anything they can do we can do better. They're for decoration really, but we sit on them for a joke sometimes.

When we renew our vows – which we're planning on doing soon after the transplant – we'll be seated on them during the ceremony. Afterwards I'm thinking of charging any friends who want to sit on them £50 a go – it will pay for the food and drinks.

The main barn seems to have become my domain in the house, but Alex has firmly put a claim on the kitchen. It is where she lives. She is always cooking in there and watching trashy soaps. EastEnders and Corrie are her top ones, but then she's also addicted to Emmerdale, Brookside and Hollyoaks. Basically, the lot. If I don't know where she is I just head for the kitchen.

The only things I'm allowed to touch in there are my own mini fridge. Alex has relegated all my chocolate, fruit and sweeties to it. She calls it my rubbish tip. The other thing in the kitchen that I'm in charge of is the wine rack. I've got a good collection in there, which I know might shock some people as I'm a recovering alcoholic, but we have this beautiful wine rack and you can't have a wine rack without wine in it. Alex says I went out and bought it all for show, but really it's for her and when guests come round. Alex likes the odd glass of Pinot Grigio and her dad loves his Shiraz and Merlot. All this might sound like I'm tempting fate too much, that shoving bottles of wine in front of my nose is self-inflicted cruelty, but I'd find it much worse if people around just drank soft drinks because I have to. I'd hate it. It would make me really uncomfortable. I have an addiction and at last I'm learning to live with it. I won't pretend alcohol isn't there. It is everywhere so it's pointless to try and avoid it. Anyway, as it's only for guests I only buy cheap wine these days!

I have always loved collecting, though. Be it wine, teddy bears, stamps, football cards, antique pens or match boxes. Unfortunately, my prized possession, the match boxes, were slung by Alex in a fit of domesticated madness when we moved in and down-sized. I'd collected them for 30 years and she just chucked the lot because they had too much dust on them. First of all it was: 'Oh, they are in the loft.' Then, 'Well, they're somewhere around.' Later, 'I think they are at my mum's.' I've never got her to finally admit it to my face. It's a shame as I picked the boxes up everywhere I went. You could probably have traced back journeys to all sorts of places I couldn't remember going to for one reason or another.

My sisters, Carol and Barbara, and my dad can't wait to come over and see Flint Barn. And Calum will be over soon to do more modelling. Though I think he'll probably stay in central London. In some ways, I think I'd rather he stayed here – it would be cheaper. We had a bit of a falling out in February when he used my credit card to pay a hotel bill without permission. I was angry and Alex was very upset. Calum dived for cover and took weeks to reappear and apologise. It was a bit sad though, as it happened around his 21st birthday, so it marred what should have been a time of celebration. But looking back on it, he's still young and if that is all the mischief he gets up to then he's a better man than me. I'm keeping my fingers crossed.

The blip with Calum aside, 2002 has been a much better year than 2001. I've now got an honorary degree from Queen's University Belfast – so everyone has to call me Doctor Best – and was recently awarded the Freedom of the Borough of Castlereagh. Castlereagh is my home town, so that was something special. There was a ceremony at the mayor's office, where lots of people said nice things about me – always a novelty – and then we all jumped in the mayor's limo and went to my Dad's house under police escort. It must have been the only time that has happened to me when I haven't been in trouble. At my Dad's we unveiled a plaque. I insisted it wasn't blue – in my book that is only for dead people and I wasn't going to tempt fate. Then we all went to lunch, and I caught up with some old mates, including one of my two best friends, Robin McCabe. I'd lost touch with him so it was nice to see his head peep round the door. He hadn't changed a bit, still a right terror. Tommy Irwin also sent his love. He now lives in America so couldn't make it.

Best of all was seeing how happy my Dad and brother and sisters were. Dad was so proud and we managed to get a little time to talk on our own. He's also under the weather at the moment and is down to have a heart bypass. I don't think he's 100 per cent sure about it, though. One lady friend he goes dancing with has had her life transformed by it. Another friend is even worse than before. So we'll see. But we sat there together and exchanged notes. It was pretty hilarious really. We were like two old women. Alex laughed her head off.

EPILOGUE
COUNTING YOUR BLESSINGS

I'm still waiting for the transplant, but am not getting down. The constant visits to hospital don't bother me. I've never been a squeamish sort. When I'm in for check-ups I always have a giggle with the nurses. They say: 'You are always happy.' And I say, ' Yeah. I've got nothing to complain about except I feel like shit.' And when the surgeon last put some more Antabuse pellets in my stomach, he decided to go in on my left side, so he made a mark on my leg with a little arrow pointing up. I looked at it and it was pointing at my cock. The whole staff were all in fits when I asked if they could double check that the people in the operating theatre knew what it meant. Alex's dream of having babies could have been cut short – literally.

Alex and I are a little stressed, though. But we just keep planning ahead. We've just got a second dog now, Rua, which means red hair in Irish, and we might start breeding setters in the future. We're planning to buy a summer house in Corfu with Alex's mum and dad. I've got some ideas for a book; my best is a story based around the whole concept of revenge. And Alex has been doing some pilots for a cookery programme. Despite the impending op, everything is so great. We feel so lucky.

It's been a hell of a life and sometimes, when I divide my life into two halves, I think 'The first 27 years were sheer bliss and the last 27 have been a disaster.'

I'm like a sailor on one of those round-the-world yachts. One day, you wake up and the sea is dead calm and the sun is shining and the next, you find yourself in the middle of a storm.

People always relate that corny old story about me when the Irish waiter delivered champagne to my hotel room, where I was sharing the bed with Mary Stavin and several thousand pounds of gambling winnings and asking, 'Where did it all go wrong, George?'

I've told the story myself and it has always got a big laugh. But, of course, it *did* all go wrong. And I can tell you where it went wrong. It went wrong with the thing I loved most of all, my football, and from there the rest of my life unravelled. When the football was great and I was playing well, I couldn't wait to get up in the morning and that was the foundation of my life.

When the game wasn't worth getting up for, then I saw no point in getting up at all.

When I look back on my career, it seems that it came and went in the blink of an eye and I think sports people in general think like that. I went to Manchester United in 1961 and I left at the beginning of 1974, so you're only talking 12 years, which in the overall picture of your life, isn't long.

But God, I packed some living into those 12 years – I lived about three lives in that time.

Now I just want to live a normal life. I've never been one to plan ten or even five years ahead. I've always lived for the day and given the *way* I've lived my life, that has probably been the most sensible option. But for the first time, I do look a little bit towards the future now. At the moment I'm planning for our next summer holiday, for instance.

And I plan relaxation now. Alex and I set aside times when the weather's going to be hot and we stop work and just enjoy ourselves. I've always liked the fact that you never know what's round the next corner, though in my case, it has often turned out to be a nasty surprise. But I've had some pleasant ones, too, in the past two years.

I was worried about how I was going to make a living when I came out of the Cromwell but workwise, the 12 months after that were phenomenal.

I did an advert for the Milk Marketing Board, I've been doing the Manchester United magazine, a video for VCI and Sky TV have asked me about doing outside reports as well as my Saturday afternoon appearances on the football panel. I've also got my own website and want to do a restaurant guide on

Northern Ireland. On top of all that, it looks as though Alex may get her own show on Irish TV on interior design, having already done a successful pilot.

We could have retired on what we have made in the last year alone and Alex was saying the other day, 'Isn't it a shame that you have to get sick and almost die before you can make a decent living?'

Of course my drink problem will never go away. No matter how long I go without drinking and not even fancying a drink, it will still be there lurking. And I'd be fooling myself if I said I would never have another drink because I could fall off the wagon tomorrow. It really is like they say at Alcoholics Anonymous, one day at a time, because I cannot imagine going the rest of my life without a drink.

It's even harder because I still have friends who insist that I don't have a problem. They say, 'I drank the same amount as you.'

But they didn't. And I've never met anyone who could drink as much as me over a period of time.

The hardest thing for me is getting my head round the fact that drink can actually kill. I never believed that was possible and I would look at people of 80 who had been drinking and smoking all their lives and think 'It hasn't harmed them.'

Now I accept not just that drink can kill me but that I'm suffering from a disease which I have to fight. After all the bad times I've had, I think I've got more reasons to live now than at almost any other time in my life. I owe Alex some good years after all she's been through and when I get fully better, to have a family of our own. I want to be there for my family, too.

I have had moments where things have seemed so bleak that I couldn't see any way out. The thought of never drinking again terrified me and I would have rather just given up trying to get better. But I have to fight my fears for the sake of Alex, my family and all the people who care about me and who hate to see me so ill. Every day is a struggle, but I intend to beat this if I can.

My dad is 83 now and I don't know how many years he has got left so I would like him to be able to spend those years in peace at last, without worrying about me. I want to enjoy seeing my nephews and nieces growing up and, of course, I want to see my son Calum become a man and perhaps make me a grandfather.

He normally comes over to stay with me for a month every summer and he seems a level-headed kid, though I do worry that he might inherit this disease called alcoholism, which killed my mother and almost killed me. He doesn't really drink now, as far as I know, but if he has inherited the genes of Mum and me, one drink could start him off. When he was about 17, he asked me what was a good age to start drinking and I said there was never a good time to start.

It won't be easy but given a lot of determination and a little luck, I am hoping to prove that it's never too late to stop.

I'm lucky that, despite all the bad press I've had over the years, the public still seems to like me and tend to remember the good things I did on the football field, rather than the mistakes I have made off it. And they seem to be sympathetic about the latter. This never came across more positively than when the *Sun* newspaper conducted a readers' poll at the end of the millennium to decide the greatest British sports person of all time, which meant readers could choose from such greats as jockey Lester Piggott, racing drivers Stirling Moss and Nigel Mansell, boxers Henry Cooper, Frank Bruno and Lennox Lewis, not to mention footballing legends like Sir Stanley Matthews, Tom Finney and my dear, late pal, Bobby Moore. Yet I was honoured not just to win that poll but to win by a mile.

There have been other polls like that and they always give me a warm glow because they say everything about what the real people think about you. And for weeks afterwards, people who have seen the poll will come up to me and start asking things like, 'What was your favourite goal?' and 'Do you remember that time you scored that goal against such and such?'

That's great, because it allows me to enjoy those moments again in my mind. All sportsmen who have performed at the highest level have that. In my case, it means remembering that fantastic night in Lisbon in 1966 when I became El Beatle and of the even greater one at Wembley two years later, when I helped United win the European Cup.

But I also recall moments which most fans wouldn't remember but which meant a lot to me, like scoring twice against West Brom in the dying minutes to win a game we were losing 2–1. West Brom will always have a special place in my memory because it was against them that I walked out of the Old Trafford tunnel for the first time and experienced that feeling of the hairs standing up on the back of my neck. They still stand up sometimes when my mind reels back to that day and other days like it.

All the bad times cannot wipe away those memories. And, despite all the ups and downs, when I look back at my life as a whole, it is impossible for me not to feel blessed.

CHRONOLOGY

1946
22nd May. George Best born in Belfast.

1961
16th August. Joins Manchester United as an amateur.

1963
22nd May. Sign professional forms with Manchester United.
14th September. Makes league debut in home fixture against West Bromwich Albion, aged 17. United win 1–0.
28th December. Scores first league goal versus Burnley at Old Trafford.

1964
15th April. Makes Northern Ireland debut in 3–2 win against Wales in Swansea.
14th November. Scores first goal for Northern Ireland in a 1–2 away defeat against Switzerland.

1966
9th March. Scores twice in a 5–1 away win against Benfica in the 2nd leg of the European Cup quarter-final tie. Many observers believe Best's performance in the match to be his finest ever.

1967
4th May. Scores a hat trick in a 6–0 home win against Newcastle United.
21st October. Plays in what many observers believe to be his finest game for his country as Northern Ireland defeat Scotland 1–0 in Belfast.

1968
4th May. Voted British Footballer Of The Year.
29th May. Scores in Manchester United's 4–1 victory against Benfica in the final of the European Cup at Wembley Stadium.

16th October. Sent off for the first time in his playing career against Estudiantes at Old Trafford.

December. Named European Footballer Of The Year.

1969

5th April. Presented with the European Footballer Of The Year trophy by Paris magazine *France Football*.

28th July. Plays for the Rest of the UK against Wales in Cardiff.

3rd December. Knocks the ball from the referee's hands at the end of the League Cup semi-final 1st leg match against Manchester City at Maine Road.

1970

2nd January. Suspended for four weeks and fined £100 after knocking the ball out of the referee's hands after the League Cup tie against Manchester City.

7th February. Scores six goals in Manchester United's 8–2 win against Northampton Town (away) in the 5th round of the FA Cup. It is Best's first game after suspension.

18th April. Sent off playing for Northern Ireland against Scotland after spitting and throwing mud at the referee.

1971

4th January. Appears before an FA disciplinary commission after acquiring three cautions for misconduct in a period of 12 months. Best arrives three hours late. He is fined £250 and given a six week suspended sentence.

8th January. Misses the train taking the Manchester United team to play Chelsea in London. Best takes a later train though but spends the weekend with actress Sinead Cusack. The episode makes the front and back pages of the National newspapers for three days.

11th January. Manchester United suspend Best for two weeks following the incident in London.

27th January. Plays and scores for a Rangers/Celtic select side in a benefit game for the 66 victims of the Ibrox disaster.

21st April. Scores his only hat trick for Northern Ireland in a 5–0 win against Cyprus in Belfast.

18th September. Scores a hat trick in a 4–2 home win against West Ham United.

13th October. Refused permission by Manchester United to play for Northern Ireland against USSR in Belfast after Best receives death threats.

23rd October. Best receives further death threats that he will be shot whilst playing for Manchester United in an away game at Newcastle United. Best plays and scores the only goal of the game. Security is tight and Best receives police protection after the match.

17th November. Best is subject of 'This Is Your Life'.

27th November. Scores his second hat trick of the 1971/72 season in a 5–2 away victory against Southampton.

1972

4th January. Misses training all week.

8th January. Dropped for the home game against Wolverhampton Wanderers after missing training. Best flies to London and spends a much publicised weekend with current Miss Great Britain, Carolyn Moore.

10th January. Best returns to Old Trafford and is fined two weeks wages (about £400). He is instructed to do extra training and ordered to move from his home to his previous digs with Mrs Mary Fullaway.

16th February. Tells Daily Express journalist John Roberts that he is fed up playing in a poor Manchester United side and as a consequence he would like to play elsewhere.

1st May. Plays for a Rest of Europe side against Hamburg SV in a testimonial match for Uwe Seeler in Hamburg.

20th May. Best is in Marbella when he announces that he has decided to retire from football. He declares that he has been drinking a bottle of spirits a day.

1st June. Rumours circulate that Best will return to football as he flies out to Majorca.

7th July. Flies back to Britain and announces he will again play for Manchester United. The Club suspend him for two weeks for a breach of contract and the Marbella affair and order Best into lodgings with Pat Crerand. This arrangement is short-lived when Best's house is put up for sale and he moves back into digs with Mrs Mary Fullaway.

10th July. Reports for pre-season training.

12th August. Plays in Manchester United's first game of the season against Ipswich Town at Old Trafford.

18th October. Sent off playing for Northern Ireland in an away match against Bulgaria for kicking an opponent.

30th October. Following Manchester United's 1–4 home defeat against Tottenham Hotspur, Best announces he will seek a transfer if his team is relegated.

18th November. Plays in the Manchester derby at Maine Road. United are beaten 0–3.

22nd November. Fined by Manchester United for missing training.

25th November. Makes his last appearance of the 1972/73 season in the home game against Southampton.

29th November. Best sees United manager Frank O'Farrell after missing training earlier in the week. He is subsequently dropped from the team as rumours prevail that Best will be transfer listed.

4th December. Leaves Manchester without permission from the Club and is later seen in a London nightclub.

5th December. Suspended for two weeks by Manchester United and transfer listed at a fee of £300,000. Derby County declare interest.

6th December. Bournemouth show an interest in Best but he announces that he would like to join Chelsea.

7th December. New York Cosmos show interest in Best.

11th December. Manchester City manager Malcolm Allison shows interest in signing Best.

14th December. Best is presumed to have been taken off the transfer list when Manchester United chairman Louis Edwards announces that the Irishman will commence training.

16th December. Manchester United are beaten 0–5 at Crystal Palace and speculation mounts that manager Frank O'Farrell will resign.

19th December. O'Farrell is sacked by Manchester United. Best sends a letter to the Club directors to say that he is finished with football. This is the second time that he announces his retirement.

1973

4th January. New York Cosmos again express an interest in signing Best.

11th January. Found guilty of assaulting waitress Stefanja Sloniecka and causing actual bodily harm during an incident the previous November in Ruebens nightclub.

16th January. Flies to Toronto to discuss the possibility of playing in the World Indoor Soccer League but it comes to nothing. New York

Cosmos approach Manchester United for permission to negotiate terms to sign Best but the proposed deal fails to materialise.

26th March. Best declares an interest in playing for Northern ireland but his Club say that they would block his intention.

11th April. Crystal Palace make a bid for Best.

13th April. Queens Park Rangers hold transfer discussions with Manchester United about a possible transfer of Best to Loftus Road.

27th April. Best resumes training four months after announcing his retirement.

7th May. Admitted to hospital in Manchester after suffering from thrombosis in Marbella whilst on holiday.

19th June. Best declares that he will not play football again and says it is his intention to write a book with Michael Parkinson.

27th August. Manchester United Chairman Louis Edwards states that the Club would like Best to start training again.

28th August. Best announces that after talks with Manchester United manager Tommy Docherty that he would like to give football another try.

10th September. Reports to Manchester United for training.

25th September. Plays for 45 minutes in Eusebio's testimonial match in Lisbon as Benfica play the Rest of the World.

3rd October. Plays in Denis Law's testimonial game for Manchester United against Ajax.

6th October. Plays for Manchester United Reserves against Aston Villa Reserves at Old Trafford. 7,126 spectators attend to watch Best's latest comeback game.

15th October. Plays in a friendly match away against Shamrock Rovers.

20th October. Plays in his first team comeback game against Birmingham City at Old Trafford.

24th October. Plays in Tony Dunne's testimonial match for Manchester United against Manchester City.

November. Opens club 'Slack Alice' in Manchester.

1974

1st January. Best plays in his last ever game for Manchester United in the fixture away at Queens Park Rangers. United lose 0–3.

4th January. Best fails to turn up for training.

5th January. Omitted from the Manchester United team to play Plymouth Argyll in the FA Cup 3rd Round tie at Old Trafford. Best walks out of the ground vowing never to play for the Club again.

12th January. Suspended for two weeks and transfer listed by Manchester United.

16th January. Tonbridge are keen to sign Best and offer Manchester United £100,000. United manager Tommy Docherty dismisses the move as a publicity stunt. Crewe Alexandra also make enquiries about Best.

21st February. Best is arrested in Manchester and later charged in London with stealing a fur coat, passport, cheque book and other items from the flat of Miss World, Marjorie Wallace. He is later released on bail of £6,000.

24th April. Cleared of all charges relating to the Marjorie Wallace incident.

May/June. Best plays in five games for Jewish Guild in South Africa including:

5th June. Hellenic Versus Jewish Guild.

5th August. Plays for Dunstable Town in a friendly fixture against Manchester United Reserves.

12th August. Plays for Dunstable Town in a friendly fixture against Cork Celtic.

29th October. Plays in Jeff Astle's testimonial match.

27th November. Plays in Tony Book's testimonial match.

1975

29th October. Plays for Dunstable Town in a friendly match against Luton Town.

7th November. Banned by FIFA from playing anywhere in the world.

8th November. Released from his Manchester United contract and FIFA lift Best's worldwide ban.

10th November. Signs for one month to play home games only for Stockport County. Best plays and scores in a friendly game for the Edgeley Park Club against Stoke City. The match attracts 8,000 spectators.

24th November. Scores twice in Peter Osgood's testimonial. Chelsea are reported to be interested in acquiring Best although refuse to meet his wage demands. Queens Park Rangers and Southampton also declare an interest in the player.

26th November. Plays in Pat Crerand's testimonial game.

28th November. Best makes his league debut for Stockport County against Swansea City and scores in front of 9,220 spectators.

4th December. Chelsea are again rumoured to be interested in signing Best on a match fee basis linked to attendances.

12th December. Plays and scores for Stockport County against Watford. The game attracts a crowd of 5,055 spectators.

26th December. Plays the last of the league games for Stockport County against Southport. 6,321 fans watch the game.

Late December. Best signs for Los Angeles Aztecs for the 1976 NASL season.

28th December. Plays in the first of three League of Ireland games for Cork Celtic in the home fixture against Drogheda.

1976
11th January. Plays for Cork Celtic in the home fixture against Bohemians.

18th January. Plays for Cork Celtic in the away fixture at Shelbourne.

19th January. Best is sacked by Cork Celtic due to his 'lack of enthusiasm'.

20th February. Arrives to play for Los Angeles Aztecs.

17th April. Makes his debut for Los Angeles Aztecs in a 1–2 away defeat against San Jose Earthquakes.

18th July. Scores a hat trick in a 8–0 home win against Boston Minutemen.

12th August. Best signs a contract to play for Fulham.

18th August. Plays his last game of the 1976 NASL season in a 0–2 play off defeat away to Dallas Tornado.

2nd September. Best is registered to play for Fulham.

4th September. Makes his league debut for Fulham in the home fixture against Bristol Rovers. Best scores after 71 seconds in front of a 21,127 crowd.

2nd October. Sent off in the away match at Southampton for using 'foul and abusive language'.

13th October. Makes 'comeback' appearance for Northern Ireland in an away fixture against Holland almost three years after his last international game.

1977

14th May. Plays his final league game of the 1976/77 season as Fulham lose 0–1 at Blackburn Rovers.

20th May. Returns to Los Angeles to play his first game of the 1977 NASL season for the Aztecs. His team lose 0–1 at Portland Timbers.

25th August. Plays his last game of the 1977 NASL season in a 0–1 play-off defeat at Seattle Sounders.

30th August. Best returns to England but is unable to appear for Fulham due to the London Club owing Los Angeles Aztecs compensation.

3rd September. Plays for Fulham in the home game against Blackburn Rovers.

8th September. Returns to Los Angeles until a problem of who owns Best's registration is resolved.

18th September. Returns to London.

24th September. Plays again for Fulham in the 1–3 defeat at Cardiff City.

12th October. Wins his 37th and final cap for Northern Ireland in the home game against Holland.

12th November. Plays his final game for Fulham in the 0–2 away defeat at Stoke City.

29th November. Best is suspended by Fulham for not attending training sessions. Best had already returned to Los Angeles.

1978

24th January. Marries Angela MacDonald Janes, aged 25, in Las Vegas.

2nd April. Best plays in his first game of the 1978 NASL season for Los Angeles Aztecs in a 2–3 home defeat against Houston Hurricane.

May. Suspended by Los Angeles Aztecs for missing training.

20th June. Plays his last game for Los Angeles Aztecs in a 0–4 defeat at Washington Diplomats.

June. Transferred to Fort Lauderdale Strikers.

24th June. Best scores two goals on his debut for Fort Lauderdale Strikers as his new side beat New York Cosmos 5–3 at home.

23rd August. Plays his last game of the 1978 NASL season for Fort Lauderdale Strikers in a 1–3 play-off defeat away to Tampa Bay Rowdies.

September. Best guests for Detroit Express on a European tour playing two games for them in Austria. Disagreement over his registration surface when Fulham announce that Best is only able to play for them outside America.

11th October. At the request of the FA, Best is banned by FIFA from playing anywhere in the world until the registration dispute with Fulham is resolved.

12th October. Best's mother, Ann, dies.

1979

28th March. FIFA lift Best's ban and he is cleared to play for Fort Lauderdale Strikers.

31st March. Best plays his first game of the 1979 NASL season for Fort Lauderdale Strikers in a 2–0 home win against New England Teamen.

25th July. Plays his last game of the 1979 NASL season for Fort Lauderdale Strikers in a 6–3 away win at California Surf.

July. Suspended by Fort Lauderdale Strikers for missing both training and matches.

October. Manchester United refuse Best a testimonial match.

13th November. Best guests for Ipswich Town in a testimonial match for manager Bobby Robson.

16th November. Best signs for Hibernian from Fulham.

24th November. Makes his Hibernian debut in the away match at St Mirren. Best scores though his new team lose 1–2. 13,670 spectators attend the game.

15th December. Best fails to appear for the away game against Morton.

1980

9th February. Best fails to appear for the home game against Morton.

11th February. Suspended by Hibernian.

17th February. Best deemed unfit to play in the home game against Ayr United in the 4th Round of the Scottish Cup. He is dismissed by Hibernian.

24th February. Best re-engaged by Hibernian.

13th April. Best signs to play for San Jose Earthquakes for the 1980 NASL season.

19th April. Plays his final game of the 1979/80 season for Hibernian at home to Dundee United before flying out to join San Jose Earthquakes.

27th April. Plays his first game for San Jose Earthquakes in the away game at Edmonton Drillers. His new side lose 2–4.

1st June. Best fails to appear for the game against California Surf.

23rd August. Scores in his last game of the 1980 NASL season for San Jose Earthquakes in a 1–2 home defeat against Los Angeles Aztecs.

September. Signs a new two year contract with San Jose Earthquakes.

9th September. Best plays his first game of the 1980/81 season for Hibernian in the away fixture against Dundee.

11th October. Plays in his final game for Hibernian in the home match against Falkirk.

1981

6th February. Son, Calum Milan Best, is born in San Jose.

29th March. Best plays his first game of the 1981 NASL season for San Jose Earthquakes in a 0–3 home defeat to New York Cosmos.

22nd July. Best scores one of his finest ever goals playing for San Jose Earthquakes against Fort Lauderdale Strikers in a 3–2 home win.

19th August. Plays his last ever game in the NASL for San Jose Earthquakes in a 1–3 away defeat to Vancouver Whitecaps.

8th September. Best guests for Middlesborough in a testimonial match for Jim Platt.

26th September. Manchester United consider re-signing Best.

October 1981. Middlesborough show interest in signing Best during San Jose Earthquakes British tour.

11th December. Middlesborough prematurely announce that a deal has been done to sign Best.

14th December. Best announces that he will not be joining Middlesborough.

1982

November. Best is declared bankrupt.

1983

24th March. Signs for AFC Bournemouth after receiving clearance from San Jose Earthquakes.

26th March. Best makes his debut for AFC Bournemouth in the home game against Newport County watched by a crowd of 9,121 spectators.

16th April. Best makes his final away league appearance in England when AFC Bournemouth visit Southend United. 4,275 spectators watch the game.

7th May. Best makes his final league appearance in England for AFC Bournemouth in the home game against Wigan Athletic 15 days short of his 37th Birthday. 4,523 spectators are present.

3rd July. Best plays in the first of four league games for struggling Brisbane Lions in Australia. His new team win 2–1 in the home game against Sydney Olympic.

8th July. Plays in the 0–3 home defeat against St. George.

10th July. Plays in the 1–1 draw away to Marconi.

17th July. Best plays in his final game for Brisbane Lions in the home fixture against Adelaide City. His side is beaten 0–4 in front of 1,600 spectators.

24th July. Best plays for Australian side Osborne Park Galeb and helps them to a 2–1 home victory against Melville Alemannia. A crowd of approximately 2,000 watch the game.

10th October. Best guests for Linfield against Everton in a testimonial game for Peter Dornan.

1984

28th January. Plays for Tobermore United in an Irish Cup match at home to Ballymena United.

5th August. Plays for Hibernian in a testimonial match for Jackie McNamara against Newcastle United.

3rd November. Best is charged and then bailed for a drink driving offence. He later fails to turn up at court, is subsequently arrested and assaults a policeman.

3rd December. Receives a three month prison sentence for drink driving and the assault on a policeman. He is bailed pending an appeal.

17th December. Best's appeal is dismissed and he is sent to Pentonville prison though eight days later he is transferred to Ford open prison in Sussex.

1985

8th February. Released from prison after serving eight weeks of a twelve week sentence.

17th May. Guests for Aston Villa in a match against West Bromwich

Albion in a benefit game to help victims of the Bradford City fire disaster.

1986
17th February. Plays in the George Dunlop testimonial match.
7th May. Plays in the Geny Peyton testimonial game.
3rd December. Best plays in a testimonial game for Pat Jennings at Windsor Park, Belfast.

1987
December. The Irish FA refuse to grant Best a testimonial game.

1988
11th January. Ulster Television screen a tribute programme entitled 'Best Intentions'.
June. Plays in a charity match in Tokyo to raise money for Aids research.
8th August. Best has his own testimonial match played at Windsor Park, Belfast. Approximately 25,000 spectators watch the game.

1989
June/July. Promotional work in Australia.
June. Working relationship ends with former agent Bill McMurdo.

1990
19th September. Appears on the Wogan show.

1992
5th May. Receives bankruptcy discharge.

1995
24th July. Marries for a second time; to Alexandra Jane Macadam Pursey, aged 23, at Chelsea Town Hall, London.

1996
22nd May. BBC2 devote an entire evening's viewing to celebrate Best's 50th birthday.

1999

May. Best's former home in Bramhall, Cheshire is put up for sale by the owners at an asking price of £450,000. He originally had the house built in 1970 at a cost of £30,000.

26th May. Best leaves the European Champions' League final four minutes early and misses Manchester United's two late dramatic goals which seal a 2–1 victory for his old team against Bayern Munich.

2000

23rd January. Best honoured by the Football Writers' Association with a unique services to football award.

9th March. Rushed to Cromwell Hospital in west London with suspected liver failure.

13th April. Leaves hospital after almost five weeks.

2001

11th April. Returns to Cromwell hospital to have anti-alcohol pellets inserted into his stomach.

20th May. Named the top Manchester footballer of the past fifty years by a Manchester Evening News Sunday Pink Panel.

28th May. Best appears at a celebrity six-a-side tournament at Chelsea's Stamford Bridge. He does not play but presents the trophies.

17th September. Best's autobiography 'Blessed' is published by Ebury Press.

22nd November. Falls ill in Cyprus from a viral infection and is admitted to a Limassol clinic.

25th November. Commences contributing a weekly column to the *Mail on Sunday*'s 'Night and Day' magazine.

29th November. Leaves the clinic in Cyprus after recovering from illness.

13th December. Best presented with an honourary degree from Queen's University in Belfast.

2002

11th March. George is one of the baton carriers for the Queen's Jubilee relay race in London.

3rd April. Awarded the freedom of Castlereagh, the area of east Belfast where Best grew up.

CAREER
STATISTICS

Team	Season	League A	League G	FA Cup A	FA Cup G	Lge Cup A	Lge Cup G	Europe A	Europe G
Manchester United (5/63 – 1/74)	63/64	17	4	7	2	-	-	2	0
	64/65	41	10	7	2	-	-	11	2
	65/66	31	9	5	3	-	-	6	4
	66/67	42	10	2	0	1	0	-	-
	67/68	41	28	2	1	-	-	9	3
	68/69	41	19	6	1	-	-	6	2
	69/70	37	15	7	6	8	2	-	-
	70/71	40	18	2	1	6	2	-	-
	71/72	40	18	7	7	6	3	-	-
	72/73	19	4	-	-	4	2	-	-
	73/74	12	2	-	-	-	-	-	-
Jewish Guild (5/74 – 6/74)	1974	5	n/k	-	-	-	-	-	-
Stockport County (11/75 – 12/75)	75/76	3	2	-	-	-	-	-	-
Cork Celtic (12/75 – 1/76)	75/76	3	0	-	-	-	-	-	-
Fulham (9/76 – 5/77)	76/77	32	6	2	0	3	2	-	-
(9/77 – 11/77)	77/78	10	2	-	-	-	-	-	-
Hibernian (11/79 – 4/80)	79/80	13	3	3	0	-	-	-	-
(9/80 – 10/80)	80/81	4	0	-	-	2	0	-	-
AFC Bournemouth (3/83 – 5/83)	82/83	5	0	-	-	-	-	-	-
Brisbane Lions	1983	4	0	-	-	-	-	-	-

CAREER RECORD IN NASL

Team	Season	Regular Season				Play Offs			
		A	G	As	P	A	G	As	P
Los Angeles Aztecs									
(4/76 – 8/76)	1976	23	15	7	37	1	0	0	0
(5/77 – 8/77)	1977	20	11	18	40	5	2	4	8
(4/78 – 6/78)	1978	12	1	0	2	-	-	-	-
Fort Lauderdale Strikers									
(6/78 – 8/78)	1978	9	4	1	9	5	1	2	4
(3/79 – 7/79)	1979	19	2	7	11	-	-	-	-
San Jose Earthquakes									
(4/80 – 8/80)	1980	26	8	11	27	-	-	-	-
(3/81 – 8/81)	1981	30	13	10	36	-	-	-	-

Key
A = Appearances
G = Goals (2 points)
As = Assists (1 point)
P = Points (Total points for goals and assists combined)

CAREER RECORD EXCLUDING NASL

Team	League A	League G	FA Cup A	FA Cup G	Lge Cup A	Lge Cup G	Europe A	Europe G
Manchester United	361	137	45	23	25	9	34	11
Jewish Guild	5	n/k	-	-	-	-	-	-
Stockport County	3	2	-	-	-	-	-	-
Cork Celtic	3	0	-	-	-	-	-	-
Fulham	42	8	2	0	3	2	-	-
Hibernina	17	3	3	0	2	0	-	-
AFC Bournemouth	5	0	-	-	-	-	-	-
Brisbane Lions	4	0	-	-	-	-	-	-
TOTALS	440	150	50	23	30	11	34	11

CAREER RECORD IN NASL

Team	Regular Season A	Regular Season G	Regular Season As	Regular Season P	Play Offs A	Play Offs G	Play Offs As	Play Offs P
Los Angeles Aztecs	55	27	25	79	6	2	4	8
Fort Lauderdale Strikers	28	6	8	20	5	1	2	4
San Jose Earthquakes	56	21	21	63	-	-	-	-
TOTALS	139	54	54	162	11	3	6	12

INTERNATIONAL APPEARANCES

Date	Opponents	Venue	Result	Goals
1964				
15th April	Wales	Swansea	3–2	
29th April	Uruguay	Belfast	3–0	
3rd October	England	Belfast	3–4	
14th October	Switzerland WC	Belfast	1–0	
14th November	Switzerland WC	Lausanne	1–2	1
25th November	Scotland	Glasgow	2–3	1
1965				
17th March	Netherlands WC	Belfast	2–1	
7th April	Netherlands WC	Rotterdam	0–0	
7th May	Albania WC	Belfast	4–1	1
2nd October	Scotland	Belfast	3–2	
10th November	England	London	1–2	
24th November	Albania WC	Tirana	1–1	
1966				
22nd October	England EC	Belfast	0–2	
1967				
21st October	Scotland	Belfast	1–0	
1968				
23rd October	Turkey WC	Belfast	4–1	1
1969				
3rd May	England	Belfast	1–3	
6th May	Scotland	Glasgow	1–1	
10th May	Wales	Belfast	0–0	
10th September	USSR WC	Belfast	0–0	
1970				
18th April	Scotland	Belfast	0–1	
21st April	England	London	1–3	1

| 25th April | Wales | Swansea | 0–1 | |
| 11th November | Spain EC | Seville | 0–3 | |

1971

3rd February	Cyprus EC	Nicosia	3–0	1
21st April	Cyprus EC	Belfast	5–0	3
15th May	England	Belfast	0–1	
18th May	Scotland	Glasgow	1–0	
22nd May	Wales	Belfast	1–0	
22nd September	USSR EC	Moscow	0–1	

1972

| 16th February | Spain EC | Hull | 1–1 | |
| 18th October | Bulgaria WC | Sofia | 0–3 | |

1973

| 14th November | Portugal WC | Lisbon | 1–1 | |

1976

| 13th October | Netherlands WC | Rotterdam | 2–2 | |
| 10th November | Belgium WC | Liege | 0–2 | |

1977

27th April	West Germany	Cologne	0–5	
21st September	Iceland WC	Belfast	2–0	
12th October	Netherlands WC	Belfast	0–1	

NORTHERN IRELAND PLAYING RECORD

Appearances	Won	Drawn	Lost	Goals Scored
37	13	8	16	9

INDEX